A Companion to the Works of Heinrich von Kleist

Studies in German Literature, Linguistics, and Culture

Edited by James Hardin
(South Carolina)

Camden House Companion Volumes

The Camden House Companions provide well-informed and up-to-date critical commentary on the most significant aspects of major works, periods, or literary figures. The Companions may be read profitably by the reader with a general interest in the subject. For the benefit of student and scholar, quotations are provided in the original language.

A COMPANION TO THE WORKS OF

Heinrich von Kleist

Edited by
Bernd Fischer

CAMDEN HOUSE

First published 2003
by Camden House

Camden House is an imprint of Boydell & Brewer Inc.
668 Mt. Hope Avenue, Rochester, NY 14620 USA
and of Boydell & Brewer Limited
PO Box 9, Woodbridge, Suffolk IP12 3DF, UK

ISBN: 1–57113–177–9

Library of Congress Cataloging-in-Publication Data

A companion to the works of Heinrich von Kleist / edited by Bernd Fischer
    p. cm. — (Studies in German literature, linguistics, and culture)
Includes bibliographical references and index.
ISBN 1–57113–177–9 (alk. paper)
1. Kleist, Heinrich von, 1777–1811 — Criticism and interpretation.
I. Fischer, Bernd, 1953–   II. Series: Studies in German literature,
linguistics, and culture (Unnumbered)

PT2379.Z5C64 2003
838'.609—dc21

                                                           2002154955

A catalogue record for this title is available from the British Library.

This publication is printed on acid-free paper.
Printed in the United States of America.

Contents

Themes and Motifs

Introduction: Heinrich von Kleist's Life and Work

Bernd Fischer

Life

BERND HEINRICH WILHELM VON KLEIST was one of the most innovative, colorful, and enigmatic authors of the turbulent first decade
of the nineteenth century. He did not belong to any particular school of
literature but explored the intellectual and aesthetic structures of his time
from a radical intellectual stance and with a unique literary voice. Many
of his works can be read as experimental case studies of the possibilities
and limits of contemporary thought and poetics. These literary experiments are of sufficient complexity to disallow simple and comfortable
results. Instead, they tend to expose troubling contradictions and to raise
fundamental questions about the capacities of language, communication,
metaphysical orders, and existential antinomies. This may be the primary
reason why Kleist's dramas and novellas have been at the forefront of the
German literary canon for 150 years. Even today they possess an uncommon staying power, having survived all twentieth-century shifts in
literary fashions and intellectual paradigms from realism to expressionism,
from political analysis to formalism, and from existentialism to post-
structuralism. As any German teacher or any analysis of the history of
German studies can attest, readers and scholars alike continue to find
immediate and personal access to Kleist's aesthetics, and many continue
to be amazed at how Kleist's works foreshadow the concerns and literary
tastes of generations of readers. Kleist achieves all of this without relying
on atemporal poetic norms (as could be said about German classicism)
and without postulating the permanence of infinite longing as the central
charge of literary modernity (as do his Romantic contemporaries).
Rather, Kleist combines exceptional literary talent and a sophisticated
sensitivity for the hidden antinomies of his world at the threshold of
modernity with a radical bent for the extreme; and he does not shy away
from scenes of shocking brutality and unsettling absurdity, as well as
irritatingly grotesque yet seductive images and narrative strategies.

Often perceived as far ahead of his time, Kleist can, nevertheless, be understood as a son of that time — albeit a uniquely radical one. Like his classicist contemporaries, he attempted to merge the mythological drama of Greek antiquity with dramatic forms of political psychology and modern realism. Like his Romantic contemporaries, he possesses a thoroughly ironic narrative voice. He is akin to authors of the late Enlightenment in that his polemical posture is deeply informed by an all-permeating skepticism. Moreover, all of his literary and essayistic enterprises engage in complex ways with concrete issues of his time. To name just a few: revolution, anticolonialism, nationalism, education, military reform and wars of liberation, economic reform and liberalism, "truth" and Kantian philosophy, God and religion, power and gender, communication and propaganda, art and reception, feeling and reason, identity and community. With Kleist, the celebrated autonomy of classical and Romantic art becomes porous, penetrable for the challenges of a recalcitrant reality. His literary skepticism allows for an irony that is no less playful than its Romantic counterpart; his ironic play, however, turns intensely serious. Kleist drives his heroes, his narrators, and his audiences into paradoxical and antinomic emotions and reflections that question overt popular convictions, as well as hidden metaphysical and political orders. In some ways he stands at the threshold of a literature that continues in the nineteenth century with authors such as E. T. A. Hoffmann, Büchner, and Heine and leads the way for the literature of high modernism. At least, this is how early twentieth-century readers, Thomas Mann and Kafka among them, have read Kleist's work.

Kleist was born on 18 October 1777 in Frankfurt an der Oder, the first son of Joachim Friedrich von Kleist and his second wife, Juliane Ulrike, née von Pannwitz. (Kleist himself believed that his birthday was 10 October.) The Kleist family had a long tradition of furnishing the Prussian military with officers, but when Joachim Friedrich von Kleist, a captain in the Leopold von Braunschweig regiment at Frankfurt, died unexpectedly in 1788, his wife and children fell into financial limbo. The mother's appeal for a pension was denied by the Prussian king, who also turned down the family's request to admit the ten-year-old Heinrich to the Prussian military academy. Instead, he received some home schooling (most importantly, from Christian Ernst Martini) and then was sent to Berlin to continue his primary education at the school of the French-reformed community. In 1792, at the age of fourteen, he entered the Prussian military as a corporal. One year later Kleist's mother died, and his aunt, Auguste Helene von Massow, became the family's guardian.

Kleist's military career is important in two ways. It was there that he met his life-long friends Otto August Rühle von Lilienstern (1780–1847) and Ernst von Pfuel (1799–1866), and it was there that he experienced fundamental contradictions between the ideals of enlightened humanism and the reality of Prussian everyday life in drastic and, finally, no longer bearable forms. In 1799 he quit the service and promised never to ask for readmittance into any military. Instead, he intended to educate himself to serve the state in an administrative career. Then twenty-two, Kleist had access to some of his family's funds and returned to Frankfurt an der Oder to begin his studies at the university there. He socialized with the neighboring family of August Wilhelm Hartmann von Zenge, tutored von Zenge's daughters, and in 1800 announced his engagement to the oldest daughter, Wilhelmine. That same year Kleist left the university after just three semesters and traveled to Berlin to apply for a position in the Prussian civil service. Toward the end of August he and a friend from his youth, Ludwig von Brockes, undertook a trip to Vienna. In Dresden, however, they decided to travel instead to Würzburg. Much has been written about the purpose of this mysterious trip. Was Kleist an industrial spy for the Prussian government? Was he on a secret trade mission? Did he undergo an operation for a sexual impediment of some nature? Did he believe that he had found a mathematical formula to break the Vienna or Würzburg casinos, as is the latest speculation? We know little about Kleist's motive for the trip, but we can learn much about the inner development he went through from the extraordinary letters he wrote to his fiancée and members of his family during it. At this time Kleist presented himself as an adherent of an early Enlightenment road map to human fulfillment: the achieving of happiness through virtue and education. But a closer reading can detect the first seeds of doubt.

Returning to Berlin, Kleist joined the Prussian Technical Commission as an apprentice in December 1800. By April 1801 he had asked for a sabbatical and traveled with his half sister, Ulrike, to Dresden and then to Paris, which hosted many of Europe's first-rate intellectuals, artists, and scientists, including a large contingent from German-speaking states. One of the official reasons for the sabbatical was that Kleist desired to continue his studies in mathematics with cutting-edge French mathematicians. We have no proof that he seriously pursued this endeavor, but during his Paris stay he was introduced to many leading scientists and intellectuals.

At the end of November the siblings were on their way home. They had a serious disagreement in Frankfurt am Main, however, and parted company. Instead of returning to Berlin, Kleist went to Basel and Bern, where he had close contact with the Enlightenment author and politician

Heinrich Zschokke (1771–1848), who, in the precarious Swiss attempts to remain independent from Napoleon's France, sided with Napoleon.

It is around this time that Kleist first seriously considered becoming a writer. At twenty-four he had full access to his inheritance. He suggested to his fiancée that they buy a farm at the shores of Lake Thun and live off the land and his writing. Wilhelmine rejected the plan, and Kleist instead rented a house on the lake's Delosea island. From there he wrote his last letter to Wilhlemine, breaking off their engagement, in May 1802. Kleist's curious letters to Wilhlemine continue to draw attention from scholars interested in biography, gender studies, and the epistolary form. More than anything they document his plunge from a somewhat naïve belief in the ideals and conceptions of the early Enlightenment to a radically skeptical view of the world. According to him, the crucial turning point was what scholars have labeled his Kant crisis. In 1801 he wrote to Wilhelmine that after reading Kant, he was shattered by the newly found conviction that human intellect was unable to decide whether what we call truth is truly the truth or only appears so to us — a fundamental cognitive dilemma that would inform much of his writing.

In May 1802 Kleist was ill and in dire need of additional funds. Ulrike came to the rescue, and the siblings traveled to Erfurt and Weimar with Ludwig Wieland (1777–1819), the son of the famous Enlightenment writer Christoph Martin Wieland (1733–1813). One of the high points of Kleist's literary career was the praise and encouragement he received from the grand old man of German literature during his stay at Wieland's estate in Ossmannstedt in January and February 1803. In Wieland's estimation, Kleist's work on the tragedy *Robert Guiskard, Herzog der Normänner* (Robert Guiskard, Duke of the Normans, 1808) revealed a talent that was more capable than Goethe and Schiller of achieving the high dramatic goal of the new century: combining modernity and antiquity.

Back in Dresden, Kleist struggled unsuccessfully with these high expectations. In July 1803 he left again for Switzerland, this time with Ernst von Pfuel, without having completed the drama. The friends traveled on to Milan and in mid-October to Paris, where Kleist experienced a complete mental collapse. He denounced his talent, destroyed the *Guiskard* manuscript, and on 26 October set off for the north of France on another strange and as yet unexplained adventure: he traveled to St. Omer to join the French army and participate in the planned invasion of England. The French commander turned his application down, however, and sent him back to Paris. On 18 November, Kleist repeated his attempt to join the invasion troops. This time he was taken into custody for traveling without permission and without a passport. The Prussian ambassador in Paris finally issued him a passport, along with an order to return to Prussia immediately. On the way Kleist fell severely ill (if, indeed, he had ever recovered from his breakdown) and was taken in for several months by the physician Georg Wedekind in Mainz, a former Jacobin. This episode has been the cause of much speculation about the development of Kleist's political convictions. Wedekind tried to find a position for Kleist in the French administration of Koblenz. Kleist, however, continued on to Berlin, with stops at Weimar to visit Wieland, Frankfurt an der Oder, and Potsdam.

In Berlin, Kleist had to endure a severe reprimand from Karl Leopold von Kökeritz, the king's general adjutant, regarding his bohemian lifestyle, neglect of duties, and attempt to join a foreign service. On 31 July 1804, during his fourth audience, Kleist was promised a position in the Prussian civil service. In December he was introduced to Karl Freiherr von Stein zum Altenstein, who admitted him into the Department of Finance as an apprentice. In May 1805 Kleist traveled to Königsberg to continue his education. He worked in the East Prussian administration and attended lectures on finance by Christian Jakob Kraus (1753–1807), a follower of Adam Smith and Prussia's leading liberal economist. He also met with Wilhelmine, who by then was the wife of the philosopher Traugott Wilhelm Krug, Kant's successor at the University of Königsberg. In February 1806 Kleist applied for a six-month extension of his studies in Königsberg. In June, however, he asked to be dismissed, citing health problems.

At the end of October, after the catastrophic defeat at Jena and Auerstedt, the Prussian court fled to Königsberg. Kleist left for Dresden in January 1807 but was arrested by French troops in occupied Berlin and accused of espionage. He and his traveling companions, Karl Franz von Gauvain and Christoph Adalbert von Ehrenberg, were taken to Fort de Joux, near Pontarlier, and later to the prisoner of war camp at Châlons-sur-Marne. Kleist was released on 13 July 1807, after the peace of Tilsit, and arrived in Dresden on 31 August. There he rejoined Rühle von Lilienstern and Pfuel and was introduced to Adam Müller (1779–1829), who had just published Kleist's comedy, *Amphitryon*. In September the friends announced a plan to open a publishing business. The financial success of this enterprise hinged on their idea of publishing the *Code Napoléon* in the German-speaking countries. The request for a concession for the publishing house lingered, however, and instead, Kleist and Müller founded *Phöbus: Ein Journal für die Kunst*. The first issue appeared on 23 January 1808; it included a fragment of Kleist's verse drama *Penthesilea*. The request for the publishing concession was finally turned down in February. Kleist contributed many pieces to the monthly journal. In all, eleven issues were published; the last one, in the middle of March 1809, was followed by a turbulent quarrel between the two editors about what assets and debts remained.

In April, Kleist traveled to Austria with the historian Friedrich Christoph Dahlmann; they visited the battlefield of Aspen on 25 May, three days after the short-lived Austrian victory over Napoleon's troops. By this time Kleist was recklessly engaged in the clandestine anti-French resistance movement. He may have served as secret courier between Prussian and Austrian resistance groups, or he may have hoped to find employment in Vienna, as had other German intellectuals with anti-Napoleon sentiments. The luck of war was soon reversed with the French victory over Austria at the battle of Wagram, however, and Kleist remained in Prague. He applied for a concession to publish a patriotic weekly, *Germania,* which never materialized. In the meantime, his friends in Berlin heard rumors that he had died in Prague. Kleist's travels in 1809 and the specifics of his entanglement with the Prussian resistance remain unknown to this day.

At the beginning of 1810 Kleist was in Berlin. Stopping at Frankfurt an der Oder on the way, he had taken out a mortgage on his parental house for 500 Taler. After yet another mysterious trip, this one to Frankfurt am Main in January, he returned permanently to Berlin on 4 February. With the death of Queen Luise (1776–1810), Kleist lost the pension that had been arranged through his cousin Marie von Kleist. Instead, he gained a concession for an innovative daily newspaper that received special privileges from the government, including exclusive rights to police reports on crime, accidents, fires, and other interesting occurrences; in return, the paper was to publish official government announcements. The first issue of the *Berliner Abendblätter* appeared on 1 October. Aside from Kleist, who as editor also wrote many pieces himself, the contributors included such illustrious names as Adam Müller, Achim von Arnim, Clemens Brentano, Friedrich de La Motte-Fouqué, Friedrich Schulz, and other prominent intellectuals who resided in Berlin. In addition to its mixture of daily news and official announcements, the paper offered reviews and short articles on the theater and the arts, philosophical essays, and polemical exchanges. It seems to have been quite successful until the beginning of December, when the police ordered a stricter censorship after the *Abendblätter* published some articles that indirectly criticized Karl August von Hardenberg's economic reforms. The last issue appeared on 30 March 1811. It was preceded by tumultuous disagreements about the government's promises to support the newspaper.

Once again without a job and without funds, Kleist applied to Hardenberg for the editorship of the *Kurmärkisches Amtsblatt* or for readmittance into the Prussian civil service. He explained his situation in a letter to Prince Wilhelm von Preussen on 20 May and in a letter to King Friedrich Wilhelm III on 17 June. On 9 September he was granted an audience with the king, who ordered that Kleist be readmitted into the military as soon as war broke out. On 18–19 September, Kleist, who believed that war with France was imminent, visited his family in Frankfurt an der Oder and asked for money to purchase an officer's uniform. Instead, he was, according to his own report, scolded and told that he was a useless parasite. On 19 September he asked Hardenberg unsuccessfully for a private loan to cover the cost of a uniform. During the autumn he entered into a close friendship with Adolphine Sophie Henriette Vogel, who suffered from incurable cancer. On 20 November the couple spent the night at the Neue Krug, an inn at the Kleiner Wannsee near Berlin. Around 4:00 P.M. the next day Kleist shot Vogel and then himself.

Works

It is safe to assume that Kleist worked on at least three of his dramas during the time he spent on the island of Delosea in the late spring of 1802: *Robert Guiskard, Die Familie Schroffenstein* (The Schroffenstein Family), and *Der Zerbrochne Krug* (The Broken Pitcher, 1811). The first to appear was *Die Familie Schroffenstein*. It was published anonymously in 1803 by the Swiss publisher Gessner, whose son Kleist had befriended in Switzerland and who prepared the book together with Ludwig Wieland. While the play's basic plot follows Shakespeare's *Romeo and Juliet*, Kleist's drama of lovers torn apart by feuding families lacks the grand pathos of a central tragic hero. Rather, the plot's development is driven by erratic decisions and false motivations, confusion and misguided reactions, violent emotions and unintended consequences. The tragic catastrophe remains incomprehensible, and a pervasive sense of incomprehensibility and uncertainty is the play's central theme. It is, therefore, tempting to read the play as an exposition of Kleist's own metaphysical crisis that accompanied his abandonment of the secure virtues of self-improvement and ethics offered by early Enlightenment philosophy in favor of a radical skepticism that laments (and, at times, almost celebrates) the incomprehensible nature of the world, as well as the individual's inner feelings. Famous is the cave scene in act 5 (often read as a play within the play) in which the lovers Ottokar and Agnes exchange their clothes, resulting in a chain of mistaken identities that leads to their deaths.

Since Kleist destroyed the manuscript of his tragedy *Robert Guiskard, Herzog der Normänner* in 1803, we have only the ten scenes he published in the *Phöbus* in 1808. Without doubt, Kleist considered this attempt to reclaim the drama of Classical Greece (Sophocles, in particular) for the modern world his most ambitious undertaking — one that was meant to establish him as one of the premier German playwrights along with Goethe and Schiller. Judging from the fragment of 1808, Kleist had, indeed, mastered a grandiose language in verse form with sublime and monumental metaphorical imagery. It was not the language, but rather self-imposed demands vis-à-vis dramatic structure and plot that must have driven him into despair. Guiskard, the unbeaten duke of the Normans, is shown at a decisive moment during the siege of Byzantium. With superhuman heroism he denies the deadly illness (smallpox) that has befallen him and confronts his troops, who wish to return home, as well as his family, who attempt to betray him. Kleist used an article in Schiller's *Horen* as his main historical source, and, following the outlines of this account, the drama would most likely have ended with Guiskard's defeat in the manner of a tragedy of character. This possibility has prompted much speculation among Kleist scholars that Kleist may have intended to write an allegorical play about Napoleon.

Amphitryon: Ein Lustspiel nach Molière (Amphitryon: A Comedy after Molière) was written in 1805–1806 in Königsberg and published in 1807 by Arnold in Dresden. Adam Müller introduced the play in a foreword that interpreted it as a Romantic adaptation of the theology of immaculate conception. The effect was that many contemporaries and some scholars counted Kleist among the authors of Romantic Catholicism. Twentieth-century scholarship has clearly parted with this assumption, as is amply documented in Jeffrey Sammons's comprehensive analysis of the vast *Amphitryon* scholarship in this volume. In contrast to Molière's work, Kleist's adaptation of the classical myth of Jupiter's seduction of Alkmene by appropriating her husband's body deemphasizes the "galant amores" of the divine seducer and stresses the challenge posed to Alkmene's belief in the certainty of her innermost feelings. The witty dialogues reach into the realms of idealist philosophy of identity, as was much debated in post-Second World War existentialist scholarship. More-recent scholarship has focused on the equally fundamental questioning of the interdependencies of patriarchal and religious orders — political orders that arrange themselves and triumph at the end of the play, leaving Alkmene behind with her famous sigh: "Ach!"

If he had done nothing else, Kleist would still have to be counted among Germany's canonical authors for having written one of the country's few lasting comedies. He was inspired to write *Der Zerbrochne Krug* by seeing, in Switzerland in 1802, a copperplate engraving by Le Veau of *La Cruche Cassée,* a lost painting by Debucourt depicting a scene in a country court. Zschokke reported in 1842 that he, Kleist, and Ludwig Wieland promised each other that each would write a literary adaptation of the engraving: Zschokke a story, Wieland a satire, and Kleist a comedy. Kleist worked on his comedy in 1803 in Dresden and in 1805 in Berlin and completed it in Königsberg. The play was not published until 1811, but Goethe attempted to produce it at the Weimar theater as early as 2 March 1808. To Kleist's deep dismay, Goethe's production was a flop. It seems that Goethe had no means of doing justice to the comedy's analytical structure. Instead, he lamented that the one-act play had no dramatic plot and divided it into three acts with two intermissions, thus breaking the crucial analytical tension. The drama unfolds as comical double-talk interspersed with biblical, mythological, as well as erotic allusions that gradually reveal the judge Adam, who is to solve the mystery of Eve's broken pitcher and honor, as the culprit.

Also in 1808 Kleist's tragedy *Penthesilea* was brought out by the famous publisher Cotta in Tübingen. This one-act verse drama about the doomed love of Achilles and the Amazon queen Penthesilea contained, according to Kleist, the whole filth as well as the splendor of his soul; it turned out to be more intense in both style and content than most of his contemporaries could bear, but *Penthesilea* has become one of the most celebrated plays on the German stage. Achilles' and Penthesilea's feelings are deeply intertwined with the conflicting political and, hence, ethical orders of their respective states. At the end the play leaves no way out but a relapse to most basic forms of violent subjugation and possession. In a chain of deceptions and self-delusions Achilles is hunted down and killed by his love, who madly joins her dogs in devouring his body. Once she comes to understand that Achilles had challenged her only as a way of surrendering to her, Penthesilea dies of her grief with a grandiose last monologue, describing how she digs up a deadly feeling out of her dark sorrows and forges it in the heat of her bosom into a dagger that takes her life.

Das Kaethchen von Heilbronn oder Die Feuerprobe: Ein Grosses Historisches Ritterschauspiel (Kate of Heilbronn; or, The Test of Fire: A Great Historical Chivalric Drama) was published in 1810 by the Realschulbuchhandlung in Berlin and was performed in the spring of the same year in Vienna. The play offers precisely what the subtitle promises but with a Kleistian twist. Although it remains a Romantic historical chivalric drama with all the ingredients of a medieval fairy tale (secret trials, somnambulism, angels, mistaken identity of the king's daughter, prophetic dreams, happy ending, and so on), Kleist cannot help but introduce a number of countercurrents that expose the Romantic trappings, such as artificially assembled bodies of great beauty and a king who may have committed a rape. According to Kleist, Kaethchen's somnambular and seemingly passive pursuit of her love for the Ritter vom Strahl, which is based on an unquestioned belief in her innermost knowledge — paradoxically, her passivity is, therefore, absolutely determined and confident — is to be understood as the opposite of Penthesilea's active but self-doubting and ultimately tragic passion for Achilles.

Die Hermannsschlacht (The Battle of Teutoburg Forest) was not published until 1821, when it appeared in Ludwig Tieck's edition of Kleist's posthumous works published by Reimer in Berlin. Kleist wrote the patriotic play in the second half of 1808 and sent it to the poet and court secretary Heinrich Joseph von Collin in Vienna at the beginning of 1809, suggesting that a production of the drama by the Viennese theater would be timely, because it was written for the current political situation: Austria was about to enter into another war with France. Kleist uses elements from Tacitus's account of the victory of Hermann (in Latin, Arminius), leader of the Cheruscans, over the Roman general Varus at the battle of the Teutoburg Forest in 9 A.D. to compose a didactic propaganda play about the political and military techniques and ethical challenges of a total war of liberation. At least, this is how the play has been perceived by most critics. A closer reading, however, reveals that the drama offers little actual propaganda but, rather, an analysis of the political structures and workings of propagandistic warfare. Furthermore, as is often the case with Kleist, its surplus of horror and brutality, with which the absolute ethics of partisan warfare of liberation are portrayed, foreshadows the catastrophes that this new political and military ideology would ignite in the coming centuries (cf. Fischer 300–320).

There is much agreement among scholars that Kleist's other patriotic drama, *Prinz Friedrich von Homburg* (Prince Frederick of Homburg), written between 1809 and 1811, is his most mature and brilliant dramatic accomplishment. It, too, was first published in Tieck's 1821 edition. Kleist dedicated and sent it through Marie von Kleist to the Princess Amalie Marie Anne, wife of Prince Wilhelm of Prussia. It would not be performed in Prussia until it was staged in Breslau in 1821, however, for one scene raised objections from the Prussian elite: Prince Frederick — a Prussian officer, after all — faints at the sight of his open grave. Kleist had taken the plot from the memoirs of Frederick II but transformed Homburg into an ambitious young officer hungry for honor and fame and introduced Natalie, the duke's niece, as his love interest and an important political voice. The dramatic action is introduced by a somnambular dream scene that reveals the prince's realm of psychological desire, and Homburg's last words are: "Ein Traum, was sonst?" (1:709)[1] The drama is neither tragedy nor comedy, but, at its core, it experiments, as do many of Kleist's works, with interconnected notions of belonging, identity, and moral or heroic principles. Following his eagerness for personal honor, the prince has prematurely entered the battle and has thus prevented a total victory over the Swedish troops. A military court condemns him to die, and the prince breaks down in view of his imminent execution. He begs for his life and gains the support of the court's women. The duke leaves the decision in Homburg's own hands: he is to decide whether the judgment is right or wrong. Homburg finds the strength to affirm the court's judgment of his own free will, and, consequently, he can be pardoned. There has been much debate about the primary message of this play over the last 175 years: is it the inflexible law of the state that yields to the feelings and desires of the young prince's ambition, or is it the prince who matures and accepts the primacy of the honor of military law, or is it Natalie who manages to mediate two unsupportable male positions into a more practical and sustainable concept of personal desire and political honor?

Among his contemporaries Kleist's novellas and stories fared much better than his dramas; the same could probably be said about his reception by recent Kleist scholars, who have taken great pains to analyze his masterfully composed stories and novellas. Several of Kleist's prose narratives appeared first in popular journals such as the *Morgenblatt* and *Der Freimütige*. Others were most likely written to fill the pages of Kleist's own journals, *Phöbus* and the *Berliner Abendblätter*. They were collected in two volumes published by the Realschulbuchhandlung in Berlin in 1810 and 1811. "Michael Kohlhaas," "Die Marquise von O . . ." (The Marquise of O . . .) and "Das Erdbeben in Chili" (The Earthquake in Chile) made up the first volume; "Die Verlobung in St. Domingo" (The Engagement in Santo Domingo), "Das Bettelweib von Locarno" (The Beggar Woman of Locarno) "Der Findling" (The Foundling), "Die heilige Cäcilie oder die Gewalt der Musik" (St. Cecilia; or, The Power of Music), and "Der Zweikampf" (The Duel) filled the second volume.

Kleist's prose style is unusually innovative and original. The sentences are often long and complex but seem precise and economical. At the same time, they include often a kind of hidden "double-talk" — literary and biblical allusions and quotations, grotesque exaggerations and borrowings from contemporary trivial literature, sexual and political innuendo, and so on — that can implicitly question much of what the narrative voice is at pains to establish. It seems that these techniques of laconic irony escaped many of Kleist's contemporary readers, and they still offer quite a challenge today. For Kleist does not limit his probing perspectivist play to his fictional characters but extends it to his narrative voice and even to his reader. Often it is the minute scenic portrayal of actual occurrences and events that do the trick and force characters, narrator, and reader alike to reevaluate what seemed so clear and convincing just a few sentences before. Sometimes it is the precise choice of words in a character's monologue or dialogue or even in the descriptions and reflections of the narrator that opens everything up for debate and reevaluation.

Famous are the beginnings of Kleist's stories that offer, often hidden in compact and factual sentence structures, much of the tension that unfolds in the stories. Take, for example, the first sentence of "Der Zweikampf":

> Herzog Wilhelm von Breysach, der, seit seiner heimlichen Verbindung mit einer Gräfin, namens Katharina von Heersbruck, aus dem Hause Alt-Hüningen, die unter seinem Range zu sein schien, mit seinem Halbbruder, dem Grafen Jakob dem Rotbart, in Feindschaft lebte, kam gegen Ende des vierzehnten Jahrhunderts, da die Nacht des heiligen Remigius zu dämmern begann, von einer in Worms mit dem deutschen Kaiser abgehaltenen Zusammenkunft zurück, worin er sich von diesem Herrn, in Ermangelung ehelicher Kinder, die ihm gestorben waren, die Legitimation eines, mit seiner Gemahlin vor der Ehe erzeugten, natürlichen Sohnes, des Grafen Philipp von Hüningen, ausgewirkt hatte. (2:229)

The sentence seems to introduce a bureaucratic, chronicle-style narration. But every word, every apposition, every characterization, and every grammatical relation is purposely chosen, and the hardly noticeable narrative tension of the first sentence will unfold into the discovery of complex political, judicial, and religious structures. Just think of the awkward specification of time, simultaneously precise and vague: around the end of the fourteenth century, at the dawn of the night of the holy Remigius. Or why these colorful names, and what does it mean that Katharina "seemed" below rank?

Kleist's first sentences are surpassed only by some of his closing sentences. Take "Der Zweikampf" again: after a complicated plot about the justice and truth-value of the medieval institution of the duel, the emperor feels the need to change the empire's statutes:

> und sobald er nach Vollendung seiner Geschäfte in der Schweiz, wieder in Worms angekommen war, ließ er in die Statuten des geheiligten göttlichen Zweikampfs, überall wo vorausgesetzt wird, daß die Schuld dadurch unmittelbar ans Tageslicht komme, die Worte einrücken: "wenn es Gottes Wille ist." (2:261)

What a paradoxical law! Furthermore, one must wonder whether the clue to the whole story may lie in the otherwise superfluous piece of information offered in the last sentence: that the emperor had just returned from business in Switzerland, another famous literary place of "divine judgment" (Schiller's *Wilhelm Tell*) that did not go in favor of the crown.

More often than not, Kleist's stories are elaborations of particularly difficult or paradoxical philosophical questions or propositions. "Das Erdbeben in Chili," for instance, tackles the theodicy problem that had been raised again under the impression of the earthquake of Lisbon by Kant, among others. But the story of the forbidden love of Jeronimo and Josephe goes beyond the question of the possibility of a "deus malignus." Just when the couple and their illicit son seem to be saved from the brutal Catholic law that had condemned them to death, the story uses the post-earthquake situation to question Rousseau's optimistic assumptions about human nature once it is freed from societal orders. Finally, the story culminates in an exploration of the church's ideological staging of precisely these questions in order to reestablish its own power.

This paradoxical proposition introduces the story of "Michael Kohlhaas": "An den Ufern der Havel lebte, um die Mitte des sechzehnten Jahrhunderts, ein Roßhändler, namens *Michael Kohlhaas,* Sohn eines Schulmeisters, einer der rechtschaffensten zugleich und entsetzlichsten Menschen seiner Zeit" (2:9). How can Kohlhaas be one of the most virtuous and, at the same time, most dreadful men of his time? Kleist unfolds this proposition as a confrontation of two conflicting ethics. The horse trader Kohlhaas is wronged by aristocrats, who abuse their privileges in a way that threatens all commerce. Since the absolutist state offers no justice and no satisfaction — Kohlhaas's wife loses her life while petitioning the Brandenburg court — the merchant becomes a political rebel and forces the state, through terror and blackmail, to abide by the law, thus affirming the ethics of the merchant class within the political order of the absolutist state. Revenge has become the virtue of Kohlhaas's righteous rebellion. Kleist uses the occasion to shed some light on Luther's position vis-à-vis the peasants' rebellion, and he does not fail to illustrate the political identity of each player through his or her actions and motives, including religion and supernatural beliefs.

A similar question of politicized ethics and love unfolds in "Die Verlobung in St. Domingo," this time set within the paradigm of an anticolonial rebellion. In 1807 Kleist had been imprisoned in the same Fort Joux in the south of France where Toussaint L'Ouverture, the black leader of the Haitian war of independence, had died three years earlier. This is the first time that questions of belonging and identity within the constraints and complexities of a race-based colonial order are raised and explored in German literature. As usual, Kleist does not paint a black-and-white picture of the dangerous love of an officer of the French occupying army and a black rebel girl, as the officer is not really French but Swiss, and the girl is not really black but has a French father.

Questions of class, family, and ethics are also investigated in "Der Findling." A most virtuous man, the pious Roman merchant Piachi, who rescues a poor foundling from the plague to take his own dead son's place and inherit the family business, becomes a murderer. Piachi's belief in his ethical framework is shuttered to such an extent by the betrayal of his adopted son that even at the moment of his execution he is still driven by a lust for revenge and commits the most blatant blasphemy. The lie that comes to bear in this conflict between old father, young wife, and son lies within the structure of the family itself, as well as in the bigotry of the Catholic political order.

The interconnection of power and religion, as well as the functionality of art, are also explored in "Die heilige Cäcilie oder die Gewalt der Musik." In addition, this "legend of a legend" exposes the psychological drives of rebellion and counterrebellion. In a scene filled with erotic tension four Dutch brothers who are planning to raid a French convent in the aftermath of the Reformation fall victim to the power of music. Or is it a miracle performed by St. Cecilia herself to save the church? The brothers go insane and spend their days in praise of the mystery of the Holy Trinity. Or have they become holy themselves?

In a similar fashion, "Der Zweikampf," seemingly a fairy tale with a miracle and a happy ending, becomes a fairy tale of a fairy tale by laying bare some of the narrative and psychological structures of fairy-tale narration. The core question is whether God reveals, through an unexpected application of the judicial institution of the duel, the political truth of the story's intricate levels of manipulation and conflict, or whether the characters are saved from an arbitrary judgment by sheer luck.

The question of political orders and the uncanny is also the topic of Kleist's shortest story, "Das Bettelweib von Locarno." This little masterpiece of concentrated narration offers in a nutshell all that is to be said, theoretically and aesthetically, about a genre that was in Kleist's time and is today one of the most popular trivial narratives: the ghost story.

Finally, "Die Marquise von O . . ." presents the question of female and male pride and gendered dominance as a modern societal tale about one of the most drastic oppositional pairs conceivable: rape and immaculate conception. In this "moral tale" Kleist's propensity for philosophical double-talk and biblical, as well as erotic, allusions moves from the realm of skeptical irony as close to humoristic narration as he ever got.

Kleist's predilection for narrative puzzles, riddles, paradoxes, and political allusions is also quite evident in the more than thirty short anecdotes and episodes he wrote for the *Berliner Abendblätter*. Many of these often quite brief texts have hidden connotations that are only comprehensible if one considers their political context. To give one example, the anecdote "Mutterliebe" (Mother Love) tells of a mother in St. Omer in the north of France who sacrifices her life strangling a rabid dog that has just killed two of her children. If one remembers that Kleist had traveled to St. Omer to catch up with Napoleon, who was planning an invasion of Britain, the little anecdote seems to answer the question of the purpose of Kleist's mysterious trip, as well as the state of mind that prompted it.

Of great importance in current scholarship are Kleist's unorthodox philosophical essays. The most famous and important ones are "Über die allmähliche Verfertigung der Gedanken beim Reden" (On the Gradual Construction of Thought by Speech), a philosophy of language that not only anticipates much of today's pragmatic and structuralist language theories but also confronts the reader with the problem of intended and unintended consequences of speech-acts in a manner that is almost reminiscent of chaos-theoretical assumptions; "Über das Marionettentheater" (On the Marionette Theater), a carefully structured essay with numerous famous Kleistian images that, together with the short pieces "Betrachtungen über den Weltlauf" (Observations on the Way of the World) and "Von der Überlegung: Eine Paradoxe" (Of Reflection: A Paradox), seem to offer an ironic recapitulation and simultaneous dismissal of the whole project of idealist philosophy of history; "Brief eines Malers an seinen Sohn" (Letter from a Painter to His Son), "Brief eines Dichters an einen anderen" (Letter from One Poet to Another), and "Empfindungen vor Friedrichs Seelandschaft" (Sentiments while Viewing Friedrich's Seascape), which question some central philosophical foundations of late eighteenth-century aesthetic theory; and, finally, "Allerneuerster Erziehungsplan" (Newest Education Plan), which turns the foundation of Pestalozzi's pedagogical theory on its head.

Even this brief introduction into Kleist's life and work illustrates that a volume such as this companion book cannot attempt to do justice to all the works and all the questions that have been and are of interest to past and current readers and scholars. What it can do is to exemplify past and current modes of reading Kleist, summarize scholarly debates, point out consensus where it exists, provide intellectual and poetological contexts, and raise some specific and some broader questions that individual contributors find of particular interest today. The eleven articles, by some of the most recognized Kleist scholars on three continents, make no attempt at the accessibility or comprehensiveness of a textbook or a work of reference. They are not meant to serve as basic introductions for the novice reader of Kleist; rather, they provide the informed and curious reader with transparent approaches to the cutting edge of today's international Kleist scholarship.

A critical edition of Kleist's works does not exist. There are, however, three well-researched and reliable editions of his complete works and letters. Most scholars use the two-volume edition by Helmut Sembdner or the four-volume edition of the Deutscher Klassiker Verlag, which builds on Sembdner's work but offers extended commentaries. Occasionally, scholars quote from the unique edition currently being undertaken by Roland Reuß and Peter Staengle, who attempt to offer a text that comes as close to the original as possible and avoids modernizations and tacit corrections.

Notes

[1] Volume and page numbers refer to the Kleist edition listed in each essay's list of works cited. All other references in the text provide the author's name (for authors with more than one publication, also the year) and page number. Volume numbers and authors' names are omitted from the citations if they are obvious from the context. The plays are, at times, referenced by act, scene, and line: e.g., 1.4.201.

Works Cited

Fischer, Bernd. *Das Eigene und das Eigentliche: Klopstock, Herder, Fichte, Kleist. Episoden aus der Konstruktionsgeschichte nationaler Intentionalitäten.* Berlin: Schmidt, 1995.

Kleist, Heinrich von. *Sämtliche Werke und Briefe.* 2 vols. Ed. Helmut Sembdner. Munich: Hanser, 1984.

Heinrich von Kleist's Works

Die Familie Schroffenstein: Ein Trauerspiel in fünf Aufzügen. Bern & Zurich: Gessner, 1803. Tr. Mary J. and Lawrence M. Price as *The Feud of the Schroffensteins.* London: Badger, 1916.

Amphitryon: Ein Lustspiel nach Molière. Ed. Adam H. Müller. Dresden: Arnold, 1807. Tr. Marion Sonnenfeld as *Amphitryon: A Comedy.* New York: Ungar, 1962.

Penthesilea: Ein Trauerspiel. Tübingen: Cotta, 1808. Trans. Humphry Trevelyan as *Penthesilea,* in *Five German Plays,* vol. 2 of *The Classic Theatre.* Ed. Eric Bentley. London: Mayflower, 1959; New York: Doubleday, 1959.

Phöbus: Ein Journal für die Kunst. Ed. Kleist and Adam H. Müller. Nos. 1–10, Dresden: Gärtner, 1808; nos. 11–12, Dresden: Walther, 1808.

Erzählungen, vols. 1–2. Berlin: Realschulbuchhandlung, 1810–11 — comprises vol. 1, "Michael Kohlhaas: Aus einer alten Chronik," Tr. J. Oxenford as "Michael Kohlhaas," in *Tales from the German.* London: Chapman & Hall, 1844; New York: Harper, 1844; "Die Marquise von O . . .," Tr. Heinrich Roche as "The Marquise of O . . .," in *Great German Stories.* London: Benn, 1929; "Das Erdbeben in Chili," Tr. Norman Brown as "Earthquake in Chili," in *The Blue Flower.* New York: Roy, 1946; vol. 2, "Die Verlobung in St. Domingo," Tr. Martin Greenberg as "The Engagement in Santo Domingo," in *The Marquise of O—, and Other Stories.* New York: Criterion, 1960; "Das Bettelweib von Locarno," Tr. Ernest N. Bennett as "The Beggar Woman of Locarno," in *German Short Stories.* London: Oxford, 1934; "Der Findling," Tr. Martin Greenberg as "The Foundling," in *The Marquise of O—, and Other Stories.* New York: Criterion, 1960; "Die heilige Cäcilie oder Die Gewalt der Musik, Eine Legende," Tr. J. Oxenford as "St. Cecilia; or, The Power of Music: A Catholic Legend," in *Tales from the German.* London: Chapman & Hall, 1844; New York: Harper, 1844; and "Der Zweikampf," Tr. Martin Greenberg as "The Duel," in *The Marquise of O—, and Other Stories.* New York: Criterion, 1960.

Das Käthchen von Heilbronn oder Die Feuerprobe: Ein großes historisches Ritterschauspiel. Berlin: Realschulbuchhandlung, 1810. Tr. Elijah B. Impey as *Kate of Heilbronn,* in *Illustrations of German Poetry.* London: Simpkin, Marshall, 1841. Tr. Frederick E. Pierce as *Kaethchen of Heilbronn or The Test of Fire: Great Historical Chivalric Drama in 5 Acts,* in *Romantic Drama,* vol. 2 of *Fiction and Fantasy of German Romance: Selections from the German Romantic Authors, 1790–1830 in English Translation.* New York: Oxford, 1927.

Berliner Abendblätter. Ed. Kleist. First quarter, nos. 1–77, Berlin: Hitzig, 1810; second quarter, nos. 1–76, Berlin: Kunst- und Industrie-Comptoir, 1811.

Der Zerbrochne Krug: Ein Lustspiel. Berlin: Realschulbuchhandlung, 1811. Tr. J. Krumpelmann as *The Broken Jug: A Comedy. Poet Lore,* 45 (1939): 146–209.

Germania an ihre Kinder. N.p., 1813.

Das erwachte Europa. Berlin: Achenwall, 1814.

Hinterlassene Schriften. Ed. Ludwig Tieck. Berlin: Reimer, 1821 — includes *Die Hermannsschlacht: Ein Drama; Prinz Friedrich von Homburg: Ein Schauspiel,* Tr. Francis Lloyd and William Newton as *Prince Frederick of Homburg,* in *Prussia's Representative Man.* London: Trübner, 1875; Tr. Hermann Hagedorn as *The Prince of Homburg,* in *The German Classics of the Nineteenth and Twentieth Centuries,* vol. 4, ed. Kuno Francke and W. G. Howard. New York: German Publication Society, 1913; and "Fragment aus dem Trauerspiel Robert Guiskard, Herzog der Normänner."

Gesammelte Schriften. 3 vols. Ed. Ludwig Tieck. Berlin: Reimer, 1826.

Politische Schriften und andere Nachträge zu seinen Werken. Ed. Rudolf Köpke. Berlin: Charisius, 1862.

Werke: Kritisch durchgesehene und erl. Gesamtausgabe. 5 vols. Ed. E. Schmidt, G. Minde-Pouet, and R. Steif. Leipzig: Bibliographisches Institut, 1904–1905.

Sämtliche Werke und Briefe. 2 vols. Ed. Helmut Sembdner. Munich: Hanser, 1985.

Sämtliche Werke und Briefe in vier Bänden. 4 vols. Ed. Ilse-Marie Barth et al. Frankfurt a.M.: Deutscher Klassiker Verlag, 1987–97.

Sämtliche Werke. Ed. Roland Reuß and Peter Staengle. Frankfurt a.M.: Stroemfeld/Roter Stern, 1988–.

Critical Approaches

Jupiterists and Alkmenists: *Amphitryon* as an Example of How Kleist's Texts Read Interpreters

Jeffrey L. Sammons

E VEN BY KLEIST'S standards of misfortune, *Amphitryon* seems to have been born under an unlucky star. Published, as the first of his works to appear under his name, by his friends while he was in a French prison, it was sold, in his own opinion, well below its value, having been thrust on a publisher by Gottfried Körner with a claim that the imprisoned author was in need of support (Sembdner 1984, 133–34). Of Kleist's five preserved comments on the play, four deal with the financial aspect (Sembdner 1969, 33–34). Interpretation does not commonly stress the fact that Kleist was virtually destitute throughout his creative years, a dependent of his relatives to a degree that was damaging to his self-esteem. It has long seemed to me that despite his intermittent suicidal moods and the existential pathos of his last days, if some congenial no-bleman had provided him with shelter, sustenance, and cultivated companionship on his estate, he might have managed much longer. The dearth of authorial guidance to our interpretive work is characteristic of Kleist generally; in the Heimeran series of authors' commentaries on their own works, the Kleist volume just cited is the slenderest. It is impossible to follow his literary and cultural reading exactly, which sometimes leads to inflated claims for his erudition and memory for texts.

Amphitryon appeared with a commentary by Adam Müller, who, in the flush of his newfound Catholic faith, gave it a Christological interpretation, which, in turn, contributed to Goethe's distaste for it — he used a copy of it for wrapping paper (Sembdner 1984, 147; see Grathoff 322). This apprehension long endured (Wegener 32), even echoing into more recent times (see, for example, Milfull 11; Zimmermann 226–40). Thomas Mann was not mistaken to characterize it as "gräßlich und beleidigend" and to charge Goethe's recoil from the pathological Kleist with a petulance inconsistent with his own imaginative range (Müller-Seidel 1967, 52, 67–68).[1] While the publication aroused some interest in the literary community, it came to be ignored, and its premiere did not occur for nearly a century, in 1899; thus, it has the shortest stage history of all of Kleist's dramas (see Reeve 53–77), and to my knowledge it has never been performed in the United States, though it has had some embarrassing musical-comedy successors. It was long thought to be unplayable (Wegener 42–45). To be sure, it is difficult to cast; as with Shakespeare's *Comedy of Errors*, a literal rendition would require as actors two sets of identical twins. Otherwise, considerable suspension of disbelief is required of the audience.

In addition, the work comes before the public as a translation, "Ein Lustpiel nach Molière" (Kleist 1:377). Molière's play, though not one of his most canonical, was well known to literary connoisseurs of the time; what was so important about a translation? When leafing through it, one must get well into act 2 before realizing that it is a good deal more than a translation or adaptation. Once Kleist's ingenuity had been grasped, criticism took the opportunity to value his German depth and spirituality at the expense of the alleged French shallowness and frivolity of Molière's court entertainment. This was still the view of Thomas Mann (while claiming to know nothing about Molière; Müller-Seidel 1967, 52–53); only relatively recently has German criticism found ways to rehabilitate Molière's work, lately in its critically ideological dimension (Szondi; Jauss 1981; Höller).

But most disconcerting has been an enduring resistance to interpretation. In 1979 a work of 300 printed — or, rather, typed — pages was entirely devoted to the history of *Amphitryon* criticism (Wegener); and after twenty more years of labor, we now have a wide-ranging, garrulous, 450-page effort recapitulating many of the problems and proposing to set them right at last, not least "um den großen Teil der Kleistliteratur beiseite zu schieben" (Fetscher 83). Perhaps we should rejoice at this indeterminability; after all, it is the infinite interpretability of texts that justifies the permanent institution of literary scholarship. "There never can be too many prayers," Kernan once remarked, "even if some of them are mumbled" (39). One might think of Wellbery's demonstration of the availability of *Das Erdbeben in Chili* to a variety of contemporary theoretical modes. But in view of the fact that Kafka is constantly and relevantly adduced in the discourse about Kleist (see Furst), one might as well think of *The Commentators' Despair*, the title Corngold gave to his arrangement, in alphabetical disorder, of the conflicting and contradictory interpretations of *Die Verwandlung* (by probably unconscious analogy, Földényi has recently sequenced ninety-six Kleistian motifs on the same principle). The problem is not peculiar to *Amphitryon;* Ribbat remarked of Kleist studies in general: "'Anything goes' oder 'Rien ne va plus'" (283). In the same vein, De Man observed of the endless discourse about the dialogue on the marionette theater:

> The spectacle of so much competence and attention producing so little result certainly puts to the test any attempt to add one more reading to those that have already been undertaken. More often than not the diversity that becomes manifest in the successive readings of a text permits one to determine a central crux that works as a particularly productive challenge to interpretation. Not so with *Marionettentheater;* this brief narrative [*sic*] engenders a confusion all the more debilitating because it arises from the cumulative effect produced by the readings. (271)

A reviewer of Wegener's survey commented mockingly that his "cosmopolitan perspective" had "apparently crippled Wegener's ability to contribute anything significant of his own to the issues of reading *Amphitryon*" (Leonard Schulze in Erdman 340). But this strikes me as an utterly reasonable and unastonishing consequence of the experience. It seems that we cannot take step one in the interpretive process: collectively agree on the simplest questions or the superficial meaning of the text.

For example, what is its genre? Most seem to agree that it is a drama; but is it a comedy, as Kleist's subtitle clearly states, "erhaben-heiter, metaphysisch-versöhnlich" (Nordmeyer 1946, 6)? Or should we just disbelieve Kleist's designation (Wegener 216) and declare it a tragedy of Alkmene, a view that seems first to have been proposed by Heinrich Meyer-Benfey in 1911 (Wegener 42)? Or is it a tragicomedy, the term that Plautus waggishly coined for his progenitor text, thus not comic but *potentially* tragic (Guthke 121–22; cf. Wegener 87)? Then: who is the hero, or protagonist? One of my eminent teachers once astonished us by declaring that a first task of interpretation was to establish who is the good guy and who is the bad guy. Contemplating Kleist makes this precept much less simple-minded than may at first appear. Most observers agree, with some exceptions or modifications (Nordmeyer 1946, 353–58; cf. Wegener 159–71; Michelsen 125; Guthke 120), that the hero of *Amphitryon* is not Amphitryon, an "eitle[r] Laffe" and "Hahnrei" (Fischer 66) whose "bare-faced dictatorship" (Allan 8) the drama exposes. Is, then, Alkmene the heroine, as was once widely thought and still often is (Lange 30)? Should not the drama have been named for her, as was Euripides' lost tragedy (Hölscher 114–16; Silz 47–48, 51)? Or, as came to be suggested, notably by Ryan, is the hero — or, at least, the elevating and educative figure — Jupiter? This view has been much disputed but continues to live on in the Reclam commentary (Bachmaier 61) and the new critical edition (Kleist 1:930, 968). Finally, if the annunciation of the birth of Herkules is not Christological, what might it mean, and how are we to read Alkmene's final "Ach!"? I should think that no other syllable in the history of German letters has generated such a corpus of incompatible exegesis; Greenberg's "Ah!" (84) cannot, of course, capture the overtones.

The history of criticism is not completely chaotic; the modes come in waves: nationalistic, idealistic, existentialist, close reading. But the 1960s brought an attempt at a marked revaluation: Alkmene, long revered as a figure of pure feeling and resolute integrity whom nobody, as Wegener has pointed out (194), had thought of as guilty, came to be regarded as the butt of the comedy: narrowly fixated on marriage, in empiricist false consciousness wrongly idolizing her husband, and in need of elevation of her spiritual horizon by Jupiter. The perspectives of reading the text came to be defined by this difference to such a degree that I began to suggest to students that interpreters could be divided, even retrospectively, into Jupiterists and Alkmenists. Silz, for example, can appear in this light as an Alkmenist, as can Graham, basically; Arntzen and Jancke as Jupiterist; Thomas Mann, while typically ambiguous, tends to the Jupiterist side when he treats Alkmene as childish (Sembdner 1967, 77). The distinction affected the generic reading: the Jupiterists tended to the comic tone, the Alkmenists to the tragic (Silz again, and, in a modified way, Guthke). This duality may have come to be less noticeable in recent criticism, which has been refined into esoteric theoretical contexts rather large for Kleist's intellectual resources and mental furniture. Yet there are still echoes of the debate, and it is indicative that Allan opened his recent general study with a reference to the dispute between Ryan and Wittkowski that made the distinction notorious (1). Wegener, for example, came down on the Alkmenist side (212–13); Jauss (1979, 226 and n.) is explicitly Alkmenist, while Schulze seems to take the Alkmenist line when he places her in the tradition of the balanced, harmonious beautiful soul (249). Stephens, an Alkmenist sympathetic to her suffering, logically sees her role as belonging to "a tragedy encapsulated within a comic context" (75–76). Nölle, on the other hand, who thinks that Jupiter steps out of his role for Alkmene's sake in order to comfort her for Amphitryon's failures as a husband, seems quite Jupiterist (171, 173), as are Oellers, who believes that Alkmene has been enriched by her experience (72), and Bachmaier, who gets quite impatient at her mulish inability to grasp Jupiter's superior claim (47). Allan, who finds Alkmene mistaken for supposing herself perfectly in love with her husband and blames her for asserting "the reality of an unreal husband in order to deny the existence of a real god," is, at any rate, not very Alkmenist (8, 123), and Gustafson, by charging Alkmene with reliance on rational rather than spontaneous use of language and, thus, failing to recognize the transcendent, is subtly not Alkmenist. The translator Greenberg is distinctly Jupiterist in a manner that suggests influence from Ryan (xxxi–xxxv). To what extent these differences indicate gender biases on the part of the critics is a question I leave to others, though it is interesting to see Fetscher argue that the *Alkmenists*, at least of the past, are the patriarchal ones, insofar as they ascribe to Alkmene "alle Klischees, welche im Patriarchat gängige Münze sind: Naturverhaftung, aber ohne Erotik, Empfängnis in Unschuld, Heimat und Herz ohne Körper, Unschuld in der Fügsamkeit, Intuition, aber nie Intellekt" (151).

In an appropriate spirit of intimidated trepidation, I should like to suggest how some of these issues appear to me as a nonspecialist observer. This will be more of a commentary than an interpretation; since originality in this case seems virtually impossible, or at least beyond my powers, I shall keep a persistent eye on a representative portion of the extant criticism. One good place to begin would be at the beginning, with the appearance of Sosias and his confrontation with his double, Merkur. This beginning is already an example of the insecurities that beset interpretation. That it closely follows the base text in Molière need not concern us much, since Kleist shows himself quite able to adapt Molière when it suits him. Somewhat more of a concern is the generic question. We seem to be in quite conventional comedic territory here, low comedy at the expense of the low-born. While a recent effort has been made to see Sosias intertextually, as a Bakhtinian carnivalesque figure who restores the Hanswurst role driven from the German stage in the preceding generation (Zeyringer), there has been a recurring interpretive strain that takes a contemptuous view of him as fatuously vain, materialistic, and, above all, cowardly, dwelling on a moral level that contrasts with the elevated realm of Amphitryon, Alkmene, and, presumably, the gods (e.g., Nölle 163–64; see also Fetscher 194–200, where Sosias is charged with failing to achieve Hegel's master-slave dialectic). Even worse things have been said about him: that he yields to force like the German people under Hitler (Nordmeyer 1947, 123) or, worst of all for today's critical fashions, that he does not understand the problem of language (Schulze 256). But it seems to me, as it has occasionally seemed to others, that one might take a friendlier view of him. It is true that his habit is to keep his head down and his rear covered, but this may not be a contemptible posture. Kleist was by no means an unambiguous admirer of heroism. At the age of nineteen he grieved at the inhumane killing the military profession required, and at twenty-one, denouncing military discipline as tyrannical, he abandoned the career as incompatible with his humane values (Kleist 4:18, 27). One might think not only of Prince Friedrich, paralyzed by the fear of death, but of even more dubious fighting men such as Count F . . . in *Die Marquise von O . . .* or Count Jakob in *Der Zweikampf,* or, contrarily, of Michael Kohlhaas's guerrillas making fools of the regular troops sent out against them or of Herrmann's victory of mind over muscle. As early as 1884 Wilhelm Scherer claimed that Kleist polemicized against stoic heroism more than anyone in his time (as cited by Fetscher 201–2). It may be true, as Fetscher suggests, that Kleist had a vision of an ideally pure heroic age, but there is a large gap in his world between wishing something were so and the way it really is. The ideal is only a memory maintained in myth, and it becomes grotesque in reality (Wickert 50).

As for the problem of language, it is true that Sosias is a literalist, as has been long observed of Kleist himself, and it is the play with words, especially his desperate efforts to protect his first-person pronoun, that supplies much of the comedy of the drama. But this literalism enables him to understand that something is happening that he does not understand; he takes the incomprehensible as reality (Oellers 75). With this incomplete understanding he is able to obtain a more adequate grasp of the situation than Amphitryon, preoccupied with his inflated sense of self, can achieve. It is true that what Sosias tells Amphitryon about the encounter with Merkur seems nonsensical — it is not intentionally hard to understand, in order to bait Amphitryon (Vohland 328) — it *is* hard to understand, as reports in Kleist tend to be, but if Amphitryon were to listen as his situation deteriorates, he might more quickly perceive the enormity of what has befallen him (see Arntzen 218). When witnessing Alkmene's bewildered reception of the real Amphitryon, Sosias thinks at first, "In ihrem Oberstübchen ists nicht richtig" (2.2.860), but then he gets it: "Was über Euch verhängt ist? Ihr seid doppelt, / Amphitryon vom Stock ist hier gewesen" (2.2.901–2); in the subsequent scene 2.3 with Charis, he sees the parallel at once. It is quite some time before Amphitryon is able to penetrate to this much cognition. The relationship of Amphitryon and Sosias is a traditional hierarchical one of master and servant; the great Amphitryon has no readiness to attend to Sosias, at least until he is forced to, reacting instead with anger and threats, while Sosias copes with apparent subservience, evasion, and partially veiled sauciness. It is probably true that he is not, as is sometimes suggested, a sort of "Jacobin" or anticipatory class-conscious proletarian, but he does defend himself (cf. Fischer 63). Nor does it seem to me fair to imply that he easily and cravenly gives up his identity to Merkur's force. I agree, rather, with Stephens: "Once

Sosias becomes aware that Merkur will enforce his claim to their joint identity by physical violence, he declares himself willing to renounce it, but in reality does nothing of the kind. He simply reverts to being himself whenever Merkur is not about" (86).[2]

As for Merkur, it seems that most interpreters would prefer to avoid him. Wegener reports (220) that Müller-Seidel (1961) was the first to give Merkur much attention and suggests a reason for the avoidance: Merkur poses a problem to any interpretation "welche die Bedeutung des Stücks darin sieht, daß sich in ihm das Göttliche in seiner Wahrheit erschließt" (222). God or not, of all of Kleist's characters he is one of the most villainous; he seems to resemble Shakespeare's Iago in unmotivated evil. Bored and resentful at his role of enabler of Jupiter's amour, he vents his brutality on the least and most vulnerable of all the beings on the scene. Although he himself is a kind of subaltern servant, treated as a utensil by his master, he rudely and meanly rejects Sosias's reasonable proposal that he acknowledge their fraternal condition. Fetscher, one of the few to comment at any length on Merkur, points out that Kleist coarsens Molière's portrayal, reducing Mercure's readiness to dialogue and playfulness, adding his boredom, and escalating his malice to malignance (52–61). Kleist seems rather to have drawn the tone from his alleged model Johann Daniel Falk, where Merkur says to Sosias: "Dem Übel ist leicht abzuhelfen . . . Ich schlag dich todt" (as cited by Sembdner 1974, 39). The inference that the interpreters seem to want to evade is that Merkur comes out of the same realm as Jupiter, whatever that may be. If Jupiter is divine and transcendent, so is Merkur, who, for all his grouchiness, serves Jupiter faithfully by keeping Sosias and then Amphitryon out of the palace, and who has also negotiated with the goddess of Night as the "gute Göttin Kupplerin" (1.5.519) to lengthen the night of Jupiter's bliss. Fetscher argues: "In Haltung, Gefühls- und Bewußtseinslage hat Kleist die beiden Götter weit voneinander abgesetzt" (54). But this is not logical. It seems to me, rather, that the radically malevolent Merkur is an index to the realm from which Jupiter also comes.

The persistent lack of consensus about Jupiter is intimately involved with the lack of consensus about Kleist's attitude toward religion, which has ranged from Müller's Catholicizing through ascriptions of modified, heterodox Christianity (Stephens 72–74) or a pantheism (or pseudo-pantheism, Silz 60) of the age of Goethe, primarily propagated by Jupiter himself, to a nonreligious or even antireligious posture regarding religion as superstition (cf. Prigge-Kruhoeffer 13), even to paganism and nihilism (cf. Maass 38, 350). The question is difficult to address in a brief space. My own suspicion is that Kleist's religious views — or, perhaps, feelings — were not entirely stable and came to expression in contradictory ways. Gearey may be incautious when he states: "Kleist is the first writer in German literature to challenge seriously the long-standing concept of the benevolence of the spirit that rules the world" (37–38), but there seems to me little doubt that he is outside the periphery of the common environmental discourse. As regards *Amphitryon*, I am not persuaded by those who, beginning in the 1960s, treated it as a drama of religious education in which all are punished with blindness for having forgotten the gods (see Wegener 108–27, esp. 113), and hold rather with those who find the religious tone of the drama critical and skeptical, as Wittkowski has "mit scharfzüngiger Vehemenz" (Wegener 145).

In the first place, it is arguable that no one in Thebes really believes in the gods (see Wegener 169). Thebans dwell within inherited conventions and expressions; they know the old stories of Jupiter's amorous visitations but have great difficulty grasping that such a thing might happen in the here and now, just as no one in "Die Marquise von O . . ." believes in virgin births, at least not in our world. When Amphitryon asks: "O ihr allmächtgen Götter, die die Welt / Regieren! Was habt ihr über mich verhängt?" (2.1.899–900), it is just a conventional turn of phrase, and he silences Sosias, who tries to give him a hint; even when he intuits something miraculous — "Doch heute knüpft der Faden sich von jenseits / An meine Ehre und erdrosselt sie" (2.2.910–11) — he is characteristically self-involved. For some time in the play, before comprehension dawns, these utterances are a form of dramatic irony that amuses the knowing audience. Alkmene, too, it has been argued, is basically indifferent to the gods (Michelsen 133). Jupiter chastises her for interposing an image of Amphitryon in her prayer, but since Jupiter cannot be gazed upon with mortal eyes and, therefore, can only be metonymically imaged, what is she to do? One could as easily say that she worships Jupiter by imagining him in the form of the man she loves and honors. Furthermore, one might ask what Jupiter is doing, and why. Although he is, presumably, the creator and governor of the world, he is unfulfilled and forlorn, unsatisfied by the company of Olympians such as Merkur — and, one supposes, the unmentioned consort Juno — and, therefore, longs for the love of his beautiful creature Alkmene and her acknowledgment of it, differentiated and elevated from her attachment to her husband.

What is going on here? Whether or not Kleist intended to satirize the quasi-Goethean pantheism, as Mommsen has pungently argued (19–22), may be undecidable, but the aporias that attend its articulation effectively deconstruct it. The notion that God is identical with his creation yet can disengage his creatures and stand over against them logically requires a

Plotinian or Cabbalistic doctrine of emanations, requiring in turn, if ascribed to Kleist, that he be made into some species of mystic. Stephens, in an expansion of what Wittkowski called Jupiter's "Weltanschauungspropaganda" (1972, 163), finds his claims for himself a sequence of incoherent, opportunistic devices to oblige Alkmene to acknowledge him,

> a verbal ordeal that will see him invoke, by turns, the divine presence in the whole of creation; the creator's separation from his creation; the divine privilege of jealousy at the conduct of his creation; the creator's need to be loved by his creation; indeed, to love himself in the love of his creation; and the divine right to tell his creation to be silent when it says something he does not like. . . . The self-representations of Kleist's Jupiter read like a haberdasher's catalogue of the concepts of the divine then in fashion. (88, 95)

Wilson finds that Jupiter gets himself into a "preposterous position" (106), and Jauss argues that Jupiter's pantheistic argument "führt sich selbst ad absurdum" (1979, 243). Wegener has pointed out, furthermore, that there is no evidence of adherence to pantheism on Kleist's part outside the text of *Amphitryon* (26). Doctrinally, Jupiter *is* Amphitryon; he says so (3.11.2293) yet impersonates him — the doubling is only an optical illusion — in order to cuckold him, and if Alkmene is also an element of his being, his infatuation with her is with himself and, therefore, narcissistic. "If he were the locus of full being," Schulze observes, "he would not find it necessary to have his identity mirrored to him" (260). God, it seems, is inordinately neurotic. This is a less comic than distressing possibility, perhaps surpassed only by the notion played with in the *Nachtwachen von Bonaventura,* almost exactly contemporaneous with *Amphitryon,* that God might exist but be crazy.[3] This might be the ultimate horror story. In the past, Gundolf blamed Kleist for these effects, because the complaint of loneliness is inappropriate to a god: "Gott hat als Gott keinen Charakter. . . . [s]o hat [Kleist] damit Gott Vater und Jupiter zugleich zerstört" (85–86); a good example, as it seems to me, of the obfuscating effect of viewing Kleist through Goethean eyes. It would be more just to accept the drama's "basic doubt concerning the governance of the universe" (Lindsay 108). Földényi argues, in an acute perspectivization, that God, by suddenly breaking into the sphere of humans and making sport of them, undermines belief in his existence (166). It is, in any case, a mistake to force Kleist into congruence with the Classical-Romantic environment: "It is in the disappearance of a regular relationship between Man and the higher reality that Kleist differs from the mainstream of German Romanticism" (Reeves 55).

The idea that Jupiter might be malign is not new. In an old but elegant essay it was argued that Kleist may have regarded God himself as evil (Prigge-Kruhoeffer 46). Silz asserted that "these gods are morally bankrupt" with "a sinister quality" and that the "major reason for the inconsistencies in Kleist's play is the shifting — not to say shifty — character of . . . its god-villain, Jupiter" (53, 65, 60). It seems the gods can be rescued only by claiming that they are outside any human moral system, so that outrage is irrelevant (cf. Nordmeyer 1946, 13, 18). A malign Jupiter is well established in Molière interpretation, with a concept derived from Descartes: "The world of Amphitryon is ruled by a capricious *mauvais génie* who has the power and the will to deceive us" (Gossman 205). Jupiter wants to be loved "*for no reason*. . . . Such a 'love' as this is inwardly contradictory and self-destructive" (Gossman 209; the argument is pursued by Neumann). Jauss has interpreted Jupiter's desire to be loved for himself as a form of an "Unterscheidung, aus der sich die moderne Identitätsproblematik der Amphitryon-Version des deutschen Idealismus ableiten läßt" (1979, 226), but I agree with Fischer that the identity problem has been overinterpreted (62) and am inclined to look in a somewhat different direction.

Jupiter exhibits less the attributes of a divine being than of a ruler of a feudal German state of Kleist's time, behaving like a "wahrer Fürst," as Wittkowski sardonically observes (1969, 51). He resembles what in the authoritarian usage of the time was called a *Landesvater,* a father to his principality. Characteristic of the posture is the demand to be obeyed and revered *and* to be loved, like God above and the *Familienvater* below. It is a neurosis of power, born of the consciousness of its fragility in an age of revolution. Allan demotes Jupiter even further, to "a sophisticated, but essentially egocentric, 'Don Juan' figure" (113). Such observations have long been made of Molière's Jupiter — for example, by Jauss, who remarks that he is a modern ruler, demanding acknowledgment, not just submission (cf. 1981, 125), and that "Molière hat den klassischen Jupiter zu einem absoluten Souverain mit modernem Bewußtsein verjüngt" (1979, 228). Nordmeyer's denomination of the style of Kleist's Jupiter as that of the *grand seigneur* (1946, 168) is a commonplace in Molière interpretation (Gossman 201, 211). Jauss sees implicit ideological-historical implications prefigured in Molière: "die beginnende Polarisation zwischen der repräsentativen Öffentlichkeit des Ancien Régime und der Sphäre einer Autonomie des Privaten, die für die sich bildende bürgerliche Gesellschaft vor allem in der Intimität von Liebesehe und Familie verkörpert ist" (1979, 230). I do not mean to impose an explicitly dissident political discourse on the play, but the metonymy of the ideologies of religious and political domination might occur easily to the imagination of a skeptical outsider such as Kleist; or, as Schulze puts it, the drama can be seen as "a meditation on the foundations of the state" (263; cf. Wittkowski 1969, 57). The melding of secular and divine personae might seem predictive of the alliance of throne and altar that, within a decade, will be installed in the Metternichian system.

It will no doubt be clear from my skeptical view of Jupiter that I count myself among the Alkmenists. I do, indeed, see Alkmene as the heroine of the drama and the node of the tragic vector of the tragicomedy, and I find the condescending and amused view of her on the part of some of the Jupiterists quite unintelligible. It may derive in part from a confidence that Kleist cannot have had an elevated view of womankind, which, in turn, may derive from a reading of his correspondence with his alleged fiancée Wilhelmine von Zenge, in which he is overbearing, manipulative, patronizing, and distrustful, while demanding absolute trust. In my opinion, the Kleist of this correspondence, requiring the impossible from her and imposing an imaginary notion of marriage (Lange 138), is not patriarchal or misogynist but preposterous; I sometimes recommend it, along with Kafka's not dissimilar correspondences with his alleged fiancées, to students as a manual of how not to get married, while pretending, even to oneself, that this is what one wishes to do: "at least as involved with subverting the dialogue he longed for as with establishing it" (Newman 102). Földényi reads a subtext of panic: "was wird sein, wenn sich diese Sehnsucht tatsächlich erfüllt und er sie heiraten muß?" (230). It is possible to interpret this disjunction as symptomatic of the strains of Kleistian discourse: the correspondence "embodies the dilemma of the modern subject: as it gains autonomy, it simultaneously suffers from the loss of connectedness with the world around it; as it seeks connection, it fears a loss of its own integrity. . . . From the beginning . . . his discourse and his actions contradict his goal of establishing intimacy through dialogue" (Newman 103–4).

In one of those embarrassing moments that sometimes attend the awarding of literary prizes, Monika Maron, on receiving the Kleist Prize in 1992, explained how difficult she found it to get past that correspondence to any appreciation of him, indicating only at the end of her acceptance speech an inkling that something rather different might be found in *Penthesilea*. But we need not turn to Kleist's superheroine to see how much strength and autonomy he was able to imagine into female figures: Michael Kohlhaas's wife giving her life in an effort to exact a civil and lawful alternative to his course of vengeance and then even returning from the other world in an attempt to save him; the Marquise von O . . . charging directly through prejudice and convention to restore her reputation; Toni unheeded and misunderstood in her desperate device to rescue the unworthy Gustav; Agnes von Schroffenstein drinking the water she believes to be poisoned (perhaps having read Schiller's *Kabale und Liebe*), thus making that leap into trust demanded of all in Kleist's world but achieved by few; Eve desperately trying to save her unworthy beau while throwing into his teeth: "Du hättest denken sollen: Ev ist brav, / Es wird sich alles ihr zum Ruhme lösen" (1171–72); Natalie, in a splendid Kleistian literalization, reifying her metaphorical command of a regiment to deploy it under the Elector's windows; even Thusnelda, for all that she is manipulated into it, feeding Ventidius to the bear, a highly comic scene that has unnecessarily worried moralistic commentators. Alkmene belongs in this company: she is proud and aristocratic; she holds her own in one of Kleist's most impossible and unbearable situations; she is prepared to cast off Amphitryon when she misreads his bewildered rage as a ruse to be rid of her or to cast herself out if she can be persuaded that she has been dishonored, god or no god. Above all, she is, or tries to be, strong in love.

Many of the interpreters have been resentful of her insistence on her love for and fidelity to Amphitryon. Allan denounces her for asserting "the reality of an unreal husband in order to deny the existence of a real god," thus encapsulating herself in contemptible social convention (123). Even Fischer, who is not a Jupiterist, criticizes her for supporting the ethos of marriage and its fetters, commenting disdainfully that she is still on her honeymoon (64). Well, no doubt we should all try to get over the honeymoon as soon as possible. But it seems to me that this view, versions of which are often encountered, fails to acknowledge the quality of Alkmene's bond with Amphitryon: it is erotic — in a word, sexual. This is quite clear in her immensely fulfilled mood after the night with the disguised Jupiter, expressed in her first, unambiguous "Ach" when asked by Jupiter, "Schien diese Nacht dir kürzer als die andern?" (1.4.506–7) Her married love is based on a satisfying sexual relationship, which Jupiter escalates; therefore, the insistence of Jupiter and the Jupiterists that she needs to distinguish between conjugal dutifulness and a higher, freer love strikes me as perverse. Alkmene herself orders this issue as graciously as she can when she responds to Jupiter's nagging about it:

> Wie kann dich ein Gesetz der Welt nur quälen,
> Das weit entfernt, beschränkend hier zu sein,
> Vielmehr den kühnsten Wünschen, die sich regen,
> Jedwede Schranke glücklich niederreißt? (1.4.461–64)

Then, as she does several times, she turns Jupiter's effort to drive a wedge between her and her husband into erotic play:

> . . . Nicht, daß es mir entschlüpft
> In dieser heitern Nacht, wie, vor dem Gatten,
> Oft der Geliebte aus sich zeichnen kann;
> Doch da die Götter eines und das andre
> In dir mir einigten, verzeih ich diesem
> Von Herzen gern, was der vielleicht verbrach.
>
> (1.4.486–92)

Even in 2.4, when, in her woman-to-woman talk with Charis, she begins to reflect on the special nature of the past night, she still does not come to the point of supposing Amphitryon incapable of this unusual sexual gratification, even if this is one of the places where she edges toward a differentiation of the doubles, which some interpreters have clutched upon as repressed acknowledgment and desire. She perceives the experience "wohl als etwas Besonderes, nicht aber als etwas Außermenschliches" (Oellers 73). Kleist did not take the hint in Hederich's lexicon (col. 178), which he, like his contemporaries, is assumed to have consulted on matters of antiquity, that the marriage was unconsummated prior to Jupiter's visit. What in all of this has caused interpreters to join Jupiter in hostility to the institution of marriage is a mystery to me.

In the past they seem to have been strangely embarrassed by Alkmene's sexuality. Gundolf sniffed at her description of the night of love as "eine Seelenwühlerei unkeuscher, von der Gesellschaft aus betrachtet indezenter als Molières schlichte Feststellung" (82); he thought Kleist in the years 1806 to 1808 caught in erotic obsession, generating *Amphitryon, Penthesilea,* and *Käthchen* (88). Allan seems to identify innocence with asexuality (117). The claim of the Reclam commentary, in keeping with its Jupiterist outlook, that Alkmene's sexual abandon cannot be spontaneous because it is within the marriage bond, strikes me as willful refusal of perception (Bachmaier 24). Whether Kleist was fearful of women and fled sexuality by attaching himself to his evidently lesbian half-sister Ulrike (cf. Zimmermann 134, 154), I leave, with relief, to the biographers, but that Alkmene is ashamed of her sexual desire for her husband (McGlathery 64, 67) I cannot accept. Sex in *Amphitryon,* according to Fetscher, is "dieses häufig tabuierte oder mit euphemistischen Formulierungen verdunkelte Thema des *Amphitryon . . .*" (5). My impression is that sexuality is positively charged in Kleist's texts. The clothes-changing scene in *Die Familie Schroffenstein,* an anticipation of the wedding night, is an assertion of value against the surrounding viciousness. There is no sinfulness in the sexual relationship of Jeromino and Josephe in *Das Erdbeben in Chili,* except as imposed by the dominant theocracy. There are powerful currents of desire, though expressed in differing ways, in both *Penthesilea* and *Käthchen*. If it is true, as some biographers tend to assume, that Kleist never had a consummated sexual relationship, the erotic glow that warms his texts feels like a wistful yearning. What is not positive is sexual assault (Count F . . ., Nicolo, Count Jakob) or manipulative deceit (Adam) or disingenuous seduction (Gustav, Ventidius, and, I am inclined to think, Achilles). I am further inclined to think that Jupiter belongs in this series.

Alkmene never accepts Jupiter's violation of her. I read the lines that have drawn so much commentary:

> Wenn du, der Gott, mich hier umschlungen hieltest
> Und jetzo sich Amphitryon mir zeigte,
> Ja — dann so traurig würd ich sein, und wünschen,
> Daß er der Gott mir wäre, und daß du
> Amphitryon mir bliebst, wie du es bist (2.5.1564–68)

as part of her increasingly tense effort to evade (Glenny 54–55) or deflect what increasingly feels like an assault on her integrity. Probes into her sub-conscious to make her mean something other than she says, such as Nord-meyer's (1947, 117, 121), I think are futile. It is true that this reasoning causes a problem with what looks like Jupiter's exclamation of triumph:

> Mein süßes, angebetetes Geschöpf!
> In dem so selig ich mich, selig preise!
> So urgemäß, dem göttlichen Gedanken,
> In Form und Maß, und Sait und Klang,
> Wie's meiner Hand Äonen nicht entschlüpfte! (2.5.1569–73)

Jauss suggests that Jupiter simply misunderstands her, unable to confront the defeat that seals his loneliness (1979, 244), Stephens that he "con-sistently pretended that all his defeats are really wins" (94). Allan thinks that he is masking a defeat that is his own fault for having created such a woman: "hoist by his own petard: defeated by a creature of his own making, a woman who so perfectly reflects the masculine fantasy of the 'infallibly' faithful wife that without actually being faithful to Amphi-tryon, can never be unfaithful with Jupiter" (129) — a good example of how an unwillingness to appreciate Alkmene can generate an eccentric result. If Jupiter's triumph is an anticipation of the final recognition scene (Michelsen 135), it would appear in retrospect to be far from promising. For Jupiter's management of the dénouement and anagnorisis is disastrous for her sense of self. He rehabilitates not Alkmene but Am-phitryon; he meets Amphitryon's demand for recompense by the birth of a hero, to which Alkmene, unlike Molière's Alcmène, does not aspire (cf. Kleist 1:939), and does so while she is unconscious. Previous to that he has at last maneuvered her into choosing him over Amphitryon.

Most critics have tended to agree that, motivated by her love, she chooses the better Amphitryon (for example, Schulze 257). Sosias does so also, immediately (3.5.1919–20). But, beyond that, she is driven to denounce the real Amphitryon in the grossest and most carnal terms: "Du Ungeheuer! Mir scheußlicher, / Als es geschwollen in Morästen nistet! . . . Solch einen feilen Bau gemeiner Knechte, / Vom Prachtwuchs dieser königlichen Glieder, / Den Farren von dem Hirsch zu unterscheiden" (3.2.2240–41, 2249–51). Wilson thinks that these lines show that Alkmene's purity is not absolute and that they parody Goethe's *Iphigenie,* reminding us that Jupiter rather outlandishly responds with: "Du Göttliche! Glanzvoller als die Sonne!" (3.2.2270) As Wegener points out, most interpreters have either simply ignored this disconcerting turn in the drama or have tried to turn the tirade against Jupiter (36, 209). But it is not surprising that, practically since the beginning of the interpretive history, observers have wondered how the marriage might survive this moment (for example, Silz 52; Lindsay 116; Michelson 139). Critics of the strict observance will admonish us that there is no warrant to speculate on anything outside the text, but Oellers's view that only philistines worry about the future of the marriage (73) is excessively severe; more persuasive to me is Földényi's observation that "das letzte 'Ach'! kündet von der Wüste, die sie erwartet" (23). As for the recompense of the birth of Herkules, which some interpreters prefer to ignore (Wegener 222–26), I cannot follow those who view it as a positive resolution (for example, Graham 92; Arntzen 245; Kleist 1:922). Even Molière's Sosie says sarcastically of it that Jupiter knows how to sugar the pill ("Le Seigneur Jupiter sait dorcr la pilule," 1.1913). "She is not to be consoled," remarks Schulze pungently, "by the genealogical booby prize of a hero-son" (262); Fetscher asserts that with the annunciation she is passed over and declared incompetent (174); Földényi that the child will "weniger Christus als einem Minotaurus ähneln" (167). But there is another consideration.

It is characteristic of Kleist to place characters in impossible situations that destroy the very structure of the self. The queenly Penthesilea becomes a cannibal; the judicious and honorable Kohlhaas turns into a homicidal maniac; the elder Schroffensteins go mad with murderous rage; after the sight of his grave the valiant Prince Friedrich renounces the last shred of dignity, even his beloved; Gustav von der Ried blows out the brains of an innocent and helpless girl; Piachi sacrifices his immortal soul to insatiable vengeance; skulls, including those of children, are smashed. I do not believe that these extreme situations are designed to expose the inner truth of the self in a "belief that they reveal more about human nature than the norm itself" (Cohn 142) or are merely situations experimenting with character (cf. Glenny 73), just as I doubt that Kleist's characters have a psychology deeper than what we are told of them. Rather, I am reminded of what one reads of death-camp inmates: the situation is so far beyond experience and habit, so resistant to understanding and coping, that the very fabric of the self disintegrates to the degree that questions as to whether one or another behaved well or ill lose their relevance. The violence in the deep places of Kleist's imagination creates an effect similar to this in kind if not in magnitude. One might recall that Penthesilea sighs "Ach Prothoe" when her sense of self is destroyed (24.2828). "Mir scheint jedoch, daß das bei Kleist unter solcher Tortur Entäußerte keine Art von Schönheit, auch keine schreckliche, an den Tag bringe, welche die Gewaltsamkeit ihrer Hervorbringung tilgen könnte," observes Fetscher (38). Therefore, I cannot see how Alkmene's final "Ach" can be an expression of gratification (Kleist 1:930), successful elevation of her religious spirit, or longing for the departing Jupiter and complete unity (Jancke 107); it is more plausibly "a refusal to participate in the ritual of public sublimation" (Schulze 259), "ein Ausdruck der Selbstentfremdung der Seele" (Földényi 20). Neumann goes even farther: saying that the end is not even tragic, he implies that the play is absurd, a form of the theater of cruelty (154).

How is it, then, a comedy? Perhaps we do not always understand Kleist's sense of humor, which may be as bizarre, or as infected with bitterness, as the rest of his "apocalyptic" mental disposition (cf. Fetscher 124–26). Not only is his comedy tragic; his tragedy is comic: Helbling has pointed out in connection with *Der zerbrochne Krug* that "the very themes and motifs central to his tragedies are equally germane to the spirit of comedy" (119). "Und spürt man darüber hinaus nicht auch in der tragischen Dichtung, wie sie die Übersteigerung des Tragischen bis an jene Grenze treiben, wo es komische Schattierung annimmt oder gar ganz ins Komische umzuschlagen droht?"(107), asks Guthke. One may recall the story that Kleist (and his listeners) broke out in uncontrollable laughter when reading the grim and gruesome *Familie Schroffenstein* aloud (cf. Sembdner 1969, 15); we may think of similar tales told of Kafka.

Perhaps the answers are not to be found where we are looking for them. I sometimes present to students as my "law" of interpretation a principle that if highly intelligent and subtle observers have failed for a hundred years to resolve an interpretive crux, something in the text is causing this failure. We will not be able to discover when the Elector decided to pardon the prince; "no interpretive effort will decipher his motivation, as the sharply discrepant criticism shows" (Swales 415). As Ellis says about the novellas, "while the critics argue over who has the better case, they do not see that the story is *about that argument*" (145).[4] The editor of the Brandenburg edition remarks: "Wahrscheinlich ist es überhaupt eine unangemessene Stellung zu Problemen, sie 'lösen' zu wollen" (Reuss 7 n. 15), and Stephens complains that *Amphitryon* is "treated with such utter seriousness in the secondary literature that the writing often resembles scriptural exegesis" (74). Without falling into the schoolmasterly disapproval of Kleist that is occasionally encountered (cf. Wegener 58), it may be permissible to conclude that *Amphitryon* does not yield a fully coherent, exhaustive, and paraphrasable interpretation because the project, for all its anchoring in Molière, came to reflect incompatible commitments in Kleist's unruly imagination. Graham, hostile to Kleist because he was not Goethe, put it tendentiously: "Into that vessel [Alkmene] a very sick mind has poured all his uncanny intimations of human wholesomeness and health" (88), while the idiom of deconstruction approaches from a different direction: "'Ach! is the consummate empty trace, available to contradictory meanings and carrying traces of the violence done to identity both personal and discursive" (Webber 229; cf. Wilson 127 and Földényi 11–12). If paradox and contradiction are to be acknowledged as structural principles, there is a temptation to see Kleist as a paradigmatic case for deconstructive reading, leaving blank spaces to be filled in by the reader's ideological commitments so that every interpretation alters its object.[5] Or, less strenuously: perhaps the *comedy* is to be found in the reader relationship — that is, the joke, reader and interpreter, is on you.

Notes

[1] "Könnte das Stücke nicht unchristlicher sein," remarks Földényi 167.

[2] Wittkowski 1972, 166, had made a similar observation; cf. also Kleist 1:930.

[3] Cf. Sammons 68–70; Fischer 66–67, remarking on the nearness of Kleist's comedy to the "negative[ ] Romantik," also adduces the *Nachtwachen*, a text that occurred to Sieck 310 in connection with the "Nihilismus" of *Penthesilea*.

[4] Allan [5] points out justly that Ellis himself is hardly a model of undogmatic interpretation.

[5] Cf. Theisen 19, 11–13, 18; on *Amphitryon*, which is said to push these effects to the limit, 77–93.

Works Cited

Allan, Seán. *The Plays of Heinrich von Kleist: Ideals and Illusions.* Cambridge: Cambridge UP, 1996.

Arntzen, Helmut. *Die ernste Komödie. Das deutsche Lustspiel von Lessing bis Kleist.* Munich: Nymphenburger Verlagshandlung, 1968.

Bachmaier, Helmut, and Thomas Horst, eds. *Erläuterungen und Dokumente: Heinrich von Kleist. Amphitryon.* Stuttgart: Reclam, 1983.

Cohn, Dorrit. "Kleist's 'Marquise von O . . .': The Problem of Knowledge." *Monatshefte* 67 (1975): 129–44.

Corngold, Stanley. *The Commentators' Despair: The Interpretation of Kafka's Metamorphosis.* Port Washington: Kennikat, 1973.

De Man, Paul. *The Rhetoric of Romanticism.* New York: Columbia UP, 1984.

Ellis, John M. *Heinrich von Kleist: Studies in the Character and Meaning of His Writings.* Chapel Hill: U of North Carolina P, 1979.

Erdman, David V., ed. *The Romantic Movement: A Selective and Critical Bibliography for 1981.* New York: Garland, 1982.

Fetscher, Justus. *Verzeichnungen: Kleists "Amphitryon" und seine Umschrift bei Goethe und Hofmannsthal.* Cologne: Böhlau, 1998.

Fischer, Bernd. "Wo steht Kleist in *Amphitryon?*" *Studia neophilologica* 56 (1984): 61–68.

Földényi, László F. *Heinrich von Kleist: Ein Netz der Wörter.* Tr. Akos Doma. Munich: Matthes & Seitz, 1999.

Furst, Lilian R. "Reading Kleist and Kafka." *Journal of English and Germanic Philology* 84 (1985): 374–95.

Gearey, John. *Heinrich von Kleist: A Study in Tragedy and Anxiety.* Philadelphia: U of Pennsylvania P, 1968.

Glenny, Robert E. *The Manipulation of Reality in Works by Heinrich von Kleist.* New York: Peter Lang, 1987.

Gossman, Lionel. "Molière's *Amphitryon.*" PMLA 78 (1963): 201–13.

Graham, Ilse. *Heinrich von Kleist: Word into Flesh. A Poet's Quest for the Symbol.* Berlin: de Gruyter, 1977.

Grathoff, Dirk. "Goethe und Kleist: Die Geschichte eines Mißverständnisses." In *Ethik und Ästhetik: Werke und Werte in der Literatur vom 18. bis zum 20. Jahrhundert. Festschrift für Wolfgang Wittkowski zum 70. Geburtstag.* Ed. Richard Fisher. Frankfurt a.M.: Peter Lang, 1995, 313–27.

Greenberg, Martin, tr. *Heinrich von Kleist: Five Plays.* New Haven: Yale UP, 1988.

Gundolf, Friedrich. *Heinrich von Kleist.* Berlin: Bondi, 1922.

Gustafson, Susan E. "'Die allmähliche Verfertigung der Gedanken beim Reden': The Linguistic Question in Kleist's *Amphitryon*." *Seminar* 25 (1989): 104–26.

Guthke, Karl S. *Geschichte und Poetik der deutschen Tragikomödie.* Göttingen: Vandenhoeck & Ruprecht, 1961.

Hederich, Benjamin. *Gründliches mythologisches Lexicon.* Leipzig: Gleditsch, 1770.

Helbling, Robert E. *The Major Works of Heinrich von Kleist.* New York: New Directions, 1975.

Höller, Hans. *Der "Amphitryon" von Molière und der von Kleist: Eine sozialgeschichtliche Studie.* (*Germanisch-romanische Monatsschrift*, supp. 3). Heidelberg: Winter, 1982.

Hölscher, Uwe. "Gott und Gatte: Zum Hintergrund der 'Amphitryon'-Komödie." *Kleist-Jahrbuch* (1991): 109–23.

Jancke, Gerhard. "Zum Problem des identischen Selbst in Kleists Lustspiel 'Amphitryon.'" *Colloquia Germanica* 3 (1969): 87–110.

Jauss, Hans Robert. "Poetik und Problematik von Identität und Rolle in der Geschichte des Amphitryon." In *Identität.* Ed. Odo Marquard and Karlheinz Stierle. Munich: Fink, 1979, 213–53.

———. "Von Plautus bis Kleist: *Amphitryon* im dialogischen Prozeß der Arbeit am Mythos." In *Kleists Dramen: Neue Interpretationen.* Ed. Walter Hinderer. Stuttgart: Reclam, 1981, 114–43.

Kernan, Alvin B. "The Idea of Literature." *New Literary History* 5 (1973/74): 31–40.

Kleist, Heinrich von. *Sämtliche Werke und Briefe in vier Bänden.* 4 vols. Ed. Ilse-Marie Barth et al. Frankfurt a.M.: Deutscher Klassiker Verlag, 1987–97.

Lange, Sigrid. *Die Utopie des Weiblichem im Drama Goethes, Schillers und Kleists.* Frankfurt a.M.: Peter Lang, 1993.

Lindsay, J. M. "Figures of Authority in the Works of Heinrich von Kleist." *Forum for Modern Language Studies* 8 (1972): 107–19.

Maron, Monika. "Nach Maßgabe meiner Begreifungskraft." *Kleist-Jahrbuch* (1993): 16–20.

Maass, Joachim. *Kleist: Die Geschichte seines Lebens.* Bern: Scherz, 1977.

McGlathery, James M. *Desire's Sway: The Plays and Stories of Heinrich von Kleist.* Detroit: Wayne State UP, 1983.

Michelsen, Peter. "Umnachtung durch das Licht: Zu Kleists Amphitryon." *Kleist-Jahrbuch* (1966): 123–41.

Milfull, John. "Oedipus and Adam — Greek Tragedy and Christian Comedy in Kleist's *Der zerbrochne Krug.*" *German Life and Letters* n.s. 27 (1973/74): 7–17.

Molière. *Amphitryon: Comédie.* In vol. 2 of his *Oeuvres complètes.* Ed. Georges Couton. Paris: Gallimard, 1971, 346–442.

Mommsen, Katharina. *Kleists Kampf mit Goethe*. Heidelberg: Stiehm, 1974.

Müller-Seidel, Walter. "Die Vermischung des Komischen mit dem Tragischen in Kleists Lustspiel 'Amphitryon.'" *Jahrbuch der Deutschen Schillergesellschaft* 5 (1961): 118–35.

Müller-Seidel, Walter, ed. *Heinrich von Kleist: Aufsätze und Essays*. Darmstadt: Wissenschaftliche Buchgesellschaft, 1967.

Neumann, Michael. "Genius malignus Jupiter oder Alkmenes Descartes-Krise." *Kleist-Jahrbuch* (1994): 141–55.

Newman, Gail. "'Du bist nicht anders als ich': Kleist's Correspondence with Wilhelmine von Zenge." *German Life and Letters* n.s. 42 (1988/89): 101–12.

Nölle, Volker. "Verspielte Identität: Eine expositorische 'Theaterprobe' in Kleists Lustspiel 'Amphitryon.'" *Kleist-Jahrbuch* (1993): 160–80.

Nordmeyer, H. W. "Kleists 'Amphitryon': Zur Deutung der Komödie." *Monatshefte* 38 (1946): 1–19, 165–76, 268–83, 349–59; 39 (1947): 89–125.

Oellers, Norbert. "'Kann auch so tief ein Mensch erniedrigt werden?' Warum 'Amphitryon'? Warum 'ein Lustspiel.'" in *Heinrich von Kleist*. Ed. Heinz Ludwig Arnold et al. (*Text + Kritik*, special issue). Munich: edition text + kritik, 1993, 72–83.

Prigge-Kruhoeffer, Maria. "Heinrich von Kleist: Religiosität und Charakter." *Kleist-Jahrbuch* (1923/24): 1–85.

Reeve, William C. *Kleist on Stage 1804–1987*. Montreal: McGill-Queen's UP, 1993.

Reeves, Nigel. "Kleist's Indebtedness to the Science, Psychiatry and Medicine of His Time." *Oxford German Studies* 16 (1985): 47–65.

Reuss, Roland. "' . . . daß man's mit Fingern läse, /.' Zu Kleists 'Amphitryon.'" *Berliner Kleist-Blätter*. Vol. 1.4: *Amphitryon*. Ed. Reuss and Peter Staengle. Basel: Stroemfeld/Roter Stern, 1991, 3–26.

Ribbat, Ernst. "Neue Kleist-Forschungen. Ein Zwischenbericht zu einigen Neuerscheinungen 1983–1984." *Zeitschrift für Deutsche Philologie* 105 (1986): 283–92.

Ryan, Lawrence. "Amphitryon: doch ein Lustspielstoff!" In *Kleist und Frankreich*. Ed. Walter Müller-Seidel. Berlin: Erich Schmidt, 1969, 83–121.

Sammons, Jeffrey L. *The* Nachtwachen von Bonaventura:*A Structural Interpretation*. The Hague: Mouton, 1965.

Schulze, Leonard G. "Alkmene's Ominous *Ach!* On Bastards, Beautiful Souls, and the Spirit in Heinrich von Kleist." *Studies in Romanticism* 19 (1980): 249–66.

Sembdner, Helmut. *In Sachen Kleist: Beiträge zur Forschung*. Munich: Hanser, 1974.

Sembdner, Helmut, ed. *Heinrich von Kleist: Dichter über ihre Dichtungen*. Munich: Heimeran, 1969.

————. *Heinrich von Kleists Lebensspuren: Dokumente und Berichte der Zeitgenossen.* Frankfurt a.M.: Insel, 1984.

Sieck, Albrecht. *Kleists Penthesilea: Versuch einer neuen Interpretation.* Bonn: Bouvier, 1971.

Silz, Walter. *Heinrich von Kleist: Studies in His Works and Literary Character.* Philadelphia: U of Pennsylvania P, 1961.

Stephens, Anthony. *Heinrich von Kleist: The Dramas and Stories.* Oxford: Berg, 1994.

Swales, Erika. "Configurations of Irony: Kleist's *Prinz Friedrich von Homburg.*" *Deutsche Vierteljahrsschrift* 56 (1982): 407–30.

Szondi, Peter. "Fünfmal Amphitryon: Plautus, Molière, Kleist, Giraudoux, Kaiser." In his *Lektüren und Lektionen. Versuche über Literatur, Literaturtheorie und Literatursoziologie.* Frankfurt a.M.: Suhrkamp, 1973, 153–84.

Theisen, Bianca. *Bogenschluß: Kleists Formalisierung des Lesens.* Freiburg: Rombach, 1996.

Vohland, Ulrich. *Bürgerliche Emanzipation in Heinrich von Kleists Dramen und theoretischen Schriften.* Bern: Herbert Lang / Frankfurt a.M.: Peter Lang, 1976.

Webber, Andrew J. *The "Doppelgänger": Double Visions in German Literature.* Oxford: Clarendon Press, 1996.

Wegener, Karl-Heinz. *"Amphitryon" im Spiegel der Kleistliteratur.* Frankfurt a.M.: Peter Lang, 1979.

Wellbery, David E., ed. *Positionen der Literaturwissenschaft: Acht Modellanalysen am Beispiel von Kleists* Das Erdbeben in Chili. Munich: Beck, 1985.

Wickert, Gabriele M. *Das verlorene heroische Zeitalter: Held und Volk in Heinrich von Kleists Dramen.* Bern: Peter Lang, 1983.

Wilson, Jean. *The Challenge of Belatedness: Goethe, Kleist, Hofmannsthal.* Lanham, MD: UP of America, 1991.

Wittkowski, Wolfgang. "Der neue Prometheus: Kleists *Amphitryon* zwischen Molière und Giraudoux." In *Kleist und Frankreich.* Ed. Walter Müller-Seidel. Berlin: Erich Schmidt, 1969, 27–82.

————. "Die Verschleierung der Wahrheit in und über Kleists *Amphitryon: Zur dialektischen Aufhebung eines Lustspiels oder über den neuen mystischen Amphitryon* und dergleichen Zeichen der Zeit." In *Wahrheit und Sprache: Festschrift für Bert Nagel zum 65. Geburtstag am 27. August 1972.* Ed. Wilm Peters et al. Göppingen: Kümmerle, 1972, 151–70.

Zeyringer, Klaus. "'Wo kömmt der Witz mir her?' Eine 'Lustspielfigur par excellence.' Zu den Sosias-Szenen in Kleists *Amphitryon.*" *Deutsche Vierteljahrsschrift* 70 (1996): 552–68.

Zimmermann, Hans Dieter. *Kleist, die Liebe und der Tod.* Frankfurt a.M.: Athenäum, 1989.

Kleist's *Penthesilea:*
Battleground of Gendered Discourses

Jost Hermand

Older Views and Interpretations

KLEIST'S OEUVRE ENCOMPASSES some of the most enigmatic works in German literature — and his *Penthesilea* is unquestionably the most puzzling among them. Here a virgin Amazon queen intends to subjugate Achilles, the most famous of all Greek heroes, in order to have him impregnate her at a nocturnal ritual orgy in Themiscyra. Yet, she falls passionately in love with this man in the middle of fierce combat, and she is unable to overpower him in the melee as demanded by the law of the land. When he, equally gripped by an intensely burning passion, charges unarmed toward her, she ultimately tears him limb from limb with the help of her bloodthirsty hounds and devours his corpse in an intoxicatingly cannibalistic and necrophilic manner. Kisses or bites: for her they suddenly become one and the same (24.2981). Afterward, as if awakening from a spell of temporary insanity, she plunges a "destructive emotion that is as cold as ore" into her breast — and sinks lifeless to the ground (24.3027).

It is understandable that such a scene has spurred hundreds of literary scholars, male and female alike, to wild interpretations. Many of them have attempted to base their arguments on Kleist's own statements about the drama. These statements are few and far between, however, and so cryptic as to obscure the genuine literary intention of the work. From the few references to *Penthesilea* in Kleist's letters we know only that (1) this work, second only to *Robert Guiskard,* must certainly have been his most ambitious project; (2) he wept from a deep shock while writing it — above all, after the death of Penthesilea; (3) he infused this drama with the "entire filth" and "brilliance of my soul"; (4) he considered the drama's "martial" spirit "not for women"; and (5) his *Penthesilea* and *Käthchen von Heilbronn* were connected to each other like "the + and – of algebra" (Sembdner 35–43). No further authorial comments have come to light.

Accustomed to grounding an analysis of classical dramas, such as those of Goethe or Schiller, on personal statements by the author, most twentieth-century scholars attempted to derive as much as they possibly could from these few sentences in order to defend this drama — so contrary to the repressive and bigoted moral views of the nineteenth century — as a work of genuine passion. After all, from the age of Goethe until the 1880s,[1] Kleist's *Penthesilea* was almost exclusively either rejected or ridiculed as an extremely unpleasant play whose exaggerations allegedly bordered on the unintentionally comical; or it was seen as a feverish attempt to depict nymphomania as sexual obsession or as a purely fantasy portrait of female sadism — in short, as the expression of hysteria. It was not until 1895, under the influence of the battle of the sexes depicted in the works of Strindberg and Wedekind, that a few representatives of so-called modernism finally supported and heralded the drama. Among them were Julius Bab, Wilhelm Stapel, and Maximilian Harden, who continued to take note of the female protagonist's abnormal sexuality but were willing to countenance it because of its intense erotic appeal (cf. Schmidt 8–15).

Penthesilea interpretations finally took a complete turn for the positive once expressionists and scholars of *Geistesgeschichte* examined the work and celebrated it as a passionate expression of a "life in overdrive" (cf. Hamann and Hermand 23, 106, 145, 237). This perspective peaked in the existentialist interpretations of Kleist around 1930, the standard-bearer being Gerhard Fricke in his *Gefühl und Schicksal bei Heinrich von Kleist* of 1929. According to Fricke, the theme of *Penthesilea* is "die das eigentliche Ich des Menschen in absoluter Hingabe zum absoluten Selbstsein befreiende existentielle Beziehung der Liebe" (112). After this point, whenever others analyzed this work, they spoke, like Fricke, almost exclusively in terms of emotion, being, tragedy, existence, fate, psyche, or ambition, so that the sexually pathological traits of the drama receded noticeably into the background.

A similar view dominated in West Germany after 1945, as well, when there was again much discussion of tragedy, fate, and mistaken being in other areas. A good example of this type of interpretation can be seen in Ingrid Kohrs's *Das Wesen des Tragischen im Drama Heinrichs von Kleist* (1951), which traces the problematic nature of this drama back to internal experience, to the original decision of emotion, and to helplessness in regard to the question of the meaning of being — in other words, back to Penthesilea's existential foundation of being, since she stands in diametrical opposition to the unnatural laws of her nation (37–39, 66, 131). In *Heinrich von Kleist oder das absolute Ich* (1960) Günter Blöcker similarly saw the main psychic impulse of this drama in the violent act of self-liberation that leads Penthesilea back to a "seinsunmittelbare Ordnung" (13).

This outlook prevailed in Western Kleist scholarship over the following two decades. Time and again, German studies in the West — crassly limiting its attention to the alleged singularity of the problematic nature of the individual ego in the work — emphasized the female protagonist's lust for revenge arising from a failure of communication (cf. Dettmering) and the competition between Penthesilea and Achilles as an allegory of Kleist's contest with Goethe (cf. Mommsen 41–47) in order to shift attention away from the erotically perverse aspects of the drama toward the theme of an egocentric outsider status. This subject-oriented perspective even continued to influence a number of post-1968 *Penthesilea* interpretations that sought to enlist the drama for an antiauthoritarian standpoint. In 1976, for example, Ulrich Vohland attempted to interpret Penthesilea's hatred of the coercive measures of the Amazon state as an individual rebellion against the absolutist character of the Prussian state, and he equated the bourgeois aspirations for emancipation around 1800 with the rebellious tendencies of his own time.

Markedly negative or critical views of *Penthesilea* surfaced in Kleist scholarship after 1930 only when German studies approached the play with nationalistic, Marxist, or Christian criteria. While the German fascists, with their overwhelmingly positive opinion of Kleist, for the most part emphasized his *Hermannsschlacht* and *Prinz von Homburg* and ignored *Penthesilea* for strategic reasons, the Marxists, for whom Kleist remained highly problematic because of his allegedly boundless egocentricity, viewed *Penthesilea* as the quintessence of the author's ideological missteps. Georg Lukács, for example, while still respecting Kleist's other works, could discern only eccentric, even monomaniacal, individual passion at work in this drama, and he did not shrink from condemning its decadent, excessive emotional exaggeration, dehumanizing barbarism, and bestial murderous frenzy in order to situate this play in the prehistory of National Socialism because of its emotional anarchy (cf. Lukács 32–35). In 1959 Siegfried Streller maintained a similar position in the *Weimarer Beiträge* when he spoke of an inversion of the humanistic image of the ancient classical period into an antihumanism, even a pathological exaggeration of the instincts to barbaric excesses. Instead of concerning himself with a deeper meaning in historical processes as had Goethe, Streller holds, Kleist valorized solely the idea of freedom and never advanced beyond an individual revolt that ignored any accepted social standards. This quality, according to Streller, is particularly evident in Kleist's degrading view of the feminine, which is depicted in the play as the quintessence of exemplary unnaturalness (508–12). An equally negative critique came from a Christian perspective in 1976 via Albrecht Sieck, who attempted to demonstrate that one must view the female protagonist of this drama as the very embodiment of evil, because all elements of morality, salvation, and catharsis in her figure are perverted into the satanic (428–30).

The Paradigm Shift between 1975 and 1985

The previously mentioned perspectives, all anchored in collectivist ideologies, have become increasingly rare in the last twenty-five years. Under the influence of poststructuralist or postmodern currents, new models of interpretation have arisen whose emphasis once again clearly relies on individual or, at most, group-specific elements. During these years any interpretation derived from overarching societal concepts, regardless of its methodology or critical aim, has come to be seen as totalizing, if not downright totalitarian. When this still prevalent perspective began to assert itself with the slogan "The personal is the political," it led to a conspicuous reduction of the terms of discussion to individual psychology, psychoanalysis, gender specificity, minority orientation, or group phenomenology and resulted in a distinct domination of specific, individuated discourses over possible supraindividual discourses. Many literary scholars hailed this development as a liberation from the inhibiting coercion of a quest for universal truth and as the onset of a democratizing methodological pluralism. To be sure, this development has had its positive aspects, but the reduction to psychological, gender-specific, or group-oriented perspectives has simultaneously been marked by an unmistakable decline of any feelings of responsibility for society as a whole. Instead of continuing to question the Weltanschauung or sociopolitical concepts of literary works, this discursive framework regarded as worthy of interpretation only those works that evidenced psychological or gender-specific resistance to any abstract system.

Seen from an ideology-critical perspective, though, the current rejection of earlier points of view has not only introduced democratic elements but has also, unfortunately, effected a decided leveling of many older concepts of education, culture, and historical thinking. Regrettably, the threat of undemocratic and totalitarian aspects — attacked in the older "master discourses" by the adherents of contemporary individualized discourses — actually persists in many of the new individualized discourses that emphasize psychology or gender while ignoring interpersonal, social, or historical issues. Confined to their *one* discourse, encapsulated within it and defending it against all others, they tend to assume a defiant stance vis-à-vis the rest of the world, so that their statements are often colored by secessionist and thereby undemocratic traits.

Over the last twenty-five years *Penthesilea* scholarship has also been swept along by this trend. Let us first examine the psychoanalytic, homosexual, bisexual-androgynistic, and pleasure-oriented postmodern perspectives on this drama. Drawing on Heinz Kohut's *The Analysis of the Self* (1977), Ursula R. Mahlendorf has stressed the specifically narcissistic elements in Kleist's *Penthesilea* and as early as 1979 drew a direct parallel between the double murder at the tragedy's end and the double suicide of Kleist and Henriette Vogel (253, 165). Similar theories are to be found in Sigrid Scheifele's *Penthesilea* (1992), which also argues that Kleist — driven by sadomasochistic tendencies — finally succumbed to a regression to self-destructive disintegration culminating in his suicide pact (313). In much the same vein, Ingrid Stipa bases her psychoanalytic interpretation of *Penthesilea* not just on Freud but also on Michel Foucault's *Madness and Civilization,* arguing that because of the author's precarious psychological balance the drama's plot proceeds from rational to irrational, from "kisses" to "bites" (37).

The homoerotic dimension of this discourse came to the fore in Hans Dieter Zimmermann's book *Kleist, die Liebe und der Tod* (1989), although he was writing not about *Penthesilea* but about *Käthchen von Heilbronn.* Nevertheless, both plays can be seen as passionate declarations of love to the courted man — in *Penthesilea* Achilles, in *Käthchen von Heilbronn* Count Wetter von Strahl. Other scholars have made claims about the androgynous traits in *Penthesilea,* manifest above all in the permutation of sexual roles. According to a 1993 article by Ruth Klüger, Achilles has girlish traits, while Penthesilea assumes an aggressive, even rapacious role that one would have ascribed until recently only to men (104). In an essay by Joachim Pfeiffer in Alice Kuzniar's *Outing Goethe and His Age* (1996), Kleist's gender identity is described as neither masculine nor feminine (221). Lilian Hoverland and Edith Borchardt had introduced the term *androgyny* into the debate as early as the 1980s, and Borchardt traced Kleist's alleged bisexuality, that is, his fear of "the feminine in himself" and his resulting latent homosexuality, back to "wishful Oedipal notions" that he could fulfill only in death — and as evidence she, too, adduced Penthesilea's sex slaying and Kleist's suicide pact with Henriette Vogel (187–89). This proximity to the dark side of Eros has also been stressed by Inge Stephan, who interprets Penthesilea's androgynistic nature as a counterfigure to Goethe's Mignon (1993, 201).

In the wake of the pleasure-oriented postmodern discourse initiated by Dietmar Kamper and Christoph Wulf's *Die Wiederkehr des Körpers* (1982), Maximilian Nutz interpreted Kleist's *Penthesilea* as an antirational drama of the body that enacts a definite revolt against that instrumentalization of the human senses that Norbert Elias described as the domesticating process of civilization. Instead of approaching the drama with a "distanzierten, entsinnlichten, von subjektiven Gefühlen gereinigten Blick" (166) — in short, with an academically blindered view — readers of this play should, Nutz demanded, simply yield to its intoxicating "Sirenengesang" (165), whose phantasmagorias, obsessions, borderline situations, and moments of insanity (cf. 164) express traces of an unrealized humanity (cf. 183). This drama, he insists, features a "resurrection of the body in the text" and thereby — as a sign of an emotional lust for the corporeal — stands in conspicuous contrast to frigid rationality, which is incapable of producing any valid cognition.

Feminist Discourses

Among these antitotalizing discourses that have repudiated an allegedly false generalization into universals and rationality, feminist interpretation has assumed a special position. After all, this discourse goes beyond dealing with specifically Freudian issues such as oedipal or narcissistic conflicts, interests specific to particular groups such as bi- or homosexuals, or even psychological reductions to androgyny or the pleasures of the body, and instead opens up a perspective that aims to speak for half of humanity. But even if this discourse is more comprehensive than other group-psychological or minority-oriented perspectives, it is certainly not always oriented toward the whole of society. Instead, despite all claims to democratic intentions (Müller-Seidel 145), it quite often neglects the other half of humanity. Whenever such views surface in unadulterated form — that is, as a separatist feminism taking a radical position against all male-dominated discourse — they tend toward a group-specific or even apartheid position.

In regard to literature, radical feminism is forced to draw the following consequences: it must approach all texts by women from a position of affirmation or identification and all texts by men that do not reflect a gender-specific identification from a position of criticism, rejection, and deconstruction. The sole exceptions are for texts by male authors who exhibit gay, bisexual, or androgynous characteristics, as well as works by men that portray especially strong, self-confident women or autonomous female kingdoms — bringing us right back to Kleist's *Pen-*

thesilea, which has played an important role in feminist literary criticism over the last twenty-five years — regardless of whether it approached this particular male-authored text in a critically deconstructive way, with ambivalent fascination, or positively.

After all, this drama offers everything for which a separatist-oriented feminist perspective could wish: a strong, self-confident female protagonist (1) who does not allow herself to be merely "taken," but, rather, seeks out her own partner and (2) who wishes to overpower the strongest man of all in order to bring him as her booty to the orgy in Themiscyra. The play deals with the queen of an Amazon kingdom who arose from a night of bloodshed, during which the Scythian women had "tickled" all Egyptians "to death" with finely polished daggers, because the Egyptians wanted to rape them after murdering their husbands (cf. 15.1951). Penthesilea summarizes what followed in self-confident words:

> Und dies jetzt ward im Rat des Volks beschlossen:
> Frei wie der Wind auf offenem Blachfeld sind
> Die Frauen, die solche Heldentat vollbracht,
> Und dem Geschlecht der Männer nicht mehr dienstbar.
> Ein Staat, ein mündiger, sie aufgestellt,
> Ein Frauenstaat, den fürder keine andre
> Herrschtsücht'ge Männerstimme mehr durchtrotzt,
> Der das Gesetz sich würdig selber gebe,
> Sich selbst gehorche, selber auch beschütze. (15.1953–61)

The fascination that such words exercised on women who were seeking independence from male oppression is easily grasped. In the beginning of this movement Kleist's Penthesilea was fervently idealized by feminist thinkers and writers primarily in two ways: (1) as the embodiment of the eternal feminine, assuming even the proportions of Earth Mother in the work of scholars such as Mary Daly and Heide Göttner-Abendroth who aimed at giving Penthesilea all the attributes of a romantically transfigured matriarch, or (2) as a feminine heroine who, although vanquished as an Amazon queen, still points to a future in which men and women will be equal.[2] The latter group based its argument either on the theme of "Amazonomachie" in ancient art, which Angelika Meyer attempted to apply productively in 1991, or on Renate Rolle's essay "Amazonen in der archäologischen Realität" (1986), which identified skeletons exhumed from Eastern European gravesites as those of female warriors.

Alongside those feminists who identify with the figure of Penthesilea, however, there are more critical, if not even more radical, representatives who have not shied away from deconstructing this tragedy and its Amazon protagonist as a product of male fantasy that affirms and promotes the patriarchal system. This camp, in which lesbianism often sets the tone,[3] sees *Penthesilea* as a drama that turns against female emancipation, because (1) it depicts a female state whose imperfect emulation of a masculine form of government is doomed to fail, and (2) the female protagonist does not embody a real woman but is merely a mirror image of its author — that is, she is a homoerotic persona invested with the "entire filth and brilliance" of Kleist's own soul.

Apart from these two perspectives, in which either identificatory or deconstructionist traits dominate, a third view can also be characterized as feminist. In terms of the history of mentalities, a highly ambivalent love-hate relationship lies at its foundation. Among the representatives of this group, which pursued neither matriarchal nor lesbian-separatist aspirations, one finds the heterosexual feminists who, given their antipatriarchal feelings, found their attraction to men somehow unsettling, simultaneously delightful and damnable — and they felt pulled in two directions by this drama, just like Penthesilea and Achilles. Following in the footsteps of their heroine, they vividly experienced as readers all the contradictions she embodies — being at once ferocious yet tender, outraged yet loving, vengeful yet ingratiating — because, despite their critical stance vis-à-vis men, they did not wish to eschew their heterosexuality; instead, they wanted to be not only conquerors but also objects of love, not only erotically stimulating but also erotically stimulated.

Certainly, the most famous statement in this regard is a 1982 essay in which Christa Wolf justifiably employed Kleist's dedication to *Penthesilea* as an epigraph:

> Zärtlichen Herzen gefühlvoll geweiht! mit Hunden zerreißt sie,
> Welchen sie liebet, und ißt, Haut dann und Haar, ihn auf.
>
> (Kleist 2:700)

Wolf's essay confronts the central contradiction in Kleist's *Penthesilea*, namely the "Kanibalismus aus auswegloser Liebesleidenschaft" (662). While the Greeks ruthlessly denied equal rights to women, banished them into the home, rendered them defenseless and unthreatening, and while even the great enlightened thinkers of the eighteenth century did little to liberate them, Wolf claims that Kleist drew on earlier myths in which women still figured as acting and self-determining agents, thus opening up perspectives that maintain their relevance to the present day. In her eyes Kleist was one of the first to protest against the encroaching crippling of human nature, a protest he could voice only through the mouth of a woman, because the rape of all that is organic, maternally life-sustaining, and femininely self-sufficient can be understood only as the unscrupulous elimination of the original matriarchal condition of humankind and the ensuing formation of patriarchal power structures. After two and a half millennia of male oppression, this protest finds frenzied expression in Kleist's *Penthesilea*. The charges of barbarism, even pre-fascism, with which Georg Lukács reproached the play (cf. Lukács 33), seem to her completely unjustified.[4] Not blood lust but the life strangulation caused by hypertrophied rationality, writes Wolf, drives Penthesilea to insanity in a male-centric society. Read in this manner, this play, more than any other, seems to her to represent the cry for a real possibility of a livable existence (cf. Wolf 670–76).

While these three distinct branches of feminist interpretation of *Penthesilea* shared a clear emancipatory appeal by virtue of confronting the current "male world" with a separate and, therefore, autonomous women's state — or, at least, the dream of progressive equal rights for the sexes — there has been a noticeable shift away from older forms of political engagement since the early 1990s. At any rate, the latest scholarly essays on *Penthesilea* contain scant commentary on the "merciless oppression" or "spiritual and sexual exploitation" of women. Instead, the poststructuralist current has redirected attention to psychological or anthropological aspects, based on the writings of Jacques Lacan and female literary scholars who have been influenced by him, such as Helga Gallas, Marianne Schuller, and Sigrid Weigel.

Particularly influential in this respect were the interpretations by Gallas in 1986 and 1990. In the former she defends the position that Achilles represents the ideal object of identification for Penthesilea, that is, that her battle with him is a battle with her own mirror image and her murder of Achilles is also, in Lacanian terms, a murder of the hybrid Penthesilea (215–17). The reference to Lacan is just as clear in her second essay. Here Gallas interprets the drama within the confines of a discourse that posits Penthesilea as an object of her own unconscious desire, which finds fulfillment only in death (212). Similar theses are to be found in Maria Kublitz-Kramer's essay "'Ja, wenn man Tränen schreiben könnte': Versagte Trauer in Kleists 'Penthesilea'" (1999), which places interpretive emphasis primarily on the male gaze and a dreamlike second reality à la Lacan (116). Even the studies "The Eye of the Beholder: Female Subjectivity in Kleist's *Penthesilea*," by Renée M. Schnell, and "Leibgericht: Herzstücke für eine Anthropologie in den Literaturwissenschaften," by Walburga Hülk, are reminiscent of Lacan.

It was not only Lacan but also other French psychologists, linguists, poststructuralists, and feminists, who by the late 1980s began to exert considerable influence on the interpretation of *Penthesilea* by increasingly emphasizing Kleist's deconstructive perspective while pinpointing the contradictory, uncanny, and irreconcilable elements within the drama. This trend is evidenced, for example, by the work of Carol Jacobs in 1989 and by the chapter dealing with Kleist in Rebecca Williams-Duplaintier's dissertation "Amazon Figures in German Literature," which — referring to Foucault and Luce Iragaray — advances the thesis that every aspiration to self-realization in a sexually deformed society such as Penthesilea's must necessarily lead to "depression, hysteria, and madness" (103). Ortrud Gutjahr, on the other hand, in keeping with Julia Kristeva, interpreted Penthesilea's desire in 1997 primarily as a battle against the stranger within us (cf. Gutjahr 220). Eleanor E. ter Horst further claimed in 1996 that Kleist deconstructed the traditional "two-sex model" in *Penthesilea* and attempted thereby to undermine the "gender polarities" that had existed for millennia (191, 214). In 1998 Birgit Hansen saw Kleist as the great inverter and indicated, with a Foucauldian twist, that a tabooed (sexual) desire necessarily leads to a sadistic will to kill (115–18). Gabriele Brandstetter went one step further when she interpreted *Penthesilea* in 1997 as a drama of transgression à la Jacques Derrida, which in its overstepping of differences advances into a third or uncharted territory (76).

Faced with these and similar interpretations of *Penthesilea*, many female literary scholars, including Kate Rigby in "The Return of the Repressed or the Strange Case of Kleist's Feminism" (1992), began to question whether the drama could actually be interpreted from a feminist point of view. They wondered whether it was helpful "for the movement for the emancipation of women," or whether the Amazonian aspirations would simply lead to new forms of "oppression and repression" (Rigby 325, 331). Since then, such voices have either fallen silent or been pushed aside by completely different discourses, such as those drawn from aesthetics or philosophy.

These four approaches to interpreting Kleist's *Penthesilea* — in terms of Amazonianism, lesbian-separatism, heterosexuality, or French deconstructionism — may be somewhat contradictory in ideology and sexual history, but they have, nevertheless, enriched the analysis of this tragedy with new points of view that make it difficult for men who are not totally bigoted to regress to a supposedly gender-neutral position and to speak only of phenomena such as being, emotion, fate, truth, etc.[5] Given the brevity of this essay, one can only highlight the following positive aspects of these new perspectives. They offer (1) a markedly better understanding for the interpretation of identificatory or deconstructive factors in the reading of literary works; (2) a problematization of certain feminine or masculine conceptions of persona; (3) insight into the enduring continuity of patriarchal hegemony and the necessary rebellion of emancipatory women against it; and (4) the legitimization of a gender-specific discourse, which was dismissed as pathological, hysterical, or, at least, unscholarly by many men and even older women when it took on a militant, even frenzied tone a quarter of a century ago.

It is solely this feminist discourse that has opened our eyes to the sheer naiveté of the drama's Achilles, who expects an Amazon queen simply to accept his superior strength and find happiness in assuming a subordinate role as his wife — and how naive it would be for Penthesilea to seek contentment within the patriarchal system's prescribed role expectations of appeasement, compassion, and motherliness, all of which Achilles would demand of her but for which he would never respect her. Because there is no possibility, within Achilles' social structure, for Penthesilea to achieve fulfillment outside the prescribed role of a loving wife and mother, the relationship would necessarily lead to mutual mistrust that would ultimately develop into hatred, if not insanity, on the part of the insulted Amazon queen. Feminist interpretations of the drama that focus primarily on this aspect, therefore, offer the reader more than a simple interpretive novelty. At any rate, such feminist views penetrate considerably deeper into the heart of this drama than any pathological, ontological, or existential interpretation ever could.

Limiting Considerations

It would, however, be appropriate to guard against overzealous feminist interpretations by keeping in mind that (1) the tragedy is not the apotheosis of an Amazon state, as some have claimed (cf. Wolff 189–206), but, rather, depicts vividly how repressive this fictive women's state is, with its militancy, self-mutilation, procreation rituals, gender-specific eugenics, etc. (cf. Hermand 1984, 649–51); (2) in sociological terms, the play deals not with problems of the feminine per se but, rather, with problems of a queen who clearly differs from someone such as the master artisan's daughter Käthchen von Heilbronn, regardless of the fact that the latter also commands an unshakable self-confidence and rebels energetically against the stern rules of her father; (3) the play is a highly calculated "hyper-tragedy" that permits no harmonious solution to the severity of its contradictions but, rather, flows from Kleist's limitless ambition and necessarily leads to a murderous finale (cf. Hermand 1988, 45); (4) the play can also be seen as a blasphemous parody of the neoreligious tendencies in Romanticism, because Penthesilea's consumption of Achilles' flesh and blood satirizes the Eucharist as much as "Marquise von O . . ." satirizes the immaculate conception; (5) ultimately, this tragedy was written by a man who, on other ideological levels, was deeply enmeshed in the patriarchal thinking of his time, and women, therefore, should regard its protagonist not simply as an object of identification but also as an object for deconstruction.

Nevertheless, all of these limitations do not diminish the central role of this drama for any feminist discourse that deals with Kleist. In one respect — its representation of a strong, self-confident Amazon queen — the drama is, indeed, unique for the time span shortly after 1800 when the ideal of the "beautiful soul" was still dominant. This fact does not mean, however, that one can approach the play from that perspective alone. Any critic who does not proceed solely from a specifically separatist strategy or a feminist-identificatory pathos but, rather, attempts to incorporate other aspects emphasizing sociopolitical change into the interpretation of the tragedy should avoid broadening feminist discourses into such universalisms as emotion, being, fate, or existence, for which male scholars have rightly been reproached. Even with group- or gender-specific perspectives, the historically grounded should take precedence over ahistorical absolutes. Anyone who shies away from such a task will inevitably end up invoking anthropological generalities, in which the specificity of Kleist's perspective — in other words, the uniqueness of his familial, educational, and cultural background — is lost. After all, these factors had just as profound an influence on the conception and composition of this drama as any psychic drives that could be derived from Freudian and Lacanian perspectives, which apparently are beyond any historical conditionality whatsoever. A perspective on *Penthesilea* that integrates both these points of view ultimately needs to come to the fore. Only investigations that aim in this direction — that neither rely solely on feminist discourse nor allow an anthropological, psychoanalytical, or poststructuralist point of view that coolly disregards historical context but, rather, make an effort to combine historical and gender-specific epistemological interests — appear to me to be the most meaningful and promising.

And now let us take up a few examples showing how female literary scholars, while applying feminist perspectives, have correctly linked *Penthesilea* with Kleist's sociopolitical and ideological position, instead of transporting the play into the airy realm of mythological, archetypal, psychological, or biological timelessness. In a highly informative manner, Ruth Angress has pointed to the highly political character of the so-called private sphere, that is, the thoroughly ideologized emotive and instinctual dynamics of the Amazon state (5–28). Inge Stephan has proceeded even more concretely by discussing the proximity of Kleist's Penthesilea to Amazon figures of the French Revolution such as Olympe de Gouges, Claire Lacombe, and Théorine de Méricourt (1984, 26–27.). She says that unlike Schiller, who endeavored to ridicule such female figures in his famous and often parodied ballad "Die Glocke" with lines such as "Da werden Weiber zu Hyänen," Kleist found these figures not only repulsive, but also fascinating (38). A similar perspective dominates in Carola Köhler's "Aktive Penthesilea — Passiver Achill: Das Aufbrechen traditioneller Geschlechterrollen in Heinrich von Kleists 'Penthesilea'" (1997), which associates the breaks within the traditional gender definitions with events during the initial stages of the French Revolution — a process with which even Kleist had never come to terms, either intellectually or spiritually (60, 72). Carola Hilmes interprets Penthesilea just as politically by seeking to distance her from the stock figure of the "femme fatale" (74). Sigrid Lange goes even further in her 1991 article, when she claims that Kleist's gender sophistry, despite all its exaggerations into the tragic, was nevertheless a response to the essential features of the usual contemporary images, which interpreted social gender differences as a kind of dialectic of nature and accordingly attempted to represent these role differences in psychological, ideological, philosophical, and aesthetic terms (705). In contrast to his Classicist contemporaries, Lange continues, Kleist did not attempt to tie his historical expectations for the future to the redeeming role of the feminine in the manner of Goethe's *Iphigenie*. What is invoked in *Penthesilea* as a possibility of meaning or even a potential for development is instead merely the hope for a completely different type of history (720). Without abandoning a gender-specific perspective, one can certainly pursue such historical links in even greater depth. Following the Battle of Jena and Auerstedt in October 1806, Kleist felt at odds with the Prussian state, which he believed was not opposing Napoleon with sufficient vigor, and he began to sympathize openly with guerilla fighters who tried to invoke their right to grassroots resistance in the conflict between the Prussian and French states. Therefore, Kleist's Penthesilea must also be seen in relation to such guerilla fighters, as well as to Queen Luise of Prussia, whose "Amazonian" character Kleist so admired (cf. Williams-Duplantier 50). In contrast to many of his contemporaries, such as Goethe, who sought pacification, Kleist recognized that whenever the political order no longer corresponds to the social and natural needs of the majority of the population, internal and external aggression can arise (cf. Horn 95–113).

Thus, Kleist's Amazon state, in which individual will is relegated to the realm of myths, can be understood as an extreme representation of the Prussian state — in other words, as an image of an ossified system of government that requires internal rejuvenation by means of greater concessions to subjectivity. Penthesilea's state is not exactly mocked, as was the case in so much eighteenth-century literature on the Amazons authored by men (cf. Hayn 7–22; Klein 7–30), yet it cannot fulfill the actual needs of humans — indeed, it forces its female citizens into unnatural perversion of their emotions and instincts by strong regimentation. It was not only Kleist's annoyance with the Prussian state, however, but also his enthusiasm for certain radical events of the French Revolution, as well as his love-hate relationship with Napoleon, that gave this drama an almost unsurpassable pathos. This is poetry of being beside oneself, an explosion of language and the heart, which, in spite of its mythological drapery, manifests much more of the reality of an era that was shaken by revolution and disappointment, the guillotine and the storming of the barricades, thirst for life and war cries, as Ernst Fischer remarked, than all the superficially realistic plays of Iffland or Kotzebue that were written at the same time (118).

While Kleist portrayed the conflict between the individual will and the *raison d'état* as inescapable within the confines of a hyper-tragedy, with which he also attempted to satisfy his "unbridled ambition" (cf. Herrmann 45), he made a second, politically more mature, and historically more concrete attempt to come to terms with many of the same issues in Prussian history in his *Prinz Friedrich von Homburg.* Just as he attempted to bring "the state" and "tender emotions" closer together here, he likewise endeavored to suggest a new synthesis in the area of gender differences, equipping Princess Natalie von Oranien — while preserving many conventionally contemporary feminine traits — with highly self-confident characteristics, including a rebellious nature, and depicting Prince Friedrich with both the militarism of a social climber and an "unmanly" attitude when faced with death. In this drama Kleist — nearly in the manner of Bloch's anticipation of utopia — finally placed on stage an androgynous, and thus equal, "noble couple," something he had depicted in *Penthesilea* only *ex negativo,* in a dystopian fashion (cf. Hofmann).

Nevertheless, Kleist's *Penthesilea* still maintains a lofty position within German drama, and not only because it presents the recurrent conflict between personal self-fulfillment and the demands of the state in an admittedly exaggerated but, therefore, all the more exciting form. May we never come to the point that all humans have become so similar that they no longer have any understanding of such conflicts. And may no state ever become so omnipotent that it can usurp the role of "Big

Brother" with dictatorial means or through a demagogically sophisticated social-engineering strategy of the type foreseen by George Orwell.

Translated by Matthew Lange

Notes

[1] Cf. the section "Wirkung" in Kleist 2:693–73 3 for reception history.

[2] In the following I refer to the major arguments of feminist students in my Kleist seminars in Madison, Bremen, Marburg, and Essen (1978–91).

[3] This group often refers to the "Amazonian" (cf., among others, Birkby).

[4] Anna Seghers defended Kleist against the reproach of reaction and decadence in her correspondence with Lukács (cf. Mayer 75).

[5] A good example of such a partial interpretation from a male perspective is the essay by Fuhrmann.

Works Cited

Angress, Ruth. "Kleist's Nation of Amazons." In *Positionen I. Heinrich von Kleist.* Ed. Peter Horn. Cape Town: Capc Town UP, 1982, 5–28.

Birkby, Phillis, ed. *Amazon Expedition: A Lesbian Feminist Anthology.* Washington, N.J.: Times Change Press, 1973.

Blöcker, Günter. *Heinrich von Kleist oder das absolute Ich.* Berlin: Argon, 1960.

Borchardt, Edith. *Mythische Strukturen im Werk Heinrich von Kleists.* New York: Peter Lang, 1987.

Brandstetter, Gabriele. "'Das Wort des Greuelrätsels!': Die Überschreitung der Tragödie." In *Kleists Dramen.* Ed. Walter Hinderer. Stuttgart: Reclam, 1997, 95–115.

Daly, Mary. *Gyn/Ecology: The Metaethics of Radical Feminism.* Boston: Beacon Press, 1978.

Dettmering, Peter. *Heinrich von Kleist: Zur Psychodynamik in seiner Dichtung.* Munich: Nymphenburger Verlagshandlung, 1970.

Fischer, Ernst. "Heinrich von Kleist." In his *Auf den Spuren der Wirklichkeit.* Reinbek: Rowohlt, 1968, 72–155.

Fricke, Gerhard. *Gefühl und Schicksal bei Heinrich von Kleist.* Leipzig: Junker & Dünnhaupt, 1929.

Fuhrmann, Manfred. "Christa Wolf über 'Penthesilea.'" *Kleist-Jahrbuch* (1986): 81–92.

Gallas, Helga. "Antikerezeption bei Goethe und Kleist: 'Penthesilea' — eine Anti-'Iphigenie.'" In *Monumentum Dramaticum*. Ed. Lina Dierick. Waterloo Ont.: U of Waterloo P, 1990, 209–220.

———. "Kleists 'Penthesilea' und Lacans vier Diskurse." In *Kontroversen, alte und neue*. Vol. 6: *Frauensprache — Frauenliteratur*. Ed. Inge Stephan and Carl Pietzker. Tübingen: Niemeyer, 1986, 203–212.

Geyer, Angelika. "Penthesileas Schwestern: Amazonomachie als Thema antiker Kunst." *Kleist-Jahrbuch* (1991): 124–154.

Göttner-Abendroth, Heide. *Die tanzende Göttin: Prinzipien einer matriarchalischen Ästhetik*. Munich: Verlag Frauenoffensive, 1985.

Gutjahr, Ortrud. "Iphigenie — Penthesilea — Medea." In *Frauen: MitSprechen, MitSchreiben*. Ed. Marianne Henn and Britta Hufeisen. Stuttgart: Heinz, 1997, 223–243.

Hamann, Richard and Jost Hermand. *Expressionismus*. Berlin: Akademie-Verlag, 1975.

Hansen, Birgit. "Gewaltige Performanz: Tödliche Sprechakte in Kleists *Penthesilea*." *Kleist-Jahrbuch* (1998): 109–126.

Hayn, Hugo. *Amazonen-Literatur: Vier neue Curiositäten-Bibliographien*. Jena: Schmidt, 1905.

Hermand, Jost. "All Power to the Women: Nazi Concepts of Matriarchy." *Journal of Contemporary History* 19 (1984): 649–668.

———. "Kleists Schreibintentionen." In *Heinrich von Kleist: Studien zu Werk und Wirkung*. Ed. Dirk Grathoff. Opladen: Westdeutscher Verlag, 1988, 40–55.

Herrmann, Hans Peter. "Sprache und Liebe: Beobachtungen zu Kleists *Penthesilea*." In *Heinrich von Kleist*. Ed. Heinz Ludwig Arnold. Munich: Text + Kritik, 1992, 87–104.

Hilmes, Carola. "'Wer bist du, wunderbares Weib?': Kleists *Penthesilea*." In *Die "femme fatale" im Drama*. Ed. Jürgen Blänsdorf. Tübingen: Francke, 1999, 59–79.

Hofmann, Hasso. "Individuum und allgemeines Gesetz: Zur Dialektik in Kleists *Penthesilea* und *Prinz Friedrich von Homburg*." *Kleist-Jahrbuch* (1987): 137–63.

Horn, Peter. "'Penthesilea': Die Neugestaltung eines griechischen Mythos aus dem Geist der Spontaneität." In his *Positionen I: Heinrich von Kleist*. Cape Town: Cape Town UP, 1982, 95–113.

Hoverland, Lilian. "Heinrich von Kleist and Luce Irigaray: Visions of the Feminine." In *Gestaltete und gestaltende Frauen in der Literatur*. Ed. Marianne Burkhard. Amsterdam: Rodopi, 1980, 57–82.

Hülk, Walburga. "Leibgericht: Herzstücke für eine Anthropologie in den Literaturwissenschaften." *Romanische Forschungen* 111 (1999): 17–20.

Jacobs, Carol. "The Rhetorics of Feminism: *Penthesilea*." In *Uncontainable Romanticism: Shelley, Brontë, Kleist*. Baltimore: Johns Hopkins UP, 1989, 85–114.

Klein, Hans. *Die antiken Amazonensagen in der deutschen Literatur*. Leipzig: Radelli & Hille, 1919.

Kleist, Heinrich von. *Dramen 1808–1811. Vol. 2, Sämtliche Werke und Briefe*. Ed. Ilse-Marie Barth et al. Frankfurt a.M.: Klassiker Verlag, 1987.

Klotz, Volker. "Aug um Zunge — Zunge um Aug. Kleists extremes Theater." *Kleist-Jahrbuch* (1985): 135–42.

Klüger, Ruth. "Die andere Hündin: *Käthchen*." *Kleist-Jahrbuch* (1993): 103–115.

Köhler, Carola. "Aktive Penthesilea — Passiver Achill: Das Aufbrechen traditioneller Geschlechterrollen in Heinrich von Kleists 'Penthesilea.'" In *Beiträge zur Kleist-Forschung*. Ed. Wolfgang Barthel and Hans-Jochen Marquard. Frankfurt a. d. O.: Kleist Gedenk- und Forschungsstätte, 1997, 60–74.

Kohrs, Ingrid. *Das Wesen des Tragischen im Drama Heinrich von Kleists. Dargestellt an Interpretationen von "Penthesilea" und "Prinz Friedrich von Homburg."* Marburg: Simons, 1951.

Kublitz-Kramer, Maria. "'Ja, wenn man Tränen schreiben könnte!': Versagte Trauer in Kleists *Penthesilea*." In *Trauer tragen — Trauer zeigen: Inszenierungen der Geschlechter*. Ed. Gisela Ecker. Munich: Fiale, 1999, 109–121.

Kuzniar, Alice, ed. *Outing Goethe and His Age*. Stanford: Stanford UP, 1996.

Lange, Sigrid. "Kleists *Penthesilea*." *Weimarer Beiträge* 37 (1991): 705–22.

Lukács, Georg. "Die Tragödie Heinrich von Kleists." In his *Deutsche Realisten des 19. Jahrhunderts*. Berlin: Aufbau, 1956, 19–47.

Mahlendorf, Ursula R. "The Wounded Self: Kleist's *Penthesilea*." *German Quarterly* 52 (1979): 252–72.

Mayer, Hans. "Gedenkrede auf Anna Seghers." *Argonautenschiff* 1 (1992): 7–14.

Mommsen, Katharina. *Kleists Kampf mit Goethe*. Heidelberg: Stiehm, 1974.

Müller-Seidel, Walter. "*Penthesilea* im Kontext der deutschen Klassik." In *Kleists Dramen: Neue Interpretationen*. Ed. Walter Hinderer. Stuttgart: Reclam, 1981, 144–71.

Nutz, Maximilian. "Kleists *Penthesilea* als Körperdrama." In *Heinrich von Kleist. Studien zu Werk und Wirkung*. Ed. Dirk Grathoff. Opladen: Westdeutscher Verlag, 1988, 163–85.

Pfeiffer, Joachim. "Friendship and Genre: The Aesthetic Constitution of Subjectivity in Kleist." In *Outing Goethe and His Age*. Ed. Alice Kuzniar. Stanford, CA: Stanford UP, 1996, 217–27.

Rigby, Kate. "The Return of the Repressed or The Strange Case of Kleistian Feminism." *Southern Review* 25 (1992): 320–32.

Rolle, Renate. "Amazonen in der archäologischen Realität." *Kleist-Jahrbuch* (1986): 38–62.

Scheifele, Sigrid. *Projektionen des Weiblichen: Lebensentwürfe in Kleists Penthesilea.* Würzburg: Könighausen & Neumann, 1992.

Schell, Renée M. "The Eye of the Beholder: Female Subjectivity in Kleist's *Penthesilea.*" In *Beiträge zur Kleist-Forschung.* Ed. Wolfgang Barthel and Hans-Jochen Marquard. Frankfurt a. d. O.: Kleist Gedenk- und Forschungsstätte, 1997, 44–59.

Schmidt, Werner. *Penthesilea in der Kleistliteratur.* Leipzig: J. J. Weber, 1934.

Sembder, Helmut, ed. *Dichter über ihre Dichtungen: Heinrich von Kleist.* Munich: Heimeran, 1969.

Sieck, Albrecht. *Kleists Penthesilea: Versuch einer neuen Interpretation.* Bonn: Bouvier, 1987.

Stephan, Inge. "Da werden Weiber zu Hyänen . . .': Amazonen und Amazonenmythen bei Schiller und Kleist." In *Feministische Literaturwissenschaft.* Ed. Stephan and Sigrid Weigel. Berlin: Argument, 1984, 23–42.

———. "Mignon und Penthesilea: Androgynie und erotischer Diskurs bei Goethe und Kleist." In *Annäherungsversuche: Zur Geschichte und Ästhetik des Erotischen in der Literatur.* Ed. Horst Albert Glaser. Bern: Paul Haupt, 1993, 283–309.

Stipa, Ingrid. "Kleist's *Penthesilea:* From Misapprehension to Madness." *Seminar: A Journal of Germanic Studies* 27 (1991): 27–38.

Streller, Siegfried. "Zur Problematik von Kleists 'Penthesilea.'" *Weimarer Beiträge* 5 (1959): 508–12.

ter Horst, Eleanor E. "The Transformation of Gender Paradigms in Lessing, Goethe, and Kleist." Diss., U of Michigan, 1996.

Vohland, Ulrich. *Bürgerliche Emanzipation in Heinrich von Kleists Dramen und theoretischen Schriften.* Frankfurt a.M.: Lang, 1976.

Williams-Duplaintier, Rebecca. "Amazon Figures in German Literature." Diss., Ohio State U, 1992.

Wolf, Christa. "Kleists *Penthesilea.*" In her *Die Dimension des Autors: Essays und Aufsätze, Reden und Gespräche 1959–1985.* Neuwied: Luchterhand, 1987, 189–206.

Wolff, Hans M. "Kleists Amazonenstaat im Lichte Rousseaus." *PMLA* 53 (1938): 189–206.

Language and Form

On Structures in Kleist

Anthony Stephens

Symmetry and Its Ambivalences

IN FEBRUARY 1808 Kleist wrote to the author and theater director Heinrich Joseph von Collin, from whom he hoped, among other things, to elicit a contribution for his journal *Phöbus.* A number of eminent literary figures had already turned a deaf ear to Kleist's appeal for contributions. *Phöbus* was clearly in difficulties, and, likely with more bravado than veracity, Kleist declares that in addition to *Penthesilea,* he has two more complete tragedies from his own pen from which he will publish extracts: "Das erste Werk, womit ich wieder auftreten werde, ist Robert Guiskart, Herzog der Normänner. Der Stoff ist . . . noch ungeheurer; doch in der Kunst kommt es überall auf die Form an, und Alles, was eine Gestalt hat, ist meine Sache" (4:413). His correspondent could scarcely have been aware of the fraught history of *Guiskard* as Kleist's first attempt at tragic drama in the grand manner, and there is also no indication in this letter that *Penthesilea,* then in the process of being published, would be the author's last completed tragedy.

Quite apart from any strategic departures from or distortions of the facts about his store of manuscripts in early 1808, what is claimed in his letter to Collin is both true and *not* true of his own command of artistic form, the clash of authorial perspectives on his own work betraying the quintessential Kleist. Confidence in his own mastery over anything possessing "eine Gestalt" sits oddly with the many contemporary perceptions of structural weaknesses or blemishes in his dramas. That *Robert Guiskard* never realized the full potential in which Kleist had placed so much hope when he had begun writing it in 1802 is balanced, from the standpoint of the early twenty first century, by the formal perfection of *Prinz Friedrich von Homburg,* in which he succeeds both in creating a well-shaped tragedy and in encapsulating it in another kind of drama altogether.

To address some of the questions surrounding structures in Kleist's work as a whole is, thus, to broach the issue of the inconstancy of his talent, an enigma as difficult to grasp for Kleist's contemporaries as it is for the abundant scholarship that thrives on expounding his works today. Much as we might wish that Goethe had never made his carping comments on those of Kleist's works he knew or deigned to mention, there is valid insight enough in their coldness. By contrast, the fervor of such a rarely enthusiastic voice among Kleist's early reviewers as is heard in Wilhelm Grimm's judgment on *Das Käthchen von Heilbronn,* "dass das ganze Werk durchweg aus *einem* Gusse ist" (2:878), remains so patently at variance with the text's patchwork quality that we could only wish Grimm had given the accolade to *Penthesilea,* which, as its scholarly reception over the last hundred years has shown, more properly deserves it.

Has the overlong tradition of misunderstanding Kleist's works anything to do with his treatment of structures? I believe such to be the case and will try to explain the basis for this conviction in what follows. To take the published fragment of *Robert Guiskard* as a starting point would, however, mean encumbering the inquiry from the outset with so many unanswerable textual questions that it is more rewarding to start with Kleist's first finished drama, *Die Familie Schroffenstein,* which has been preserved in two full versions, the earlier of which is styled *Die Familie Ghonorez.*

Common to *Die Familie Ghonorez* and its later revamping with "Swabian" dramatis personae and locations is, on the one hand, the clear delineation of a dominant structural principle, and, on the other, its deliberate breaking. This principle is one of symmetrical correspondence, both in thematics and plot-building: its breaking leads, among other things, to a final scene whose dissonances make it well-nigh impossible to integrate into productions that do justice to the finely tuned tragic symphony that the first four acts have composed.

Symmetry was never again to engage Kleist as fully and obtrusively as it does in this first tragedy; and yet, he was never to compromise his own realization of form with such apparent disregard for aesthetic convention as he does in both versions of this first dramatic essay from the end of act 4 onward. Both *Die Familie Ghonorez* and its later reworking, through impossible turns in the plot, destroy their own credibility, beginning with Rodrigo/Ottokar's surviving a suicidal leap from a tower window unscathed: "Der Turm / Ist funfzig Fuss hoch, und der ganze Boden / Gepflastert" (1:217). At the core of the conception of this play is a scene in which two main characters — the young lovers — perform the symmetrical action of exchanging clothes and, thus, their apparent gender and identities. The bulk of the plot, however, has demonstrated the symmetry of the decline of communication between the two branches of the same aristocratic clan to the point where the destruction of the future of the Houses of Rossitz and Warwand by murder is a well-prepared outcome.

In Rodrigo/Ottokar and Juan/Johann, sons of the same father in each version, Kleist also created his first set of alter egos, a frequent symmetrical device in his later works but one in which the imperfections of symmetry, often intensified by his characters' false perceptions of each other, are exploited to tragic or ironic ends. Thus, he was to establish similar structural patterns joining Toni and Mariane Congreve in "Die Verlobung in St. Domingo" and Nicolo and Colino in "Der Findling." Hermann and Ventidius, Homburg and Hohenzollern, Kohlhaas and Nagelschmidt offer further evidence for his liking for discrepant paired figures. Already in his first tragic drama there is, as well, some use made of *inverse* symmetries of character. The cautious and well-meaning Eustache is placed in chiastic symmetry to the spiteful and credulous Gertrude. The skeptical and humane Sylvester presents, in the early scenes in which he appears, an inversely symmetrical contrast to Rupert's intolerance and blood lust, until another more powerful and plainly negative symmetry asserts itself. Thus, the two fathers increasingly mirror one another in their actions as the play nears its end in the gratuitous destruction by murder of those same dynastic futures for which both have lived.

Where Kleist scholarship first encounters obstacles is where symmetry is potentially present but the text disappoints expectations by producing something different. Agnes is drawn with a fineness of detail that foreshadows the greatness of Alkmene in *Amphitryon;* yet, in scene after scene she is mere clay in Ottokar's hands. The young lovers could, indeed, be equivalent in insight and determination, since Kleist had a pronounced talent for creating "larger-than-life" women characters, but Agnes is relegated again and again to subordinate positions. Their ritual of drinking the water Agnes believes to be poisoned points up the lack of equal sophistication between the two lovers and signals its baneful consequences at an early stage, for Ottokar knows that what they are about to drink is nothing but water, and he thus demonstrates that superior insight vis-à-vis Agnes that parallels every omniscient narrator's superiority to the figures he manipulates in conventional narrative genres.

In Kleist's first drama there is enough asymmetry in this love relationship for the reader or audience to be disturbed by the fact that Agnes has, on the one hand, no trouble at all in grasping the foolishness of the family quarrel or the mental instability of Johann, while, on the other, she reveals herself more than once as a mere marionette controlled by

Ottokar. The scene in act 5 where Agnes and Ottokar exchange clothing in a cave, for example, has been interpreted as an epiphany (Harms 309–11); but it is hard to escape the knowledge that Ottokar invents the whole interlude and directs Agnes through it, as if he were trying to get an inexperienced actress to comprehend what love's fulfillment might be like so that she might imitate it for an audience.

One gap in the otherwise pronounced symmetry of the plot that Kleist scholarship has never managed to explain is Ottokar's long scene with the peasant girl Barnabe (4.3). Gerhard Neumann has pointed up the grotesque complementarity of "Hexenküche" and "Abendmahl" (26–28). One might posit an inverse symmetry between the harmless magic practiced by Barnabe, with its beneficent intent, and the destructive will behind the perverted eucharistic ritual with which the play opens, but this aspect of the text exhibits too many unmotivated discrepancies to make a chiastic reversal plausible.

For an inverse symmetry to be visible enough to be effective in this drama, it would need to be plotted within the sphere of the feuding branches of the same aristocratic family — the region where all the power relationships play themselves out. Yet, the cottage of Ursula and Barnabe is outside this region in every way: the peasant women know nothing of the feud working itself through in the main plot, and Barnabe's revelation to Ottokar of the true circumstances of his young brother's death comes too late to have a decisive impact on the tragic action. Symmetries, in Kleist's first drama, shape or undo themselves in the region between the polarities of the two opposed noble households, dominated by the fathers Graf Rupert and Graf Sylvester. In other words: symmetries highlight powers, then twist them toward a finale that should be tragic but verges on black comedy.

To open now a quite different perspective on symmetry as a structural fundamental in Kleist's work, let us return to his letter of February 1808 and scrutinize the term *Gestalt* more closely. Symmetries are one of a variety of formal elements that may help to provide the basis for an experience of "Gestalt" on the part of the recipient of a work of art. But for Kleist it is the subjective apprehension, the event in the consciousness of the audience, reader, or critical observer, that has primacy. The sentence concerning *Robert Guiskard* begins by conceding that the matter of the play is "yet more monstrous" than the thematics of *Penthesilea* — surely Kleist could have had few doubts as to the challenge these posed to popular taste! — but it then asserts the dominance of form over content in literary craftsmanship and ends with a rhetorical flourish that proclaims his own mastery over the ultimate touchstone of artistic realization, "Gestalt." This latter is an event in the consciousness of the recipient of art, which here amounts to a recognition of the successful interplay of "Stoff" and "Form."

The primacy of events in the consciousness over what the senses may apprehend had already been asserted in a letter to Marie von Kleist of June 1807. Here Kleist writes of a painting by Simon Vouet of the dying Magdalene in the Church of Saint-Loup in Châlons-sur-Marne. The religious subject itself is not even identified in his evocation, and the judgment he passes on aspects of the artistic execution is harsh: "schlecht gezeichnet zwar" (4:378). But his consciousness creates an artistic triumph out of the interplay between his own creative imagination and the "invention" he intuits beyond its own imperfect realization: Vouet's daub is "doch von der schönsten Erfindung, die man sich denken kann" (378). From this comment he moves on to a logical, though quite surprising, generalization: "Denn nicht das was den Sinnen dargestellt ist, sondern das was das Gemüth, durch diese Wahrnehmung erregt, sich denkt, ist das Kunstwerk" (378).

The function of structures is, in these terms, to mediate between the artist's raw material — "Stoff" — and the inner event, at once intellectual and emotional, that is the experience of "Gestalt" and of which Kleist writes at the end of his account of viewing Vouet's painting: "Ich habe nie etwas Rührenderes und Erhebenderes gesehen" (380).

From the perspective of Kleist's whole work, with all its contradictions and modulations of negativity, it is ironic that the example he chooses to define "das Kunstwerk" as such is so unlike most of his own productions. In his evocation of the painting all the formal elements work together harmoniously to produce an effect that is sustained by a balance of inverse symmetries and that Kleist has no hesitation in describing in terms of conventional Enlightenment aesthetics. The bulk of his own writings, by contrast, far from opening any simple perspectives onto utopian "Gefilde unendlicher Seligkeit" (380), are notorious either for ending in a play of ambivalences that overtaxes the educated audience's or reader's powers of conceptualization or else for culminating in moments of suffering, such as Alkmene's state of mind at the end of *Amphitryon*, for which there is no saving transfiguration as counterpoise.

Underlying an aesthetic that we glimpse in scant detail through Kleist's few preserved theoretical statements and precariously deduce from his "Erfindungen" from *Die Familie Schroffenstein* onward is, thus, the interplay between the principle of symmetry and its Other. The identity of this Other is revealed in the letter already quoted by the sentence that functions as prologue to the evocation of the painting:

"Erscheinungen rings, dass man eine Ewigkeit brauchte, um sie zu würdigen, und kaum wahrgenommen schon wieder von anderen verdrengt, die eben so unbegriffen verschwinden" (379). It is from this experience of temporal chaos that Kleist's consciousness finds refuge in the ordered contemplation of the painting of the dying Magdalene exhibited in the church. In this context, at least, symmetry's Other is transience.

At the end of the eighteenth century concepts of symmetry in the sciences would have been formulated either in terms of stasis or of predictable repetition. Such static structures or patterns of regularity need not be free of tension, as Kleist was to observe more than once in the case of the vault built of masonry. As he points out in a letter to Wilhelmine von Zenge in November 1800: "Warum, dachte ich, sinkt das Gewölbe nicht ein, da es doch *keine* Stütze hat? Es steht, antwortete ich, weil alle seine Steine aufeinmal einstürzen wollen" (4:159). When the image returns seven years later in the text of *Penthesilea*, it becomes clear that the Other of symmetry is that randomness of which the surrender to the purposeless flow of time is emblematic: "Stehe, stehe fest, wie das Gewölbe steht, / Weil seiner Blöcke jeder stürzen will!" (3:191).

What is most asymmetrical, in Kleist's terms, is the self's chance motion in time. It is significant that one of the most quoted and most negative images of human existence in his early letters foregrounds precisely this: "ein Spiel des Zufalls, eine Puppe am Drahte des Schicksals — dieser unwürdige Zustand scheint mir so verächtlich, und würde mich so unglücklich machen, dass mir der Tod bei weitem wünschenswerter wäre" (4:40). Events in "profane" time with no salving entelechy — the fortuitous dislodgment of one stone in the structure of a vault, or the mischance that makes Toni decide not to wake the sleeping Gustav to explain her stratagem to save them both in "Die Verlobung in St. Domingo" — are what make symmetry the prelude to chaos. Indeed, so many of Kleist's characters, from his first play onward, experience moments in which death appears as the only sure defense against the vagaries of transience that the intensity of them resonates throughout his whole work. Agnes's impassioned cry in act 3 of *Die Familie Schroffenstein*, "O wär es Gift, und könnt ich mit Dir sterben!" (1:178), finds an echo in Penthesilea's darkest of visions of an eternal bond with Achilles that will liberate them from time and chance — "der Zeit nicht und dem Zufall mehr zerstörbar" (2:211). But the factual conditions of such a bond have been anticipated in her earlier words in scene 5:

Hier, dieses Eisen soll, Gefährtinnen,
Soll mit der sanftesten Umarmung ihn,
(Weil ich mit Eisen ihn umarmen muss!)
An meinen Busen schmerzlos niederziehn. (2:173)

In Kleist's whole oeuvre words that may, in the context of their first utterance, seem mere hyperbole, take on again and again — once grasped in retrospect — anticipatory overtones of death as the only effective freeing of the self from symmetry's Other. Thus, in "Die Verlobung in St. Domingo" Gustav's apparently gauche attempt at flirtatiousness in his first encounter with Toni can be read, from the perspective of the final catastrophe, as a first presage of mutual destruction: "Der Fremde, indem er den Arm sanft um ihren Leib schlug, sagte verlegen: . . . Hätte ich dir . . ., indem er sie lebhaft an seine Brust drückte, ins Auge sehen können, so wie ich es jetzt kann, so hätte ich, auch wenn alles Übrige an dir schwarz gewesen wäre, aus einem vergifteten Becher mit dir trinken wollen" (3:231). For one interpretation of the inconsistencies in Gustav's behavior and of his astonishing blind spots is that his statements and actions are unconsciously gravitating toward a death that will free him from the guilt with which he is laden since Mariane Congreve atoned with her life for his own "Unbesonnenheit" (237). That Toni then, in effect, sets out in her own actions to mirror those of Gustav's first betrothed, and thereby complements her lover's death wish, is one of the deceptive symmetries of characterization at which Kleist so excelled but which render his figures so vulnerable to time and chance.

To return to Kleist's beginnings as a creative writer, we must ask: why are structural and thematic symmetries so persistently evoked in his first completed drama — only to modulate into the destructive mode? For as *Die Familie Schroffenstein* nears its closure, Sylvester and Rupert, whom the first act presents as antitheses of one another, come to resemble each other more and more. An obtrusive signal on the dramatist's part that this process is underway is that Rupert, setting off to find and kill Sylvester's daughter, perceives the reflection of his own face in a stream as that of a devil (cf. 1:211).

I suggest that the answer lies in the paradox that all lesser symmetries fall short of the most exalted one, that of Narcissus in loving contemplation of his own image, but that this, too — as the myth is at pains to emphasize — is deceptive, since symmetrical love involves complete possession, and this, in turn, is at odds with that undoing force that is mortality. Whether it be Penthesilea's longing for a union with Achilles that is immune to time and chance, or Homburg's anticipation of a narcissistic fulfillment beyond his impending execution in the monologue "Nun, o Unsterblichkeit, bist Du ganz mein!" (2:642), complete possession of the beloved object stands in Kleist's works as a metaphor for a perfection that cannot be lasting before death itself has become factual, hence timeless, and thus no longer a mere rhetorical flourish.

When, in *Die Familie Schroffenstein,* Agnes and Ottokar achieve the momentary conviction that they have crossed a threshold to a region beyond time, the complete surrender of the self and the claim to immunity from transience are blended in their dialogue:

> OTTOKAR: Willst Du's? Kann ich Dich ganz mein nennen?
>
> AGNES: Ganz Deine, in der grenzenlosesten Bedeutung.
>
> OTTOKAR: Wohl, das steht nun fest, und gilt
>
> Für eine Ewigkeit. Wir werden's brauchen. (1:176–77)

But the beloved simulacrum of the self is never grasped — even in metaphor — for more than an instant, and such instants of "sacred time" are overshadowed by Kleist's inveterate ironies, whether they be the course the family feud has already taken in *Die Familie Schroffenstein* or the Prussian court poised to drag a reluctant Homburg back from his euphoric anticipation of immortality into his questionable role as institutional hero with a job still to do. In such ways an apparently perfect symmetry of desire glosses over latent but ultimately fatal imperfections — be these the discrepancy between god and mortal in *Amphitryon* or the unresolvable contradictions between the heroine's divinely prescribed roles in *Penthesilea.*

Mirroring, both as a formal device and as a state of consciousness, is bedeviled in Kleist's works by a fatal incapacity to hold still as the plot advances. Such symmetries distort the dramatic or narrative action toward catastrophe — not merely because "profane" time and chance effect discrepant and irreversible transitions, such as Lacan was later to postulate between the Imaginary and Symbolic, but also because they leave the fictional characters in the erroneous belief they are still seeing those same incarnations of reflexive desire that they may once have seen, embracing images they have embraced before, whereas time and chance have radically shifted the focus.

The fate of Elvire in "Der Findling" shows this delusion at its cruelest. Believing that her love for Colino is safeguarded forever by her repeated erotic devotions before his image, which she segregates in place and time from her everyday domestic life, she is a totally helpless victim when she undresses and falls into ecstasy before the live and lustful

Nicolo, who has usurped the place of her icon and, thus, intruded into her "sacred" time. In such ways symmetrical structures in Kleist's work become mechanisms of destruction, because correspondences, in his plots, elude permanence and betray perfection.

We may see this point more clearly by placing Kleist's destructive symmetries in an historical perspective. Since the Renaissance, pronounced symmetries were the trademark of the closures of comedies: the twins, whose physical resemblance has wrought confusion among the other characters, are revealed to be brother and sister and, hence, may be married off to other characters with general satisfaction and acclaim. In other variants, misdirected passions that have made the path of true love thorny are resolved by symmetrical rearrangements that send the audience home cheerful.

Symmetry in this sense is also commonly used in comic endings to take the sting out of social inequality in the real world by mimicking its opposite on stage. The august and divinely ordained marriage of Tamino and Pamina in *Die Zauberflöte* gains in humanity by its parallel in that of Papageno and Papagena. In Shakespeare's *Twelfth Night* the marriage of the quick-witted servant girl Maria to Sir Toby Belch, while scarcely plausible in terms of social class, serves, within the comic fiction, as a symmetric pendant to the dual matches made for the aristocrats Orsino and Olivia.

Kleist knew the trope well from his reading of Shakespeare and such works in German as Lessing's *Nathan der Weise*. Not only does he radically alter the emotional force of this structural device from his first drama onward; he also often reverses its positioning in the plot. In *Die Familie Schroffenstein* he deploys symmetries of imagery and action from the outset to intensify the play's negative themes. With the apparent murders of the children Peter and Philipp he further projects deceptive mirrorings into the time before the play commences. For all that the "Erbvertrag" ceases to interest the characters after the end of act 2, what else is it but a device for heightening hostile feelings between the two branches of the family feelings whose relation to one another is, by turns, that of echo to voice?

Genre as Improvisation

No serious study of Kleist's dramas and prose ignores the fact that he plays at times unfathomable games with the expectations of contemporary audiences and readers, and nowhere is this practice more evident than in his use of structures. That he persisted in this course is all the more remarkable when we recall that he defines the work of art — in the midst of his most creative period — not as an autonomous entity on the page, to which the reader must adapt as well as he or she may, but as an event in the receptive consciousness of the individual: "was das Gemüth, durch diese Wahrnehmung erregt, sich denkt, ist das Kunstwerk" (4:379). The pressures on Kleist to achieve success with the public were great, as he was an intensely ambitious genius, many of whose gifted contemporaries reacted to his major works with incredible obtuseness. Equally strong were the temptations to give audiences what contemporary formulae for success dictated; and yet, on those few occasions when Kleist sees himself as succumbing, his self-reproaches are bitter, as when he writes of *Das Käthchen von Heilbronn* to Marie von Kleist in 1811: "Es war von Anfang herein eine ganz treffliche Erfindung, und nur die Absicht, es für die Bühne passend zu machen, hat mich zu Missgriffen verführt, die ich jetzt beweinen möchte" (4:484).

At the beginning of the nineteenth century, in the context of the heady formal experiments and even more audacious theoretical adventures of early Romanticism, the only restraints on Kleist's freedom to improvise, in individual works, on whatever basis in conventional structures from which he began were twofold: first, his recognition that the expectations set up by genre-based patterns were tenacious among the educated readership and audiences of his day; second, that he had chosen the most prestigious literary genre, high tragedy, as the field in which he would excel — indeed, would prove himself a talent comparable with Goethe. Failure to realize the exalted ideal of tragedy he had conceived led to the burning of an incomplete manuscript of *Robert Guiskard* in Paris in October 1803. Uninhibited improvisation with other genres, however, sets in motion a constant process of alluding to conventional models, while — at the same time — producing innovative variants of them that, in turn, introduce elements of interference into the receptive process. In other words, Kleist's characteristic technique is to subvert genre-based expectations in ways whose underlying intentions are extremely difficult to define; hence the wide disparities in the ways they are even today understood by scholars.

The prime function of Kleist's structural innovations is to provide cues which alert the audience or reader to the presence of a creative disturbance of patterns that had grown all too familiar and predictable. The question underlying much writing on Kleist is whether his disappointment of conventional expectations is driven by a consistent ideological program, such as the vision of a reformed Prussia, or whether it is experimentation for its own sake. I incline to the latter opinion and see in it the prime reason why many of Kleist's minglings of genres tend toward parody.

This is no less a feature of the narratives than of the dramas. Kleist's narrators, so prompt with dogmatic moral judgements that subsequent events throw into question or refute, are, in the main, parodistic variants on the omnipotent narrator of eighteenth-century popular fiction who guides the reader with consistency and reliability through such moral dilemmas as the plot may pose. In similar mode, the plots of Kleist's stories frequently play on the device of the deferred ending: a story reaches a point where conventional narrative technique would bring it to a close, but Kleist rings the changes on what his readers expect by developing fresh narrative sequences. The reputed death of the Graf F . . . in "Die Marquise von O . . ." and his unexpected reentry into the plot are a case in point. The scene in which the heroic rescuer of the Marquise from rape by the common soldiers, who has reportedly died of his wounds, makes an unexpected reappearance both defers the ending his real death would have imposed on the story and also satirizes the expectations of contemporary readers by introducing dissonances into one of those tableaux of "Rührung" so common in the popular art forms of Kleist's age:

> Der Commendant sprang sogleich selbst auf, ihm zu öffnen, worauf er [Graf F . . .], schön, wie ein junger Gott, ein wenig bleich im Gesicht, eintrat. Nachdem die Szene unbegreiflicher Verwunderung vorüber war, und der Graf, auf die Anschuldigung der Eltern, dass er ja tot sei, versichert hatte, dass er lebe; wandte er sich, mit vieler Rührung im Gesicht, zur Tochter, und seine erste Frage war gleich, wie sie sich befinde? Die Marquise versicherte, sehr wohl, und wollte nur wissen, wie er ins Leben erstanden sei? (3:149)

The reasons for the dissonances later become obvious: the Marquise's savior has raped her while she was unconscious. Therefore, the ironic undertones in "die Anschuldigung der Eltern" and the reason why the scene does not dissolve into unalloyed "Rührung" on all sides but takes a quite different turning can only become intelligible at a further stage of the plot. Allowing the scene to edge toward a parody of conventional "Rührung" is the author's way of signaling that the deferred ending will bring further shocks and breaches of conventional expectations.

Penthesilea appears to mark a watershed in Kleist's struggle with tragic form. Nothing in it resembles the Shakespearean mixing of genres alluded to by the final scene of *Die Familie Schroffenstein*. Rather, the interaction of tragic convergence with conventional retarding factors does much to "normalize" the play's overall structure, despite Kleist's discarding of the classic five-act division and his protraction of the action well beyond the death of Achilles. Where violence is done to contemporary expectations is in the thematics. Written in conscious opposition to Goethe's rendering antiquity so innocuous in *Iphigenie auf Tauris,* Kleist's heroine convincingly invokes "Begierden, die, wie losgelassne Hunde, / Mir der Drommete erzne Lunge bellend, / Und aller Feldherrn Rufen, überschrei'n!" (2:187) The symmetries active in the imagery surrounding both main characters in the speeches of other characters and recurring in their own language converge in the image of the violent death of the Trojan prince Hector and the inhuman treatment accorded his corpse (cf. Stephens 1994, 110–12).

If we consider the extent to which Kleist was willing in the letter of June 1807, written while he was still engaged on *Penthesilea,* to delegate the ultimate creative completion of the work of art to its assimilation into the consciousness ("was das Gemüth . . . sich denkt" [4:379]) of the observer, reader, or audience, then the hostile or patronizing incomprehension that was the common response to this tragedy — not least Goethe's tactless rejection of the text Kleist sent him "auf den 'Knieen meines Herzens'" in January 1808 (4:407) — had to be intensely embittering. Thus, Kleist parodies the misprision of his work in epigrams that emphasize that the reception of the play effectively destroys the very "Gestalt" it is meant to bring to realization: "Heute zum ersten Mal mit Vergunst: die Penthesilea, / Hundekomödie; Acteurs: Helden und Köter und Fraun" (3:412).

After the completion of *Penthesilea* and the painful recognition that his tragic masterpiece would have none of its achievements acknowledged by the reading public at large, the imperative to excel in this genre appears to lose its force for Kleist. It may also be that he takes a more aggressive stance to the idea of the work of art's attaining its culmination in the complementary process of its reception and, thus, increasingly presents challenges to readers and audiences to which their conventional expectations provide them with no adequate responses.

Improvisation thus becomes dominant in his dramatic structures. For example, in *Das Käthchen von Heilbronn* genre becomes a genuinely game-playing medium, as the text works with a congeries of popular dramatic fashions, indulging in a sprawling plot, far-fetched characterization, and a goodly amount of literary satire and parody. The one structural principle that does recur obsessively within this improvisational mode and tends to stabilize it is that underlying the many anticipatory elements in both plotting and characterization.

Prinz Friedrich von Homburg takes this principle to its furthest realization with the repetition in the closing scenes of the "dream" sequence at the beginning of the play, in which the Kurfürst and his court play a cruel game with Homburg's visions of his own future glory. At the conclusion the sequence is reenacted, but it has now become reality — albeit one that is greeted with less than joyous acceptance by a hero who has declared "Mit der Welt schloss ich die Rechnung ab!" (2:640) and has already anticipated an alternative, narcissistic apotheosis in the monologue beginning: "Nun, o Unsterblichkeit, bist Du ganz mein!" (642)

Anticipatory sequences and motifs are so common in Kleist's work that the technique becomes an important structural principle in its own right. Adam's dream, which he narrates to Licht at the beginning of *Der zerbrochne Krug,* not only anticipates the course the trial will take but also signals how one may understand what follows: Adam as judge condemns himself as miscreant in his own dream; in the play's later action Gerichtsrat Walter acts out the part of Adam's own moral alter ego — the Adam who exposes the wrongdoing of the "old Adam" but is surprisingly merciful in his enactment of judgment.

Beda Allemann, in an extract from a longer work that remains unpublished, explores anticipation as a factor that structures the psychological fixity of Kleist's heroines and heroes: "Es ist ein Bild der höchsten Erfüllung, das seine Helden leitet" (48). It is necessary to point out that Kleist's main characters are equally susceptible to images of their own humiliation or destruction, as evidenced by Penthesilea's fixation on her vision of the desecration of the corpse of the slain Hector, with which she is as prone to identify as with any positive self-representations. Christian Moser takes the theme of anticipation further in that he both integrates it into the problematics of perception that beset Kleist's characters and also traces its origin back to fundamental ambivalences in the thinking of Rousseau on the subject (43–44).

Whether seen in psychological or purely formal terms, anticipation has the effect of creating a real or apparent symmetry across a span of time. The time may be real or imaginary, profane or sacred: the interval between the opening and closing sequences of *Prinz Friedrich von Homburg* or between Adam's dream and his actually fleeing the courtroom in *Der zerbrochne Krug* is the "profane" time in which the rest of the plot unfolds. Toni in "Die Verlobung in St. Domingo," as she hastens through the night to find Gustav's party in an attempt to save him, is effectively living in an imaginary "sacred" time that synthesizes that of the death Gustav's first betrothed, Mariane Congreve, whose tragic story she has heard and with whom she now clearly identifies as an ideal self, with the moment of her own impending death at the hands of Gustav: "es mischte sich ein Gefühl heisser Bitterkeit in ihre Liebe zu ihm, und sie frohlockte bei dem Gedanken, in dieser zu seiner Rettung angeordneten Unternehmung zu sterben" (3:252).

I have argued elsewhere that it is necessary to distinguish between anticipation in Kleist's works as a psychological state — be it the narcissistic self-fulfillment of Homburg's "Nun, o Unsterblichkeit, bist Du ganz mein!" (2:642) or the anticipatory distortion of perception that renders Elvire unable to distinguish the expected painting of Colino from the live and present Nicolo at the climax of "Der Findling" (cf. 3:280) — and anticipation as a structural patterning of the text that has an aesthetic function but is initially neutral in psychological terms (1999, 464).

To pursue the ambivalences of anticipation as a structural principle in Kleist further one needs to return to the problematical question of symmetries and time. Throughout Kleist's literary works one may glimpse that phantom of human time as entelechy that dominates the outline of his early "eigne Religion" (4:204) and that serves as a prelude to the crisis he alleges has followed on his acquaintance "mit der neueren sogenannten Kantischen Philosophie" in the letter to Wilhelmine von Zenge of 22 March 1801 (4:205). A similar confidence in the possibility of purposeful human experience, guaranteed by a cosmos teleologically structured by a benevolent creator, informs the text of 1799, "Aufsatz, den sichern Weg des Glücks zu finden[. . .]." The idea of attaining a perfection of the human self through a divinely grounded entelechy of experience stands here in a not quite logical relationship to the overtly narcissistic concept of fulfillment: "Ich nenne nämlich Glück nur die vollen und überschwenglichen Genüsse, die . . . in dem erfreulichen Anschaun der moralischen Schönheit unserers eigenen Wesens liegen" (3:519). If the beauty is there already, what need is there for the whole process of "Vervollkomnung" through several reincarnations, as sketched for Wilhelmine in the letter of March 1801? The answer the essay suggests is an implicit allegiance to Leibniz's monadology whereby each monad bears within it an image of the totality of the cosmos, which is also supratemporal. Thus, Kleist writes:

> Und wo, mein Freund, kann dieser Wunsch erfüllt werden, wo kann das Glück besser sich gründen, als da, wohin die ganze Schöpfung sich bezieht, wo die Welt mit ihren unermesslichen Reizungen sich wiederholt? Da ist es ja auch allein nur unser Eigentum, es hängt von keinen äusseren Verhältnissen ab, kein Tyrann kann es uns rauben, kein Bösewicht kann es stören, wir tragen es mit in alle Weltteile umher. (3:516)

Kleist clearly began writing literary works in the wake of the collapse of a teleological philosophy that entails a harmony of inner and outer worlds and thus permits an anticipatory contemplation of the "Schönheit unseres eigenen Wesens." Kleist's characters become fixated on ideal images of fulfillment at their own risk, as the plot of the tragedy encapsulated within *Prinz Friedrich von Homburg* demonstrates. Indeed, a belief in a benevolent, teleologically structured cosmos is satirized often by Kleist, as, for example, when Jeronimo and Josephe in "Das Erdbeben in Chili" make the fatal mistake of assuming that their own preservation and the apparent transformation of society in the wake of the earthquake is the unmistakable signature of a Special Providence.

The prevalence of anticipatory structures in Kleist's works serves the function of counterpointing the "sacred time" of a universe governed by personal and historical entelechies, such as his early essay and his summation of his "eigne Religion" posit, with the profane time of European history in the age of Napoleon. While "sacred time," in the fantasies of his characters, pursues an entelechy that would ideally culminate in a state which — to quote *Penthesilea* once more — must be "der Zeit nicht, und dem Zufall, mehr zerstörbar" (2:211), the flow of profane time in the plots of his works reveals the full vulnerability of such illusions. As a result, the ultimate entry of a character into "sacred time" is usually associated or identified with the moment of death — anticipated or actual — as the endings of *Prinz Friedrich von Homburg* and *Penthesilea* each implies in a different manner.

Kleist's diagnosis of contemporary historical time in his letter to Rühle von Lilienstern of December 1805 stresses that the present appears to him as the antithesis of a well-ordered teleological cosmos: "Die Zeit scheint eine neue Ordnung der Dinge herbeiführen zu wollen, und wir werden nichts, als bloss den Umsturz der alten erleben" (4:352). An even more desolate vision of contemporary history as chaos and destruction is evoked in "Das letzte Lied" of April 1809.

The crisis of March 1801, whatever it may or may not have to do with Kant's philosophy, is presented to Kleist's closest confidantes as a loss of faith in a personal entelechy that his later condemnations of the Napoleonic era in Europe simply echo: "Mein *einziges* und *höchstes* Ziel ist gesunken, ich habe keines mehr" (4:208). When Kleist begins working on his first literary projects in Switzerland in April 1802, it is against the background of his disillusioning encounter with the "profane" legacies of both the Enlightenment and the French Revolution, as he had found them exemplified in Parisian society.

His first drama to be completed, *Die Familie Schroffenstein,* is already equipped with the full repertoire of anticipatory motifs and symmetrical devices that Kleist uses throughout his whole work. The work of art can thus counterfeit a well-ordered cosmos, but the very structural characteristics that in his "Aufsatz, den sichern Weg des Glücks zu finden

[. . .]" are emblematic of a universal harmony into which the individual may be integrated by virtue of the homology between the external order of things and an inner sphere "wohin die ganze Schöpfung sich bezieht, wo die Welt mit ihren unermesslichen Reizungen im kleinen sich wiederholt" (3:516) are turned into their opposites. The symmetrical patterning in the thematics and structure becomes a self-destroying process.

Anticipatory devices in Kleist's works as a whole have a similar function, hinting at symmetrical linkages of "sacred" or meaningful moments across the profane time in which his plots elapse but usually introducing a factor of distortion, effecting false matches or inexact correspondences that may visit themselves on the characters as the cruel ironies or deceptive coincidences so familiar to readers of his texts. The attribute common to both symmetries and entelechies in what Kleist writes before March 1801 is purposeful order. Anticipatory devices in aesthetic form are ideally suited to *imply* the presence of such order, while rarely offering any tangible proof. Rather, Kleist's technique is to allow such anticipations to arouse an expectation of order, which is then either subjected to overt negation or simply left hanging.

In an analogous manner, the overall structures of Kleist's works imitate the conventions of the genres in which they purport to be located or to which they allude but which they subvert at the same time, often with an intention that verges on parody. Thus one may read "Der Findling" as a parodistic refutation of the premises of the Bildungsroman or see the characterization of Graf Wetter vom Strahl in *Das Käthchen von Heilbronn* as fading in and out of a parody of the ideal knight — as popular literature in Kleist's time was wont to present such figures.

One may understand these parodies, in turn, as a mirroring of Kleist's primal disillusionment, first documented in March 1801, with the teleological worldview that had sustained him up to that point. Literary genres are, in effect, formal entelechies that complete themselves by fulfilling sets of expectations on the part of the reader or audience. Kleist's works notoriously play fast and loose with such expectations, improvising on the genres they mimic in ways that allow a plurality of readings from various perspectives and make Kleist scholarship, nearly two centuries after his works were written, markedly lacking in consensus as to how they are to be understood.

In Kleist's ten years as a creator of literary works, relentless experimentation takes the place of the ideological certainties that inform his early letters and his "Aufsatz, den sichern Weg des Glücks zu finden[. . .]." Certainties belong to the Lost Paradise, which first appears in 1802 in the manuscript of *Die Familie Ghonorez* — "Hinaus ins Elend aus dem Paradiese / Aus dem des Cherubs Flammenschwerdt uns treibt" (1:504) — and remains a presence in Kleist's writing till the end. It is the paradise of a teleological worldview with an assured specular harmony of inner and outer worlds. The structures of Kleist's literary works are, in this sense, the traces of a lasting exile.

Works Cited

Allemann, Beda. "Heinrich von Kleist: Ein dramaturgisches Modell." In *Nin gyoshibai* (*Marionettentheater*): *Kleist-Blätter*, vol. 3. Sendai: Sendai UP, 1987, 27–62.

Harms, Ingeborg. "'Wie fliegender Sommer': Eine Untersuchung der 'Höhlens-zene' in Heinrich von Kleists *Familie Schroffenstein*." *Jahrbuch der Schillerge-sellschaft* (1984): 270–314.

Kleist, Heinrich von. *Sämtliche Werke und Briefe in vier Bänden*. 4 Vols. Ed. Ilse-Marie Barth et al. Frankfurt a.M.: Deutscher Klassiker Verlag, 1987–97.

Moser, Christian. *Verfehlte Gefühle: Wissen — Begehren — Darstellen bei Kleist und Rousseau*. Würzburg: Könighausen & Neumann, 1993.

Neumann, Gerhard. "Hexenküche und Abendmahl. Die Sprache der Liebe im Werk Heinrich von Kleists." *Freiburger Universitätsblätter* 91 (1986): 9–31.

Stephens, Anthony. *Heinrich von Kleist: The Dramas and Stories*. Providence: Berg, 1994.

———. *Kleist: Sprache und Gewalt*. Freiburg: Rombach, 1999.

Strange News: Kleist's Novellas

Bianca Theisen

"IN DER KUNST KOMMT es überall auf die Form an, und alles was eine Gestalt hat, ist meine Sache" (Kleist 2:810). Kleist's narratives have been seen as exemplary for the revival of novelistic form in German nineteenth-century literature after the Renaissance genre was rediscovered by Goethe and the Romantics. Organized around semantic oppositions with a moralistic bent — the violation of law and just punishment in "Der Zweikampf" and "Michael Kohlhaas," erotic desire and superior moral sense in "Die Marquise von O . . .," magnanimity and slyness in "Der Findling," trust and treason in "Die Verlobung in St. Domingo," the suspension of a social order and its restitution in "Das Erdbeben in Chili" — Kleist's stories seem to adopt the basic structural model of the novella and of the novella's revision of its immediate precursor, the exemplum. With a clear reference to that literary tradition, Kleist had even contemplated titling the first edition of his collected stories, to be published in 1811, "Moralische Erzählungen" (2:835). Kleist's fierce poetic imagination — the baby held to be Jeronimo and Josephe's illegitimate son is smashed against the edge of a church pillar, Piachi crushes Nicolo's brains out against the wall — however, does not mark the departure from the older genre conventions (Marx 9). Disturbing as it may have been to a late-eighteenth-century sensibility, literary fantasies of gruesome outrage or brutish revenge are characteristic of novelistic material in general (in the variations on the *Herzmaere,* for instance, the duped husband or upset father serves up the torn-out heart or cut-off head of the lover to his wife or daughter) and directly derive from the sources on which Kleist draws for "Das Erdbeben in Chili" and "Der Findling." The seventh novella told on the fifth day in Boccaccio's *Decamerone* reports the fate of the slave Teodoro, who had fallen in love with his master's daughter Violante. When Violante's pregnancy is discovered, Teodoro is sentenced to death; her outraged father wants to force Violante to chose between poison and dagger and to have her illegitimate child "smashed against the wall" (Boccaccio 494, my translation). By coincidence, Teodoro's father, an influential Armenian diplomat, recognizes his long-lost son on the latter's way to the gallows and has the verdict suspended, and the lovers, now no longer different in social standing, can be happily and legitimately reunited. In "Das Erdbeben in Chili" Kleist appropriates the basic plot elements of Boccaccio's story: the unlawful liaison across social differences, the overstated outrage and the — in Kleist only intermittently — suspended verdict; the many coincidences in Kleist's narrative, however, certainly no longer rest on the providential machinations that grounded chance and mischance in the older novelistic tradition and sanctioned the exemplarity of such tales of illicit love. "Der Findling" is based on a story of adultery in Matteo Bandello's *Novelliere* (Baumann). Niccolò da Este marries the fifteen-year-old Parsina in a second marriage; neglected by her old but, nevertheless, philandering husband, the girl seduces his sixteen-year-old son, Ugo. When Niccolò discovers the adultery, he has the lovers thrown in jail; Parsina does not repent and, like Piachi in Kleist's narrative, refuses the hypocritical solicitations of the clerics, whom she knows to be ready administrators of her husband's cruel whims. After three days, the lovers are beheaded. Kleist splits and doubles the narrative elements of this common novelistic plot, ultimately derived from the burlesque or the *beffa,* in which the adulterous lovers are in conspiracy against an aging, cruel, miserly or jealous husband for whom the reader can have little sympathy, to the point that the lover's illicit liaison seems justified, after all. Kleist doubles the figure of Bandello's old husband, when the foundling Niccolo inherits the traits of the bigot philanderer that characterize the husband in Bandello, and when Piachi becomes, like Bandello's Niccolò, the raging murderer of his own (adoptive) son. The issue of illegitimate genealogical succession and appropriation — which seems to anger Piachi even more than Nicolo's adulterous assault — is not only an intertextual reference to Molière's *Tartuffe,* explicitly named in Kleist's text; it is also already implicit in Bandello's novella, where Niccolò da Este forcefully seized a cousin's estate (Baumann 459). Doubling the narrative elements found in preceding novelistic material or multiplying the chance encounter as the novella's structural axis, Kleist alters the story grammar of the novella altogether. He introduces an ambivalence into the grid of semantic equivalences in the novella that explodes the genre's structural closure. Does Kleist thereby modernize the genre, creating the form that will become exemplary for the nineteenth century, as has been argued (Klein 49)? Can his narratives still be seen as successors to the genre of the novella, even if they offset its genealogy, or do they partake in another discourse of newness? Kleist, I will argue, levels the distinction between the fictive and the factual, between novelistic and journalistic writing. Multiplying, even serializing the turning point, Kleist empties out the supersemantic event that constitutes the novella's structural axis and opens it up to the contingency of the factual.

Sensational News: The Novelistic Tradition

With Boccaccio's innovation, the novella takes leave of older narrative forms such as love casuistry and the exemplum. His novellas supplant the typical, general, and normative that had characterized the exemplum with a focus on the singular event and the individual case. Boccaccio still draws on the narrative material of the exemplum — for instance, on the fable of the magnanimous groom who passes his own bride on to his friend when he becomes aware of the friend's lovesickness. For the older narrative form, the groom's action constitutes an unquestionable ideal: it typifies magnanimity. In Boccaccio's version of this often modified plot, however, the gesture of friendship becomes problematic, since it neglects to solicit the bride's opinion about the exchange. The novella draws on the exemplum only to doubt its simple casuistry: whether a behavior is morally exemplary or not is no longer a question of ideal intention alone but a matter of factual circumstances and context. Exemplary behavior and social norm have become conditional — dependent on their context and perspective, and relative. In Boccaccio's novellas the preordained system of moral values on which the exemplum was based disintegrates into a set of open questions and problems that can now only be explored in a singular case, established to disquiet the reader and to prompt him or her to make his or her own judgment, rather than merely to accept the sententious decree of an exemplary general truth (cf. Neuschäfer 47–49). The novella replaces the closed order of providence with an open and increasingly complex world of possibilities. Investigating various possibilities from various perspectives, the novella reflects on its own narrative play on the probable and the improbable. The departure from the older narrative form of the exemplum — a form still vital in the moralistic tales that were popular in the eighteenth century — a departure credited to Kleist as one of his innovations (cf. Marx), is, thus, already achieved by the form's displacement in Boccaccio's novellas.

From its beginnings the novella is a self-reflexive genre. The interpretive literature has often recruited the dramatic and dialogic character of Kleist's novellas (cf. Swales) as an indicator of his outspoken preference for drama; the dramatic and dialogic, however, are generally characteristic of the novella and not specific to Kleist. The close alliance between novella and drama was often noted by Kleist's contemporaries:

August Wilhelm Schlegel and Ludwig Tieck both perceived *peripeteia,* the reversal or turning point (Wendepunkt), as constitutive of the novella. The framing techniques of novella collections evolve from dialogue; for example, unlike earlier collections such as *A Thousand and One Nights* and the *Historia Septem Sapientium,* where the frame constitutes a narrative in which the collected narratives are embedded, the frame of Boccaccio's *Decamerone* is structured as a conversation about the embedded stories. His narrators comment and reflect on what has been narrated; the frame is no longer constructed as narrative but as description (Jolles vii–xcvi). More significant, the dialogic framing technique now consciously reflects on a change of media from oral to written discourse. Self-reflexive dialogue is fictionally staged so as to introduce a temporal index of the present that can refer back to, alter, and renew what has been narrated as being past. For Paul Ernst, who advocates a genre that at his time had lost its nineteenth-century popularity and been transmuted into the short story, the novella revolves around an incident that refracts time (71). The insistence on recentness is the most significant trait of the genre: the process of narration, the framing technique suggests, happens here and now; it does not just recapitulate what occurred long ago. Even though the novella often directly lifts well-known tales and jests from earlier collections or draws on material reprinted so often that it has merged with the folk tradition, the genre asserts that the story it now has to tell is new and unheard of. Before *novella* (Novelle) came to denote a specific narrative genre in the late eighteenth century, "cent nouvelles," "novelas ejemplares" or "nouvelles" were translated into German as "neue Fabeln," "neue Beispiele," or simply "Neuigkeit." Derived from the Latin *novellus,* a diminutive of *novus,* the terms *nouvelle* and *Novelle* indicate the new and the extraordinary. *Newes* and *novel* were used interchangeably for narrative material as diverse as tales of felony, jokes, love intrigues, and the news ballad. Nouvelles, novels, and news could all connote fictional tales, as well as journalistic news reports, Lennard J. Davis has suggested. The semantic indifferentiation indicates an "undifferentiated matrix" in which fiction was not yet distinguished from fact, in which literary tales of ill-fated lovers or repenting criminals could be taken to be as true as sensational accounts of supernatural or freakish events and journalistic reports of earthquakes, wars, or executions. Davis interprets the calculated overstatement of newness in these discourses as the token of a new technology: the printing press facilitated "the rapid and relatively instantaneous publication of matters of public interest," made them available to the lower classes, and thereby constituted "a radically new discourse in the European information system" that undermined what had until then been royal and ecclesiastical pre-rogatives of dispersing information (46, 48). Breaking down the tempo-ral distance between reader and event, the new type of narrative allegedly guaranteed an immediacy and recentness the older oral discourse was never able to warrant. As Davis stresses, novellas and news imply their reader in their ambiguous self-reflexive discourse and make him or her a partial — and voyeuristic — witness to its simultaneous assertions and denials of "neweness" and "trueness."

The stress on recentness and newness not only pertains to the wide thematic scope of the novella but is the key determinant of its formal structure. Since Goethe's remark that the novella is built around an "uner-hörtes Begebnis" (Eckermann 225), theoreticians of the genre have em-phasized the extraordinary, the unusual, the strange — in short, the new — as its formal characteristic. In *Unterhaltungen deutscher Ausgewan-derten* (1795), a collection of novellas with which Goethe revived the Renaissance and Early Modern tradition, he has his group of narrators ponder the genre's peculiar features: neither the significance of an event nor its impact account for its appeal; its newness does. "Was gibt einer Begebenheit den Reiz? Nicht ihre Wichtigkeit, nicht der Einfluß, den sie hat, sondern die Neuheit. Nur das Neue scheint gewöhnlich wichtig, weil es ohne Zusammenhang Verwunderung erregt und unsere Einbildungs-kraft einen Augenblick in Bewegung setzt" (22). Even at the end of the eighteenth century — an era that imposed a poetics of originality — nov-elistic newness does not come to stand for innovation. The revived novella still takes up older narrative material and reframes it in a different way or tells it from a new perspective (cf. Goethe 25). In his novella collection Goethe appropriates orally transmitted ghost stories and Weimar gossip and rewrites two stories from Bassompierre's *Mémoires,* as well as the ninety-ninth novella from the *Cent Nouvelles Nouvelles* (1486). For the Romantic theory of the genre, newness also is a relative, somewhat am-biguous concept: novellas have to be "neu und frappant" (F. Schlegel 1967, 250), but they may be old in letter as long as their spirit is new — "Novellen dürfen im Buchstaben *alt* sein, wenn nur der Geist *neu* ist" (F. Schlegel 1980, 110).

This strange conjunction of superannuated material and current "spirit" finds its structural realization in the coincidences and chance encounters that are so eminent in the novella. The "unheard-of event" is extraordinary because it could not have been predicted, because it runs counter to what was to be expected and anticipated. The novella's un-heard-of event formalizes a structure of coincidence that, in historically differing and variable ways, couples the expected with the unexpected, the ordinary with the extraordinary, the old with the new. Indeed, the microstructure — or what Heyse calls the "silhouette" (75, my translation) — of the novella appears to be modeled on the concessive clause. Thus, Boccaccio's famous falcon novella can be outlined by one concessive clause: even though Federigo degli Alberighi has courted Donna Giovanna in vain, she finally marries him (cf. Pötters). The sacrifice of the falcon here marks the ambiguous and accidental instance by which the expected course of events — Giovanna does not marry Federigo, who has even fallen into poverty through his fruitless courting — is suddenly negated and overturned. The incidental functions as the generator of unforeseen consequences and outcomes. It undercuts the causal nexus established so far in the narrative and supplants it with a new, unexpected, and striking plot development. Chance, whether theorized as the unheard-of event or as turning point, thus annuls the anticipated relation of cause and effect that would have conformed to the discursive and narrative norms. What was to be expected can fail to occur — the novella undermines causality by opening it up to a horizon of possibilities. Already in Boccaccio chance is no longer a mere tool of providence. The novella's semantic axis of order and disorder, norm and transgression finds its syntactical correlative in the coupling of causality and concessivity and has its pragmatic analogue in an agreeably disillusioning play on reader expectations, because the very disappointment of the reader's expectations in the novella then comes to be expected of the genre. Semantically, syntactically, and pragmatically, the novella operates on the countercurrent of the expected and the contingent.

The Turn on the Novella: Kleist's "Verlobung in St. Domingo"

Kleist's writing is premised on the countermovement of causation and concessiveness characteristic of the novella and on their point of convergence in the unheard-of event, the chance encounter, or the turning point. His overstated use of chance and of the entire semantic field of *Fall* (which can mean both "fall" and "case"), with its composites *Zufall* (chance), *Zusammenfall* (coincidence), *Vorfall* (incident, event), and *Unfall* (accident), bears witness to his willful play on the supersemantic event around which the novelistic form revolves. The incident in "Die Marquise von O . . .," eclipsed from narrative sequence by the prominent dash and referred to as "Unfall" (2:106), couples the quotidian with the supernatural and spawns explanations of the inexplicable that range from medical pragmatism and the belief in divine force to the fantastic tale, only to find its final solution through a newspaper ad. Chance has left Jeronimo Rugera in "Das Erdbeben in Chili" with a rope with which he is about to hang himself, when the earthquake shatters his prison and, at least temporarily, overturns his fate. In "Der Findling" the substitution of the dead son by the adopted foundling, the story of Elvire's savior Colino, Constanze's death, Nicolo's public humiliation after being caught with Xaviera, Elvire's secret idolization of Colino's portrait, and Nicolo's assault on the unconscious Elvire are all referred to as "Vorfall," while "Zufall" doubly and conspicuously indicates the logogriphic correspondence between the names and couples the lofty role of the lover as savior to the abject impersonation of the assailant: "fand er — zufällig, in der Tat, selbst, denn er erstaunte darüber, wie er noch in seinem Leben nicht getan — die Verbindung heraus, welche den Namen: *Colino* bildete. . . . Die Übereinstimmung, die sich zwischen beiden Wörtern angeordnet fand, schien ihm mehr als ein bloßer Zufall" (210). By chance, Toni finds a rope with which she can bind Gustav and save him from the instant death Congo Hoango's unexpected return might have meant for him; interpreted as a sign of providence, the instance of binding employed not to betray but to save brings together the semantic opposition of the traitor and the savior that constitutes the narrative grid of "Die Verlobung in St. Domingo." "Zufall" and "Zusammenfall," also marked by the often used formula "es traf sich" or by the syntactical construction "eben — als," are, however, entirely given over to interpretation. Josephe boldly presumes that the earthquake happened to facilitate her and Jeronimo's happiness; driven by desire and revenge, Nicolo doubts that the logogriphic correspondence is merely accidental; and Toni's firm but gullible pragmatism even enlists God as her ally: "Gott selbst, meinte sie, indem sie ihn herabriß, hätte ihn zu ihrer und des Freundes Rettung dahin geführt" (185). Even though in Kleist chance and coincidence still indicate the unexpected and unheard-of and partake of the compressed motivational nexus of novelistic form (cf. Köhler 22), his narrative logic no longer binds them to a closed order guaranteed by divine providence (as is still the case in Cervantes), nor does it incorporate them to exemplify the unity of the general and the singular in an individual instance (as in Boccaccio and in the German Romantics' discussion of the novella in terms of an aesthetics of the general and the singular). By virtue of its sheer multiplication, the force of chance consumes itself in Kleist's narratives and, turning into complete contingency, no longer breaks up causal determination for a turn to the better but only engenders further entanglements, misrecognitions, and catastrophic outcomes.

In "Die Verlobung in St. Domingo" Kleist triples the novella's turning point and thereby creates a highly complex play on reader expectations that overturns the semantic closure of novelistic writing altogether. The narrative was published three times in 1811: first under the title "Die Verlobung" in the journal *Der Freimüthige oder Berlinisches Unterhaltungsblatt für gebildete, unbefangene Leser* in March, then in the Vienna journal *Der Sammler* in July, and finally in the second volume of Kleist's *Erzählungen* in August. The narrative's publication history attests to the seriality (specific for the news discourse) with which Kleist infuses and modifies the genre of the novella that by his time had become purely literary. The historical events that frame Kleist's narrative hold up to the requirement of recentness: the ill-fated love story of the Swiss officer Gustav von der Ried and the mestiza Toni is set during the colonial war (1791–1803) in which the black slave population in Haiti successfully fought for liberation from their white oppressors. Even though the narrative's beginning states its historical setting vaguely and generally and as if to introduce a moralistic tale biased against the blacks ("zu Anfang dieses Jahrhunderts, als die Schwarzen die Weißen ermordeten" [2:160]), its second paragraph specifies 1803 as the decisive year in which the military successes of the black general Dessalines brought about the final defeat of the French troops. The National Convention had abolished slavery in 1794, but Napoleon wanted to reestablish colonial supremacy by military force. The fact that Kleist seems to take sides with the clichéd views of enlightened European civilization, offsetting them in a crude woodcut fashion against the dark barbarity and inhuman cruelty of the blacks, labels the liberation from slavery "murder," and speaks of "die unbesonnenen Schritte des National-Convents" (161) has led critics to read the narrative as the problematic and ambiguous product of racist and colonialist prejudice (Bay; on the disputed and difficult issue of race discourse, a calculated oversight in older criticism that foregrounded the universal affective appeal of the love story, see also Gilman, Fischer, Weigel, Uerlings, and Werlen). But Kleist overturns the semantic equivalencies typical of the novelistic fiction on which the racial discourse of his narrative at first appears to be based.

The obvious opposition white/black finds its semantic equivalence in a studied and increasingly ambiguous metaphorics of light. On a stormy night the Swiss officer Gustav von der Ried seeks help at a plantation. He asks whether Babekan, who answers his call, is a Negress, stretching out his hand toward her as if he could determine her skin color by touch rather than sight. When Babekan replies: "nun, Ihr seid gewiß ein Weißer, daß Ihr dieser stockfinstern Nacht lieber ins Antlitz schaut, als einer Negerin!" (162), she ironically asserts the color-coded threat that blackness entails for Gustav. Although the night is too dark for Gustav to see Babekan at the window, the moonlight enables him to spot a black boy who rushes to close the gate. Suspicious and reluctant, Gustav is, nevertheless, easily lured into the house with cunningly staged lighting effects. Drawing him into the door, Toni is careful "das Licht so zu stellen, daß der volle Strahl davon auf ihr Gesicht fiel" (163), so that Gustav can see her "yellowish" complexion. The clear opposition between black and white is suspended by a given third, a median status. A "mulatto" and a "mestize," Babekan is supposed to be one half black, and Toni, conceived in Paris by a merchant from Marseilles, only one fourth. Gustav eagerly trusts the two women merely on the basis of their appearance: "Euch kann ich mich anvertrauen; aus der Farbe Eures Gesichts schimmert mir ein Strahl von der meinigen entgegen" (164). To lull Gustav into a false sense of security, Babekan hypocritically claims that the "Schimmer von Licht, der auf meinem Antlitz, wenn es Tag wird, erdämmert" (165) sets her at odds with and solicits the jealousy and mistrust of the blacks. At night, however, the phrase implies, she is plainly black; and the entire story is set at night or in the darkness of barred interiors. Toni, on the other hand, transforms the "yellowish" complexion, "repelling" to Gustav, a color that associates her with the betrayal of the black slave girl who intentionally infected her former master with yellow fever. After she perceives herself as Gustav's fiancée and has arranged everything for his rescue, Toni even changes color altogether; she declares that she is white: "ich habe euch nicht verraten; ich bin eine Weiße, und dem Jüngling, den ihr gefangen haltet, verlobt; ich gehöre zu dem Geschlecht derer, mit denen ihr im offenen Kriege liegt" (191). Gustav, who had been groping in the dark about Toni's ambivalent attempt to save him and takes her to be a traitor, changes color just before he shoots her; according to the narrative's overdetermined semantics, he converts from white to black: "Gustav wechselte bei diesem Anblick die Farbe" (192). At the end of the narrative the mestiza who had used her charms to lure whites to the plantation, where they would find certain death at the hands of Congo Hoango, has become white. Meanwhile, the white officer, misreading her, becomes black and is, according to the narrative's logic, "at war" with her. Blackness here marks race much less than it designates the forces of darkness — mistrust, deceit, betrayal, and revenge. Whiteness, likewise, functions as a (pseudo-) moralistic indicator of trust, love, and unconditional salvage even at the price of self-sacrifice.

The glaring exemplarity of such moralistic indicators of the "enlightened" and the "barbaric," of "whiteness" and "blackness" was frequently evoked in contemporary journalism — Kleist's otherwise liberal friend

Heinrich Zschokke had published several articles on this issue and branded the Haitian revolution as a bestial, inhuman barbarity, a fall back into the wild state of nature, in his journal *Miscellen für die Neueste Weltkunde* in 1807 (cf. Fischer). Kleist's novella takes up the collective symbolism typical of journalistic discourse (cf. Link) — Zschokke's journalistic symbolism betrays a propagandistic and moralistic bend still reminiscent of the exemplum — only to dissipate it in a confusing play on novelistic form and journalistic practice. The genre of the novella, I have argued, does not conform to the discursive and narrative norms that model our expectations of cause and effect; rather, it positions the chance encounter or the turning point so as willfully to overturn such expectations of causal determination. The expected is countered by the unexpected. Kleist serializes such turns for the unexpected.

If we try to formulate the "silhouette" of "Die Verlobung in St. Domingo" according to the structure operative in Boccaccio's tale on the falcon sacrifice, we encounter a complex narrative structure premised on three turning points: Even though Gustav is surrounded by war and deceit, he is saved, precisely by being betrayed, but nevertheless dies, even though everything had been arranged to save him, because he misinterprets his rescue as betrayal. Kleist disrupts reader expectations at three pivotal points in the narrative.

(1) *Even though Gustav finds himself surrounded by war, betrayal, and murderous revenge, he is saved.* The beginning of the story draws the sinister picture of unrelenting war and ubiquitous mistrust: Gustav trusts the black of night — the only time it is safe for him and his family to travel — more than a Negress. He presents the anecdote of the slave girl with yellow fever that carries for him the moral of abhorring treachery in order to test Toni. Toni, in turn, is afraid of the white officer and can only be persuaded to lure him into the house when she is reassured that he is alone. Informed of Babekan's bitter grudge against whites — Toni's father repudiated paternity, and Babekan suffered cruel punishment on the orders of her allegedly humane master, Monsieur Villeneuve — and of Congo Hoango's fury against all whites and his request that the two women delay white strangers seeking help until he returns to kill them, the reader is led to expect Gustav's certain doom. That Toni, up to this point fully participating in the deceptive plan, is overcome by human compassion ("übernahm sie . . . ein menschliches Gefühl" [175]) after Gustav tells her how his former fiancée sacrificed herself for him during the Terror of the French Revolution and surrenders to the "last favor" forbidden to her on penalty of death must, consequently, come as a novelistic surprise. The secret "betrothal" across racial and social differ-

ences and across the gulf of two warring parties, modeled on Shake-speare's *Romeo and Juliet,* reverses the narrative sequence built up so far, and the narrator's ironic comment on the eclipsed love scene confirms his willful play on such expectations: "Was weiter erfolgte, brauchen wir nicht zu melden, weil es jeder, der an diese Stelle kommt, von selbst liest" (175). Gustav engages in fantasies of an idyllic life with Toni on neutral ground in Switzerland, trusts his new bride completely, vows his love for her, and feels safe: "wie durch göttliche Hand von jeder Sorge erlöst" (173). But while older novellas in the wake of Boccaccio or Cervantes would have led this sensational turn of affairs toward a happy, if unlikely, outcome (a racially mixed couple living happily ever after in a Swiss idyll at the beginning of the nineteenth century), Kleist disappoints this genre expectation with additional reversals that lead into fateful misrecognition and final doom.

(2) *Even though Gustav seems safe, Toni betrays him* — in order to save him. A proliferation of contingencies surrounds this second turning point: Congo Hoango returns unexpectedly, and Toni saves the sleeping Gustav by binding him with a rope that chance — or, according to her interpretation, "God himself" — provides her. Her lover would either be executed immediately, she reasons, or, mistaking her for a traitor, ignore her advice and muster up a futile fight against Congo Hoango and his men. The narrative fully exploits the ambivalence of this ruse with its oscillation of perspective between the true and the treacherous. Congo Hoango believes that Toni has, indeed, bound the foreigner to deliver him into his hands; he takes her actions and statements to be true. Gustav believes the same, but from his perspective she must, therefore, seem to be a traitor. Babekan mistrusts her daughter's sincerity, since Toni had taken sides with the foreign officer before, and takes her to be a traitor to the black cause and a secret violator of the "Rache der bestehenden Landesgesetze" (178). This true and treacherous ruse constitutes a logico-temporal turn in the narrative that moves backward in order to move forward: it couples two anecdotes told earlier, that of the slave girl who infects her former master with yellow fever and that of the fiancée who saved Gustav from the guillotine by disavowing him; it brings together a story of univocal betrayal and a story of contrived rescue. Toni's actions and gestures, perceived against the backdrop of these two models through changing narrative perspectives, are charted on the slave girl as the archetype of disloyalty for Gustav, while Toni herself and the Strömli family see them as a true copy of Mariane Congreve's exemplary martyrdom. The providential nature of chance — Gustav feels relieved of his anxieties as if by a divine hand, and Toni takes the tool of her ruse to be

provided by God himself — is retrospectively then shown to be utterly treacherous itself.

(3) *Even though Gustav is saved, he dies.* Toni not only risks and then gives her life for Gustav, like Mariane Congreve; she must renounce her family and betray her identity in order to be acceptable to him. But her ultimate sacrifice, the declaration that she is white, paradoxically sets her at odds with a lover whose irremediable mistrust and skeptical doubt has turned him into an Othello, has made him change color (on Kleist's frequent intertextual references to Shakespeare, see Theisen 1999). The contrary course typical of novelistic structure is made explicit in the contradictory nature of Gustav's movement just before he shoots Toni: "indem er aufstand, als ob er umsinken wollte" (192), a contrary course that is also already implicit in the events surrounding Mariane Congreve's death (cf. Reuß). Gustav's gesture graphically illustrates the narratological turn of the novella: it is fully subservient to the enigmatic structure of the novelistic event that Kleist reapplies to itself in "Die Verlobung in St. Domingo," thereby giving it over to utter contingency (on the contingency of the gestures "standing" and "falling," see Schneider). Realizing his brazen misrecognition — "ich hätte dir nicht mißtrauen sollen; denn du warst mir durch einen Eidschwur verlobt, obschon wir keine Worte darüber gewechselt hatten!" (193) — Gustav shoots himself, blowing his brains out so that pieces adhere to the surrounding walls, as if to eradicate the prejudiced European reasoning that misled him. This event dissipates the Christological and moralistic implications that had governed the conjunction of providence and chance in the earlier tradition of the exemplum and the novella and that is ironically taken up in Kleist's narrative (in the exchange of the cross, the implicit references to Christ and St. Peter, see Hoverland 156; Theisen 1996, 207). Moreover, it explodes the novelistic structure of the calculated suspense of causality. With this third "turn" of events, the narrative is premised on a formula that is no longer that of disillusioned expectation: *Even though Gustav is surrounded by war and deceit, he dies.* The end fulfills the expectations raised by the narrative sequences set up at the beginning. Serializing the turning point and forcing the "even though" of its narrative logic into paradox, Kleist's narrative no longer accounts for a novella. It is modeled on the news report, attesting to the fact that the contingency of the real has come to be expected.

Anecdotal History: Kleist's Novelistic Journalism

Breaking down the framing technique of the novella collection to a single narrative, Kleist embeds three anecdotes in "Die Verlobung in St. Domingo": the story of the sick slave girl who infects her former master, the story of Babekan's betrayal by her lover, and the story of Mariane Congreve's self-sacrifice. The situation in which these embedded stories are told faintly resembles the older narrative technique of the "Halserzählung," where narration and the information retrieved from it, the solution to a riddle or a problem before a fateful date, was a matter of life and death (cf. Jolles). In the older tradition the framing narrative posed the problem to which the embedded narratives tried to give an exemplary answer. The Halserzählung often suspends a death sentence. Sheherazade's tenuous situation, cunningly deferred in 1,001 nights of continuous narration, constitutes such a Halserzählung. Boccaccio takes it up with the threat posed by the plague but modifies it: his narrators, who retreat to the country and narrate to reconstitute the social order threatened by a natural force that levels all social distinctions, return to a still plague-stricken Florence, and it is left open whether or not they survive. Boccaccio's frame no longer poses a (moral or legal) problem that could find an exemplary solution, and it suspends the threat of death only temporarily.

In *Unterhaltungen deutscher Ausgewanderten* Goethe revives traits of the older Halserzählung when he has his narrators escape from the threat of French occupation in the postrevolutionary wars and define narration as their form of supple social interaction against the political chaos of the French Revolution and the ideological strife it has brought into their circle. Frame and embedded stories are here set up as a discursive metareflection on the moralistic journals of the eighteenth century, the tradition of the novella, the French fairy tale, and the baroque historical novel (cf. Damann). Goethe redefines the previously moralistic, exemplary character of the embedded narratives with what he calls "parallel stories"; the baroness opts against the theoretical discussion of the moral tale and prefers a correlation of stories in which one narrative refers to, mirrors, and explains the other. Goethe employed parallel stories as a mirroring technique able to elucidate those mysteries of experience that evaded explicit explanation. He thus retold the narrative material found in the ninety-ninth novella of the *Cent Nouvelles Nouvelles* and supplemented it with a parallel narrative that renewed the triangulation of love and its solution in moral desistance in the earlier novella by shifting it onto a constellation of identity-constitution and subjective self-constitution proffered by the family triangle (cf. Damann 21–22; Neumann 451). In the case of the two solid Röntgen desks that miraculously crack at the same time, parallel stories, moreover, bring to bear the contingency of novelistic structure. The inexplicable and even uncanny coincidence, however, does not allow us to assume a hidden causal nexus: "daß, wenn zwei Dinge zusammenträfen, man deswegen noch nicht auf ihren Zusammenhang schließen könne" (Goethe 82). The mystery presented by the parallel event is of interest, because it is "true" in its very contingency, whether it can be explained or not (cf. Goethe 39). With such a focus on the anecdotal character of the particular and contingent parallel event, Goethe stages the novella as a historiography of the quotidian; history at large, too confusing to be surveyed at one glance, is locked into the private lives that run parallel to and mirror it. Goethe's project of an anecdotal historiography does not stand alone. Friedrich Schlegel repeatedly stressed the proximity between anecdote and novella; for example: "Novelle in der ältesten Bedeutung = Anekdote" (1980, 110). August Wilhelm Schlegel saw the novella as a particular genre of historiography meant to tell what remained untold in official historical accounts; where history proper charted the teleological progress of humankind, the novella caught the voice of the quotidian, captured the singular significance of things that happened everywhere, everyday. The anecdotal character of the novella presents "eine Geschichte außer der Geschichte" (50), tells what has happened "behind the back" of bourgeois norm and legislation, seizes a side view of history, and casts light on the obscurity of a contingent moment that runs askew to the monumentalization and universalization of history advocated by the Idealist philosophies of Goethe's and Kleist's time. "Geschichte ist eine große Anekdote," Novalis believed, welded together from a series of anecdotes (Hardenberg 356).

Kleist's technique of embedding, indebted to Goethe's replacement of the exemplary with the parallel, realizes the program of such an anecdotal historiography and radicalizes its moment of contingency. In contrast to Goethe, who defines novelistic narration *against* the current political events, abiding by Schiller's request that politics were to be excluded from his journal *Die Horen,* Kleist employs the anecdote both in his fiction and in his journalism as a highly politicized historeme or "historisches Molecule" (Hardenberg 356). The embedded anecdotal narratives in "Die Verlobung in St. Domingo" are no longer told to reconstitute a social order threatened by a natural force or a political event. They are told as news. When Toni asks about the recent political events in Fort Dauphin, Gustav details the military situation and responds to her additional question about the political causes — "wodurch sich denn die Weißen daselbst so verhaßt gemacht hätten" (170) — first with some overly general remarks, then with a singular case. According to Gustav's biased and narrow view, the Haitian colonial war has its roots in a revenge for the "tadelnswürdige Mißhandlungen" the black population had to suffer at the hands of individual white plantation owners. The anecdote of the slave girl stricken with yellow fever who treacherously invites her unsuspecting former master into her bed — a favor he had sought earlier, only to subject her to harsh mistreatment when she refused — illustrates Gustav's overly broad political comments on the socially explosive situation with a singular case meant to carry all the weight of blatant evidence. Gustav's overstated reactions to the story may lure the reader into reading it as reference to the tradition of the exemplum and the novelistic frame in the wake of Boccaccio — like a pestilence, the revolution has infected all human relationships to the point of complete dissolution of all "human and divine order" — and the story, indeed, serves as one of the two model behaviors Gustav outlines for Toni: deception and truthfulness. But Kleist subtly shifts the moralistic semantics of exemplary types onto the level of discourse itself: throughout "Die Verlobung in St. Domingo" it is never clear whether discourse is treacherous or truthful, whether the news is reliable or not. Babekan pretends that according to a report she just received, General Dessalines and his army are about to march through the district, so it would be too dangerous to send for Gustav's family right away. She makes Gustav believe that the fires flickering through the night on the surrounding hills are those of Dessalines, even though his army is, in fact, advancing toward Port-au-Prince. Kleist here even seems to reappropriate fictionally and invert a palliative news report he had translated for his *Berliner Abendblätter,* "Über den Zustand der Schwarzen in Amerika"; in that piece, however, the campfires flickering over the hills at night do not indicate an immediate threat but function to guard the white owners' properties. Published in the issues of 12, 14, and 15 January 1811, the translation of the article for the *Berliner Abendblätter* is concurrent with Kleist's composition of "Die Verlobung in St. Domingo" in early 1811. The narrative also intersects with a news report titled "Kurze Geschichte des gelben Fiebers in Europa," published in the *Abendblätter* on 23 and 24 January 1811. Kleist adapted the report from the Hamburg *Politisches Journal,* where it had appeared in December 1810 (Sembdner 311). The topic was of immediate interest, and the *Abendblätter,* as well as other newspapers, had been reporting on new outbreaks of the epidemic in Spain and Italy. The article traces the origins of the disease to the West Indies, argues that it is even more devastating than the "black death" of the plague and that it destroys social order altogether, and alerts the readers to the medical imperative of quarantine. Kleist copies the article almost to the letter but departs from it by significantly altering the last sentence (Sembdner 314–15). Where the report in the *Politisches Journal* ends in wishful thinking — may the disease never hit the Spanish coast or another part of Europe again — Kleist's version concludes with a political statement that may not have passed censorship had it not been hidden in the reprint of an article that had already passed and been published: the (Napoleonic) war in Spain, he suggests in the last sentence, obstructs measures of quarantine, so that the disease threatens to spread even further.

The indistinction between fictional and journalistic discourse that Kleist reintroduces into a genre that at his time had lost its original conjunction with the news report and become purely fictional is also already evident in "Die Marquise von O . . .," a narrative Kleist wrote in 1807 and published in his journal *Phöbus* in 1808. The Marquise's advertisement, in which she publicly and scandalously seeks for the father of her unborn child in the paper, finds its reply in the "unerhörten Artikel[s]" in "einem Intelligenzblatt, das eben ganz feucht von der Presse kam" (131). Kleist here couples the marker of the novelistic genre, the extraordinary or the "unheard-of," with that of the news discourse, recentness, and passes off the news ads as the novelistically new (cf. Theisen 2001). But Kleist not only infuses his fiction with traits of the news report, he also instills fictional elements in his journalistic practice. The distinction that Walter Benjamin drew between narrative (bound by experience, concerned with the supernatural and extraordinary, and valid over time) and information (made possible by the printing press and relying on recentness, resting on the true and plausible, and valid only for the moment) does not hold for Kleist; nor, indeed, does it hold for the indifferentiation between news and fiction characteristic of the Early Modern period, if we think of Harsdörffer's novelistic claims of having been an eyewitness to events he had most likely lifted from newspapers such as the *Mercure François* (cf. Krebs).

The usual avowal of the probable, plausible, and true is evident when Kleist (ironically) assures his readers that his novellas — as if they were news reports — are retold "nach einer wahren Begebenheit" (104) or that there are eyewitnesses who can testify to the truth of what has been reported, in the anecdotal essay "Über das Marionettentheater," as well as in the anecdote "Der Griffel Gottes." What is fictional artifice in Kleist, consciously employed to confuse the gullible reader about the status of such anecdotal accounts, was a common practice in Early Modern news reports; affirmations, affidavits, and testimonies were often attached to signal that the printed news was endowed with the authority of the true and the reliable, which the former information system of unofficial hearsay lacked (cf. Davis 55). The simultaneous assertion and denial of trueness characteristic of the early news discourse is apparent when Kleist introduces the highly accidental and improbable in "Michael Kohlhaas" and in "Unwahrscheinliche Wahrhaftigkeiten" with the disclaimer that "die Wahrscheinlichkeit nicht immer auf Seiten der Wahrheit ist" (2:96, 2:278). And the frequent and sudden changes of narrative time into the present tense that Kleist employs in his anecdotes and novellas create the effect of a scenic plasticity that draws the reader into the description of events as if he or she were actually there with the reporting narrator.

After he edited the literary journal *Phöbus* with Adam Müller in 1808, and plans for a political weekly, *Germania,* failed in 1809, Kleist published the first daily to integrate local news, the *Berliner Abendblätter,* in 1810–1811 (cf. Aretz). This innovation, premised on the daily publication of the latest police reports, which Kleist obtained because he was acquainted with Gruner, the chief of police, guaranteed the high initial popularity of the paper; the issuing office was swept by frantic Berliners who had to be kept in check by the police. The paper promised a series of extra editions that would serve the following function:

> über Alles, was innerhalb der Stadt, und deren Gebiet, in polizeilicher Hinsicht, Merkwürdiges und Interessantes vorfällt, ungesäumten, ausführlichen und glaubwürdigen Bericht abzustatten: dergestalt, daß die Reihe dieser, dem Hauptblatt beigefügten Blätter . . . eine fortlaufende Chronik, nicht nur der Stadt Berlin, sondern des gesammten Königreichs Preußen, bilden werden. (*Berliner Abendblätter* 5)

Thus, the paper kept its subscribers in suspense for weeks with the latest news of what was suspected to be the work of an infamous gang of incendiaries and murderers. But Kleist took liberties with the claim of reliability when he freely engaged in free-floating rumors along with matters of record, even though the paper explicitly professed its aim to present authentic reports in order to amend the public confusion and to quiet the unnecessary alarm created by the distorted and gossipy narratives circulating in the city (*Berliner Abendblätter* 18). Kleist bids on sensationalism, whether the events reported are reliable and authentic or not.

The day's curious events appeared under the headline "Tagesbegebenheit" or "Polizei-Rapport," later "Polizeiliche Tages-Mittheilungen": fires, robberies, arrests, suicides, accidents, and petty fraud in local markets. But such remarkable events could also be rendered in the form of anecdotes, and they then fulfilled the paper's double objective of offering "Unterhaltung aller Stände des Volkes" and "Beförderung der Nationalsache" (*Berliner Abendblätter* 75). Anecdotes, highly popular at the time, circulated in virtually every newspaper and were also compiled in voluminous collections such as the ten-volume *Sammlung von Anekdoten und Charakterzügen aus den beiden merkwürdigen Kriegen in Süd- und Nord-Deutschland in den Jahren 1805, 6 und 7*. Kleist tends to give such anecdotes, mostly adapted from police reports, gossip, other newspapers, or collections, a decisively political or sociological twist and handles them as if they accounted for the metaphorical "Pfeile" he threatens to draw from his "Köcher der Rede" in the fictional article that opens the *Berliner Abendblätter* (*Berliner Abendblätter* 1). In the column "Tagesbegebenheiten" Kleist reports on the peculiar survival of Captain Bürger. Bürger and a worker named Brietz sought shelter from a thunderstorm under a tree on the new promenade. Brietz rudely ordered Bürger to seek out another tree, as the one under which they were standing was too small for both of them. The moment Bürger left, lightning struck the tree and killed Brietz. Gruner's police report had noted Brietz's death three days earlier, and other newspapers — the *Vossische Zeitung*, the *Spenersche Zeitung*, and the weekly *Beobachter an der Spree* — had informed their readers of the incident, giving detailed accounts of the oddity that lightning struck a smaller tree rather than a larger one close by, of the injuries Brietz suffered, and of his widow and three orphaned children without mentioning the episode with Captain Bürger. It seems that Kleist published the story as "Tagesbegebenheit" rather than "Polizei-Rapport" because it no longer counted as the latest news (cf. Dotzler 50). But Kleist also shifts the focus from an oddity of nature to social impertinence and suggests that the sheer contingency of the lightning functioned as its instant, overly stark reprimand. As in his novellas, Kleist here plays on his readers' expectations and organizes his version of the news report around a contingent moment (being struck by lightning) that can both dissociate and associate cause (social impertinence) and effect (reprimand). Whether the events surrounding Captain Bürger are ultimately fictional or factual, whether they are Kleist's invention or derive from an oral source, remains unclear (Sembdner 138; Moser 188), but they were certainly sold as factual to a gullible public. Other newspapers appropriated them as such and modeled their reports on Kleist's: his version reappears in *Der Freimüthige*, the *Nürnberger Korrespondenten von und für Deutschland*, the *Allgemeine Modenzeitung*, and the *Archiv für Literatur, Kunst und Politik*.

Kleist's novellas and anecdotes are characterized by a style modeled on the news report; narrated as if from a neutral perspective, they are weighed down with incidental details to present an unheard-of event in all its immediacy. Kleist's writing dwells on the sheer contingency of the factual; his style is modeled more on what Aristotle called *tò pathos*, the scene of suffering, than on *peripeteia*, the reversal often claimed to be the key element of the novella. The unforeseen catastrophes and violent deaths in his fictional and journalistic writings repeatedly fed into the public's taste for the sensational, the new, the uncanny, and the strange. The narratives circle around a "scene of suffering" — for instance, the uncanny death of the Marchese in "Das Bettelweib von Locarno" is presented as if monstrously to avenge his earlier moral offense; but even though his white bones, scattered in the ruins of the burned castle, are said to carry all the evidence of true fact, the spooky event remains entirely unexplained and continues to haunt. The narrative is tightly knit around the scene of suffering, but this scene remains strangely empty: the ghostly appearance never becomes visible, and the uncanny madness that drives the Marchese to his doom appears in all its contingent factuality. Kleist's writing, focusing on (fictional) factuality, empties out the super-semantic event constitutive of the novella and replaces it with an aperture that attempts to cut into the raw reality of his time. Kleist finds the fictional and anecdotal openings and orifices that allow him to bypass censure and to make his anti-Napoleonic political points: with terrible wit, a Prussian drum major who is to be executed by the French asks to be shot in his anus so that his skin will not be riddled with bullets. Kleist significantly alters this anecdote, which he found in a collection (it was published in its original form in *Beobachter an der Spree* one day after it appeared in *Berliner Abendblätter;* Steig 88), tacitly to voice his political stance against the French. The anecdote, Joel Fineman observes,

> is the literary form that uniquely lets history happen by virtue of the way it introduces an opening into the teleological, and therefore time-less, narration of beginning, middle, and end. The anecdote produces the effect of the real, the occurrence of contingency, by establishing an event as an event within and yet without the framing context of histori-cal successivity, i.e., it does so only in so far as its narration both com-prises and refracts the narration it reports. (61)

With his anecdotal style and journalistic techniques, Kleist opens up the condensed supersemantic event of the novella to the contingency of the real.

Works Cited

Aretz, Heinrich. *Heinrich von Kleist als Journalist: Untersuchungen zum Phöbus, zur Germania und den Berliner Abendblättern.* Stuttgart: Akademischer Verlag Hans-Dieter Heinz, 1983.

Baumann, Hans-Heinrich. "Kleists 'Findling' und die Parisina-Novelle des Bandello. Bemerkungen zur intertextuellen Dynamik." *Brandenburger Kleist-Blätter* 13 (2000): 457–75.

Bay, Hansjörg. "'Als die Schwarzen die Weißen ermordeten': Nachbeben einer Erschütterung des europäischen Diskurses in Kleists 'Verlobung in St. Domingo.'" *Kleist-Jahrbuch* (1998): 80–108.

Boccaccio, Giovanni di. *Das Dekameron.* Trans. Albert Wesselski. Frankfurt a.M.: Insel, 1967.

Damann, Günter. "Goethes 'Unterhaltungen deutscher Ausgewanderten' als Essay über die Gattung der Prosaerzählung im 18. Jahundert." In *Der deutsche Roman der Spätaufklärung: Fiktion und Wirklichkeit.* Ed. Harro Zimmermann. Heidelberg: Winter, 1990, 1–24.

Davis, Lennard J. *Factual Fictions: The Origins of the English Novel.* New York: Columbia UP, 1983.

Dotzler, Bernhard. "Federkrieg: Kleist und die Autorschaft des Produzenten." *Kleist-Jahrbuch* (1998): 37–61.

Eckermann, Johann Peter. *Gespräche mit Goethe in den letzten Jahren seines Lebens.* Ed. Ernst Beutler. Zurich: Artemis, 1948.

Ernst, Paul. "Zum Handwerk der Novelle." In his *Der Weg zur Form: Abhandlungen über die Technik vornehmlich der Tragödie und Novelle.* Munich: Georg Müller, 1928, 68–76.

Fineman, Joel. "The History of the Anecdote: Fiction and Fiction." In *The New Historicism.* Ed. H. Aram Veeser. London: Routledge, 1989, 49–76.

Fischer, Bernd. "Zur politischen Dimension der Ethik in Kleists 'Die Verlobung in St. Domingo.'" In *Heinrich von Kleist: Studien zu Werk und Wirkung.* Ed. Dirk Grathoff. Opladen: Westdeutscher Verlag, 1988, 248–62.

Gilman, Sander L. "The Aesthetics of Blackness in Heinrich von Kleist's 'Die Verlobung in St. Domingo.'" *Modern Language Notes* 90 (1975): 90, 661–65.

Goethe, Johann Wolfgang. "Unterhaltungen deutscher Ausgewanderten." In his *Gesamtausgabe.* Vol. 20. Munich: dtv, 1974, 7–112.

Hardenberg, Friedrich von. *Werke, Tagebücher und Briefe.* Vol. 2. Ed. Hans-Joachim Mähl. Munich: Hanser, 1978.

Heyse, Paul. "Jugenderinnerungen und Bekenntnisse: Berlin 1900. Bekenntnisse. II. Aus der Werkstatt, 2. Meine Novellistik." In *Novelle.* Ed. Josef Kunz. Darmstadt: Wissenschaftliche Buchgesellschaft, 1968, 74–78.

Hoverland, Lilian. *Heinrich von Kleist und das Prinzip der Gestaltung.* Königstein/Ts.: Scriptor, 1978.

Jolles, André. "Einleitung zur deutschen Ausgabe 1921." In Giovanni di Boccaccio. *Das Dekameron.* Trans. Albert Wesselski. Frankfurt a.M.: Insel, 1967, vii–lxxxvii.

Klein, Johannes. *Geschichte der deutschen Novelle von Goethe bis zur Gegenwart.* Wiesbaden: Steiner, 1954.

Kleist, Heinrich von. *Sämtliche Werke und Briefe.* 2 vols. Ed. Helmut Sembdner. Munich: Hanser, 1985.

Kleist, Heinrich von, ed. *Berliner Abendblätter.* Ed. Helmut Sembdner. Wiesbaden: VMA-Verlag, 1980. Rpt. of the ed. by Georg Minde-Pouet. Leipzig: Klinkhardt & Biermann, 1925.

Köhler, Erich. *Der literarische Zufall, das Mögliche und die Notwendigkeit.* Munich: Fink, 1973.

Krebs, Jean Daniel. "Journalismus und Novelle." *Wolfenbütteler Barock-Nachrichten* 14:1 (1987): 6–8.

Link, Jürgen. *Die Struktur des Symbols in der Sprache des Journalismus: Zum Verhältnis literarischer und pragmatischer Symbole.* Munich: Fink, 1978.

Marx, Stefanie. *Beispiele des Beispiellosen: Heinrich von Kleists Erzählungen ohne Moral.* Würzburg: Königshausen & Neumann, 1994.

Moser, Christian. *Verfehlte Gefühle: Wissen Begehren Darstellen bei Kleist und Rousseau.* Würzburg: Königshausen & Neumann, 1993.

Neumann, Gerhard. "Die Anfänge Deutscher Novellistik: Schillers 'Verbrecher aus verlorener Ehre' — Goethes 'Unterhaltungen deutscher Ausgewanderten.'" In *Unser Commercium: Goethes und Schillers Literaturpolitik.* Ed. Wilfried Barner et al. Stuttgart: Cotta, 1984, 433–60.

Neuschäfer, Hans-Jörg. *Boccaccio und der Beginn der Novelle: Strukturen der Kurzerzählung auf der Schwelle zwischen Mittelalter und Neuzeit.* Munich: Fink, 1969.

Pötters, Wilhelm. *Begriff und Struktur der Novelle: Linguistische Betrachtungen zu Boccaccios Falken.* Tübingen: Niemeyer, 1991.

Reuß, Roland. "'Die Verlobung in St. Domingo' — eine Einführung in Kleists Erzählen." *Berliner Kleist-Blätter* 1 (1989): 3–45.

Schlegel, August Wilhelm. *Vorlesungen über schöne Litteratur und Kunst, Dritter Teil (1803–1804).* Excerpts republished in *Novelle.* Ed. Josef Kunz. Darmstadt: Wissenschaftliche Buchgesellschaft, 1968, 44–50.

Schlegel, Friedrich. "Athenäum." In *Kritische Friedrich-Schlegel-Ausgabe.* Vol. 2. Ed. Ernst Behler. Paderborn: Schöningh, 1967, 165–255.

————. *Literarische Notizen 1797–1801 / Literary Notebooks.* Ed. Hans Eichner. Berlin: Ullstein, 1980.

Schneider, Helmut. "Standing and Falling in Heinrich von Kleist." *Modern Language Notes* 115:3 (2000): 502–18.

Sembdner, Helmut. *Die Berliner Abendblätter Heinrich von Kleists, ihre Quellen und ihre Redaktion.* Berlin: Weidmann, 1939.

Steig, Reinhold. *Heinrich von Kleist's Berliner Kämpfe.* Berlin: Spemann, 1901.

Swales, Erika. "The Beleaguered Citadel: A Study of Kleists's 'Die Marquise von O. . . .'" *Deutsche Vierteljahresschrift* 51:1 (1977): 129–47.

Theisen, Bianca. "Der Bewunderer des Shakespeare: Kleists Skeptizismus." *Kleist-Jahrbuch (*1999): 87–108.

————. *Bogenschluß: Kleists Formalisierung des Lesens.* Freiburg: Rombach, 1996.

————. "Gerahmte Rahmen: Kommunikation und Metakommunikation in Kleists Marquise von O. . . ." In *Kleist und die Aufklärung.* Ed. Tim Mehigan. Columbia, SC: Camden House, 2001.

Uerlings, Herbert. *Poetiken der Interkulturalität: Haiti bei Kleist, Seghers, Müller, Buch und Fichte.* Tübingen: Niemeyer, 1997, 158–68.

Weigel, Sigrid. "Der Körper am Kreuzpunkt von Liebesgeschichte und Rassendiskurs in Heinrich von Kleists Erzählung 'Die Verlobung in St. Domingo.'" *Kleist-Jahrbuch* (1991): 202–17.

Werlen, Hans Jakob. "Seduction and Betrayal: Race and Gender in Kleist's 'Verlobung in St. Domingo.'" *Monatshefte* 84, no. 4 (1992): 459–71.

The Eye of the Beholder:
Kleist's Visual Poetics of Knowledge

Hinrich C. Seeba

T HE IMAGERY OF THE EYE," Fredric Jameson remarks in *The Prison-House of Language,* "has often seemed to furnish a privileged language for the description of epistemological disorders" (206). To prove his point in an argument for self reflexive criticism, Jameson relates an episode by James Thurber in which a student of botany is told that if he does not properly adjust the microscope he will only see his own eye rather than what he is supposed to see. But what to the scientist seems a limitation, if not a failure, of perspective is a welcome analogy for postmodern critics to proclaim the loss of the referent to self-referential language; for the linguistic window to the world has become opaque, a screen onto which the image of the viewer/speaker is projected. Looking for truth outside, the metonymic eye ends up seeing only itself. Truth is in the eye of the beholder.[1]

Heinrich von Kleist was obsessed with seeing and employed eye imagery to confront the perception of truth throughout his oeuvre, which spans only one decade — from 1801 to his suicide in 1811. Even those who are barely familiar with his work would immediately be able to connect, however vaguely, the famous ocular image of "green glasses" with Kleist's own version of an epistemological disorder, better known as the so-called Kant crisis. As the formulaic connection, which will be discussed later, obviously combined a poetic and an existential aspect, it was ideally suited for explaining why and how Kleist became a writer (cf. Seeba 1991) once the biographical approach to literature began to favor anecdotes about the deciding moment of poetic inspiration. Unlike the popular fantasies of inspiration about Schiller smelling rotten apples and Hofmannsthal's hand running through precious pearls, the Kant crisis served to place Kleist's muses, these dark forces of the abyss that lured him frequently to consider and eventually to commit suicide, in a broader existential context of Faustian dimension. For many critics the creative despair of an inadequate truth seeker was so good an image that they were disinclined to look beyond the biographical scintillation and explore in Kleist's oeuvre the literary manifestation of the paradigm shift from the mind to the eye, from the cognitive to the physiological aspect of perception. Only after the literary and critical trend of the 1970s, New Subjectivity, rediscovered the body, which is as much "inscribed" as the mind, and started reading it as a cultural text did sensual perception receive, once again, the credit it deserved (cf. Hart Nibbrig; Ohlschläger; Utz; Jay). The growing interest in cultural anthropology has moved the act of seeing as an alternate mode of knowing into the center of critical concerns. Against this background another look at Kleist's visual poetics of knowledge may provide new insights into the premises of his writing.

Kleist created one of the most compelling and, at the same time, disturbing instances of the eye metaphor — in characteristic reference to a painting whose subject is visual contemplation. When Kleist saw Caspar David Friedrich's painting *Der Mönch am Meer,* which was first exhibited in Berlin in 1810 (and immediately acquired by the king of Prussia, Friedrich Wilhelm III), he felt "als ob Einem die Augenlider weggeschnitten wären" (3:543).[2] Kleist identified with Friedrich's tiny figure of a monk contemplating the abyss of unlimited expanse: "so ward ich selbst der Kapuziner"(3:543). But as this seascape has no frame to hold onto and no objects on which to fix the gaze, the contemplation cannot rest on the visual relief usually provided by central perspective and a layering of depth. Unlike his religious stand-in, the secular viewer's contemplation is devoid of any redeeming promise. Instead, the viewer finds himself under a frightening spell, as if he were condemned to see what is not there. There is no escape from seeing the vast empty space — in fact, from seeing the very emptiness Friedrich was determined to represent (as infrared analysis has revealed; cf. Börsch-Supan 68–69) when he deliberately removed all previously envisioned objects, such as two sailboats, that could have guided and comforted the unprotected eye. Marie Helene von Kügelgen, the wife of the Dresden portrait painter and friend of Friedrich's, Gerhard von Kügelgen, best described the shock effect that the painting caused among contemporaries: "Aber es gibt ja nichts zu sehen" (*Galerie der Romantik* 29). While Friedrich's painting may suggest, as was pointed out in a catalogue of the Metropolitan Museum in New York in 1990, the Romantic origin of abstract painting a century later (Asvarishch 32), the bewilderment it elicits implies another theoretical aspect of nonmimetic representation. Feeling as if his eyelids were cut off, the viewer, thus brutally injured, is forced to engage in a painful act of seeing even when there is nothing to see. Because he can no longer close his eyes nor see anything in particular, he only sees what has become thematic here: the process itself. The switch from the object of knowledge to the mode of perception, of course, is the epistemological turn associated with Kantian philosophy that informed Kleist's writing as much as his contemporary Friedrich's painting. Literally against the painted background of an abyss in which nothingness is lurking, Kleist has made the eye a central motif in his unrelenting effort to confront the tortured perception of truth.

The role of the eye — the real one and, as we will see, its metaphorical referent, language — in defining what we see and believe to be true has always elicited both positive and negative comments. Whereas Goethe, in a classic tribute to idealism — "Wär nicht das Auge sonnenhaft, / Wie könnten wir das Licht erblicken?" (324) — could employ the image of the eye to argue the God-given nature of man, because we are what we see, skeptics, even among his contemporaries, have conversely claimed that we can only see what we are. For we ourselves are involved in generating and shaping the sight and may see in what we believe to be true nothing but the eye, our own eye, and the language we are bound to use for representing the sight. This view seems prevalent today, ever since Velázquez's painting *Las Meninas* (1656), made famous again by Michel Foucault,[3] became the icon of the prison-house of imagery, of representation representing only itself: the screen of the painting is no longer a window through which we look out into the world; instead, it represents the mirror behind the easel, with the painter, who seems to look at us, looking at himself while painting the mirror image of his subject, the king's children. But the insight into such complex nonreferentiality has not come about easily. In fact, it proved rather painful — as if the eyelids had been cut off.

Kleist caught the pain of self-reflexive knowledge in the image of a young man who suddenly becomes aware of himself and, in this psychologically fraught instance of development, loses the innocence of his childhood. The anecdote of the youth seeing himself in the mirror is told in the essay "Über das Marionettentheater" (1810) to demonstrate both the visuality of cognition at the plot level and the cognitive power of the visual example at the metacritical level. Only by looking into the mirror can the boy, who happens to dry his foot on a stool, recognize and start questioning his individuality; he sees his unintentional pose, which seemed to be entirely his own, modeled on an artistic original, the famous sculpture of a boy pulling a thorn out of his foot.[4] With his eyes fixed on the mirror image, he becomes obsessed with recapturing the pose, which, as he realizes, he had re-created unconsciously; but the fleeting "aura" (as Walter Benjamin would call it) of the original is forever lost in the repetitive reproduction. The framed view offers him insight, however disturbing, into the visual construction of his own self, as if it were a piece of art.[5] But the artistic allusion the youth tries to retrieve becomes invisible the very moment it is recognized. What is left for him to see reflects, more than anything else, the seeing subject in a futile attempt to recapture its originality. The fifteen-year-old ephebe loses his charming innocence — in other words, the very grace that is at issue in this philosophical dialogue — because he realizes: "welche Unordnungen, in der natürlichen Grazie des Menschen, das Bewußtsein anrichtet" (3:560). Phrased as if Fredric Jameson had taken his cue from Kleist, it is this lesson of epistemological disorder that the young man must learn, thus anticipating the reader's irritating understanding of this remarkably visualized treatise: only through his gaze does he attain the painful self-awareness that expels him from the paradise of childhood. Only because he discovers what he sees is his own image inscribed with an aesthetic model does he lose his naive way of looking at reality. The ephebe sees himself interpreted by the only referent possible in this hall of mirrors, an aesthetic reflection, a work of art as disappearing signifier that renders him the signified. In this semiotic reversal of roles the observer becomes the observed, as art tends to look back with a vengeance: "Denn da ist keine Stelle," says Rilke in his poem "Archäischer Torso Apollos" of another famous Greek sculpture, "die dich nicht sieht. Du mußt dein Leben ändern" (313). The loss of grace is a philosophical trope for the epistemological irritation, as it is becoming visible in the bodily image of an injury; for the attempt to remove the biblical "thorn in the eye" (Genesis 33:55) will most likely be in vain. The realization of this irreversible transformation is indeed life-changing, if not, in the case of the author, even life-threatening. But Kleist has managed to ban the horror of the epistemological moment in a highly visualized and erotically charged anecdote (cf. Hart), which serves as an argument in the philosophical discourse. It metacritically proves that knowledge can best be attained in metaphors, images, anecdotes, and poetic stories. The performative quality of truth is dramatically staged in the image and theoretical discussion of the theater of marionettes; it is visually staged time and again in Kleist's dramas and dramatic narratives.

If we assume that all of Kleist's works follow a visual poetics of knowledge, its origin can be found in one of the most celebrated "epistemological disorders" in German intellectual history. Returning once again to Kleist's so-called Kant crisis of 1801, this favorite mystery among critics, we find the occasion for the critical and, at the same time, existentially threatening account of restrictions to the mind and its representational faculties the subject of much debate. Kleist derives his alleged despair, which is often understood as the major stimulus for his subsequent tormented writing, from his recent familiarity with the "neueren sogenanten Kantischen Philosophie" (letter to Wilhelmine von Zenge, 22 March 1801; 4:205). But it is not known whether it was the reading of Immanuel Kant's *Kritik der reinen Vernunft* (1781) or of his *Kritik der praktischen Vernunft* (1790) or of a tract by the predecessor of Fichte as professor of philosophy in Jena, the Kantian Karl Leonhard Reinhold (1758–1823), *Versuch einer neuen Theorie des Vorstellungsvermögens* (1789), that caused the first of Kleist's many suicidal plunges into the often evoked abyss; for it was Reinhold from whom Kleist may have borrowed his famous metaphor of the "green glasses" that literally taint the perception of reality. If we cannot decide, Kleist writes to his fiancée, Wilhelmine von Zenge, in the same letter, "ob das, was wir Wahrheit nennen, wahrhaft Wahrheit ist, oder ob es uns nur so scheint" (4:205), the question of truth has begun to oscillate between "being" and "seeming," moving from absolute knowledge to relative perception, from the cognitive to the sensual, from noumena to phenomena, from the mind to the eyes, and from philosophy to the arts. This change, whether or not it could be attributed to Kantian theory of knowledge, was widely perceived as a paradigm shift of historic proportions because it coincided with the turn of the century, when the breakthrough of something entirely new was to be expected. Even the discourse of crisis, as Kleist experienced and announced it in 1801, is part of what has appropriately been called "Schwellenrhetorik" around 1800.[6]

The critical shift proved central to the poetological program of Romantics such as Novalis and Friedrich Schlegel but an existential challenge to others such as Kleist, who were less theoretically inclined and not prepared to develop a new philosophical design for what Philippe Lacoue-Labarthe and Jean-Luc Nancy defined as "l'absolu littéraire," the literary precursor of abstract painting. Novalis — who, incidentally, died one day after Kleist wrote his famous letter of epistemological despair — had already argued in his short essay on nonreferential language, *Monolog*, that language is abstract like mathematical formulae, which do not refer to anything: "Sie spielen nur mit sich selbst, drücken nichts als ihre wunderbare Natur aus, und eben darum sind sie so ausdrucksvoll" (Novalis 2:672). When Novalis adds, self-reflexively, that it takes a special sensitivity, "Ohr und Sinn genug . . . Wahrheiten wie diese [zu] schreiben" (673), he points to the direction of sensual perception Kleist was eventually to pursue dramatically rather than philosophically. Novalis was not thrown into an existential crisis like Kleist; instead, he explicitly welcomed the liberation of creativity from rational constraints and the subsequent shift from Enlightenment philosophy to Romantic fantasy. The programmatic poem "Wenn nicht mehr Zahlen und Figuren," which Novalis intended to use in the continuation of his novel *Heinrich von Ofterdingen* (published posthumously in 1802), celebrates the utopian hope for truth based on poetic sensitivity rather than logical discourse: "Wenn die so singen, oder küssen / Mehr als die Tiefgelehrten wissen" (Novalis 1:344). Novalis's long list of conditions for establishing truth pits positive features associated with artistic perception against negative features associated with rationalist definitions of truth to imply that alienation, this modern state of a mind that has forever forfeited the bliss of paradise, can be overcome only through sensual cognition. Separated from its prelapsarian origin, "die Welt" can return to itself, the poem suggests, only by trusting the cognitive power of song and love, poems and fairy tales — only through poetic reenchantment.

Before Kleist could resort to such utopian therapy for cognitive injury and epistemological disorder, he was only able to see the claim to truth, this enlightened concept of universal validity of knowledge, completely shattered and reduced to a localized point of view, the very "Sehepunkt" that Johann Martin Chladenius (1710–59) had introduced long before Kant as the central concept of his foundational work in historical hermeneutics, *Einleitung zur richtigen Auslegung vernünfftiger Reden und Schrifften* (1742). He writes: "Aus dem Begriff des Sehe-Puncts folget, daß Personen, die eine Sache aus verschiedenen Sehe-Puncten ansehen, auch verschiedene Vorstellungen von der Sache haben müssen" (189). The multiplication of viewpoints and, subsequently, of perceptions effectively undermined any assertion of the one and only correct view. Seeing and perception, *aisthesis* in Greek, are, of course, the domain of an emerging field of philosophical investigation, aesthetics, which evolved in concept and name from Alexander Gottlieb Baumgarten's commitment to sensual knowledge in his *Aesthetica* (1750–58). It is in this philosophical context of epistemological aesthetics, with Karl Philipp Moritz's *Grundlinien zu einer Gedankenperspektive* (1789) being one of the better-known examples, that the surge of perspectivism in the late eighteenth century generated an abundance of visual metaphors (cf. Seeba 1984). Time and again, the significance of the individualized point of view is emphasized in references to the eye as well as to glasses, binoculars, microscopes, camera obscura, and other optical devices to adjust and enhance the limiting personal view (cf. Langen) and, with the craze for Etienne-Gaspard Robertson's phantasmagoric shows culminating around 1800 (cf. Castle), to tease "the eye of the mind" with optical illusions. One of the early writers to chastise prejudice as a literally tainted view was Lessing. Referring to "das gefärbte Glas seiner vorgefaßten Meinungen" in his drama *Der Freigeist* of 1749, Lessing implored his readers to recognize preconceptions as tainted opinions far removed from the truth they proclaim (546). But while the critical mind, as it was widely perceived in the Enlightenment, could easily remove such tinted glasses and thus overcome the prejudice that taints knowledge and understanding, Kleist's generation was not as optimistic.

Obviously, Kleist was only following a common practice of his time when he tried to explain the epistemological problem to his fiancée in optical terms: "Wenn alle Menschen statt der Augen grüne Gläser hätten, so würden sie urteilen müssen, die Gegenstände, welche sie dadurch erblicken, *sind* grün — und nie würden sie entscheiden können, ob ihr Auge ihnen die Dinge zeigt, wie sie sind, oder ob es nicht etwas zu ihnen hinzutut, was nicht ihnen, sondern dem Auge gehört. So ist es mit dem Verstande" (22 March 1801; 4:205). The message of the simile is simple enough for the pedagogical exercise Kleist never tired of assigning to his fiancée: the mind can play tricks as much as the eyes. The moral lesson von Zenge was supposed to learn from the rhetorical experiment, even if Kleist did not consider her capable of grasping the full extent of its meaning, was skepticism about her own perception. Paradoxically, the apodictic reminder presupposes the very certainty whose irreversible loss it is lamenting.

And indeed, the statement would be self-canceling if it would not shift the focus, however slightly, from knowledge to language and, within the judicial rhetoric of knowledge, from unambiguous judgment ("urteilen müssen") to doubtful discernment ("nie entscheiden können"). In the court of language we cannot decide whether what we see and hold true is real and really true or whether "die Wahrheit" is only in the eye of the beholder. This inability renders any statement about truth problematic. Language of certainty appears fundamentally flawed. As the green glasses, which in Kleist's image assume the quality of a linguistic screen coloring our judgment, are no longer used as a mere optical device to modify and enhance the function of the eyes, language can no longer be seen as merely embellishing thoughts, as a rhetorical ornament for presenting thoughts in a "colorful" way. While Laurence J. Peter, in his famous book *The Peter Principle* (1969), facetiously stated that "Competence, like truth, beauty and contact lenses, is in the eye of the beholder" (43), suggesting that truth and beauty (and competence) can be removed like contact lenses, Kleist's use of the image is much more radical when he has the green glasses take the place of eyes ("statt der Augen"), as if they were implanted in a person without eyes. If there is no option other than glasses or blindness — in other words, a tainted world or no world at all — not seeing the coloring verges on blindness. As coloring the perception of reality, rather than being incidental and

ornamental, has become constitutive of seeing, all knowledge is fundamentally tainted; it is conditioned on the language of perception. As
metaphorical language, which seems to make the world more "colorful,"
is essentialized, there is no escaping from the linguistic screen. In Kleist's
totalizing statement "alle Menschen," including those who insist on the
possibility of unmediated access to truth, are prisoners of language, most
of them without even knowing it. For the mind allows us to know — or
to "see" — only "was wir Wahrheit nennen." If we believe to be true
only what we can *call* true, only sensitivity to such a naming process can
rescue us from total blindness. Thus, the real lesson to be learned from
Kleist's so-called Kant crisis is that language, in order to shape knowledge, has to precede it. Nurturing the sense of language emerges as the
pedagogical mission on which Kleist wanted first his fiancée and eventually his readers to embark.

Kleist later elaborated on this hypothesis in an essay, programmati-
cally entitled "Über die allmählige Verfertigung der Gedanken beim
Reden" (1806), claiming that words generate, rather than merely express,
thoughts. Convinced that "mancher große Redner, in dem Augenblick,
da er den Mund aufmachte, noch nicht wußte, was er sagen würde"
(3:536), Kleist, not unlike Herder one generation before him, believes in
the creative power of language and, thus, even relies on rhetorical tricks
"zur Fabrikation meiner Idee auf der Werkstätte der Vernunft" (3:535).
Ideas are verbal fabrications, because reason follows language. Johann
Gottfried Herder, who arguably was the founder of philosophy of language in Germany, had categorically stated the interdependence of language and reason in his *Abhandlung über den Ursprung der Sprache* (1772):
"Ohne Sprache hat der Mensch keine Vernunft und ohne Vernunft keine
Sprache" (37). Later polemically turning against Kant, Herder in his
Ideen zur Philosophie der Geschichte der Menschheit (1784–85) claimed
even the primacy of language: "eine reine Vernunft ohne Sprache ist auf
Erden ein utopisches Land" (357). This thinly veiled reference to the title
of Kant's *Kritik der reinen Vernunft* was a provocation Kant could not
leave unanswered. While Herder blamed Kant for advocating reason without language, Kant conversely blamed Herder for employing language
without reason. In his condescending review of Herder's *Ideen* Kant asks:
"ob nicht der poetische Geist, der den Ausdruck belebt, auch zuweilen
in die Philosophie des Vf. eingedrungen; ob nicht hier und da Synony-
men für Erklärungen, und Allegorien für Wahrheiten gelten" (799).
Unshaken in his conviction that language is not much more than an em-
bellishment and that it only distracts from the purity of reason, Kant sus-
pects anyone, who, like Herder, argues metaphorically of careless, if not

willful, corruption of truth. When it was Herder's turn to strike the next blow, in his *Metakritik zur Kritik der reinen Vernunft* (1799), he wonders aloud how a "Vernunftrichter" of Kant's caliber could so completely disregard language, through which alone "die Vernunft eben ihr Werk hervorbringt, festhält, vollendet" (183–84). After teaching his erstwhile teacher a lesson in the cognitive power of metaphorical language, Herder concludes his invective by saying that anyone who cannot see the obvious strikes a comic figure, because he tries to locate "den Strom außer dem Strom, 'das Ding an sich,' den wahren Wald, hinter den Bäumen" (217). In other words, Kant suffers from the very blindness that Kleist would later invoke as the flip side of the green glasses, when he was trying to cope with Kantian epistemology by giving it a Herderian twist.

At issue in the Kant-Herder controversy is the possibility of a poetics of knowledge. Kant's rhetorical question whether metaphors constitute or corrupt truth — whether, as Novalis put it, poets really "know" more than philosophers — is later answered by Nietzsche in his essay *Wahrheit und Lüge im außermoralischen Sinn* (1873). At the opposite end of the spectrum from Kant, Nietzsche goes so far as to assert that truth is nothing but metaphors:

> Was ist also Wahrheit? Ein bewegliches Heer von Metaphern, Metonymien, Anthropomorphismen, kurz eine Summe von menschlichen Relationen, die, poetisch und rhetorisch gesteigert, übertragen und geschmückt wurden und die nach langem Gebrauch einem Volke fest, kanonisch und verbindlich dünken: die Wahrheiten sind Illusionen, von denen man vergessen hat, daß sie welche sind, Metaphern, die abgenutzt und sinnlich kraftlos geworden sind, Münzen, die ihr Bild verloren haben und nun als Metall, nicht mehr als Münzen, in Betracht kommen. (314)

What is needed, Nietzsche implies, is to restore the cognitive distinction of metaphors by redrawing on the coins of truth their lost image or, more precisely, by raising sensitivity to the connotative rather than the merely denotative power of language. What seems to be needed is a renewed currency of truth in the kind of epistemological poetics that Herder devised, Novalis announced, and Kleist practiced. Anticipating Nietzsche's exhortation, Kleist kept investing in the currency of metaphoric truth, which derives its value from the distinct image on its coins. At the end of the "Variant" — a long passage edited out by Kleist after the first and unsuccessful performance of *Der zerbrochne Krug* in 1808 — Eve, who withheld the truth in silence to test her fiancé's trust, finally recognizes and accepts the long-denied truth: "Ob ihr mir Wahrheit gabt? O scharfgeprägte, / Und Gottes leuchtend Antlitz drauf. O

Himmel! / Daß ich nicht solche Münze mehr erkenne!" (12.2375–77). "Erkenntnis der Wahrheit," the coin metaphor suggests, is conditioned on the distinct visibility of its representation: knowledge depends on the ability to see the redeeming value of the image.

Obviously, Kleist began to agree with Herder rather than with Kant in 1801. Against the background of the conflict of the two philosophers, which had just been played out openly, Kleist's attempt to deal with Kantian philosophy takes on new significance. Starting with the famous letter to his fiancée, he is beginning to deal with and eventually to overcome the crisis of knowledge by turning it into an issue of language. Only when the episte-mological predicament, as Kleist experienced it, helps to problematize the words we use to define something as true can the creative sensitivity to language, as it guides fictional accounts of the crisis of representation, emerge as a redemptive power. Therefore, Kleist might eventually have concurred with the last lines of Novalis's programmatic poem: "Dann fliegt von Einem geheimen Wort / Das ganze verkehrte Wesen fort" (Novalis 1:345). The trust in the power of language could hardly be any stronger. In fact, "das eine Wort" was to become an important, though not always redeeming, topos in Kleist's poetics of knowledge, ranging from *Die Familie Schroffenstein,* where the entire maze of deadly mistrust hinges on "das *eine* Wort" (1.1.233), which appears to be a forced and misinterpreted admission of guilt, to *Amphitryon,* where in the confusion of identities it is hoped that "ein entscheidend Wort . . . / Das Rätsel lösen wird" (3.10, 2084–85). Kleist's word is as powerful as that of Novalis, but it typically oscillates be-tween revelation and its apocalyptic failure. The answer to the most fre-quently asked question in the judicial structure of his dramas and narratives, "Was ist geschehen?"[7] often hinges on just one word and its ambiguous interpretation. In Kleist's dramatic court of truth, it seems, the cognitive power of metaphorical language is constantly being tested. Its most power-ful structure is, of course, the dramatic trial, a truth-finding interrogation that, most famously in *Der zerbrochne Krug,* does not even spare the judge when it turns against the language of judgment itself.

The age-old choice between "realist" and "nominalist," "essential-ist" and "constructivist" perceptions of reality is so central to the episte-mological problem that only twenty years after Kleist's personal crisis of representation, Leopold von Ranke, at the other end of the spectrum, could base the entire project of historicism on the assumption that the historian should merely reproduce "die Dinge wie sie sind": "er will blos zeigen wie es eigentlich gewesen" (vii). However reductionist this view may appear today, such deictic objectivism was the unquestioned core of nineteenth-century scientism and was hardly affected by the kind of doubts that had tortured Kleist. In Kleist's own deictic image, the eye is tested as to whether it can show "die Dinge wie sie sind" or whether the eye, being no longer mimetic but a creative sensory medium, adds ("hinzutut") something to what in the Enlightenment — and in historicism, for that matter — the mind was expected to point out, to represent, and to reproduce without any subjective — that is, aesthetic — interference. While in most of pre-Kantian epistemology it was only beauty, not truth, that was seen in the eye of the beholder, Kleist unknowingly followed Chladenius when he made the eye — both the act of seeing and the point of view — the critical issue of the search for truth: "Ja, wenn wir den ganzen Zusammenhang der Dinge einsehen könnten! Aber ist nicht der Anfang und das Ende jeder Wissenschaft in Dunkel gehüllt?" (letter to Adolfine von Werdeck, 29 July 1801; 4:249). Because "Wissenschaft," which here still means totalizing knowledge rather than science, is shrouded in the dark, it would fall upon the eyes, if they only could, to bring it out into the light and thus to engage in the project of Enlightenment by making seeing ("sehen") the preferred mode of knowing ("einsehen").

If Kleist has been praised for developing a dramaturgy of language taken literally, his performative attention to linguistic ambivalence may well have started with the semantic switch between *sehen* and *einsehen, greifen* and *begreifen, Klarheit* and *Aufklärung* — that is, between the literal and the metaphorical meaning of a given word, specifically between the physical and the abstract connotations of insight, understanding, and knowledge. Pushing even the sensual mode of knowing into the counterfactual statement of wishful thinking ("if we only could see the truth"), Kleist further exacerbates the paradigm shift that he had experienced as an existential crisis. If the eyes are as inept as the mind to reflect, and to generate insight into, "den ganzen Zusammenhang der Dinge" (cf. Gebhard) — or, as Goethe's similarly desperate Faust would say, "was die Welt im Innersten zusammenhält" (20) — then, Kleist implies, we are left with only one alternative. If we cannot, either rationally or visually, know and represent reality as it really is, we have to create our own and invent the ordered coherence that we assign to reality. Blurring the borderline between philosophy and aesthetics, Kleist's Kant crisis has opened up the question of truth to the possibility of its aesthetic construction. Without this crisis setting free the creative energy that is entailed in visual invention, it can be assumed, Kleist could not have become the gripping writer of modernity and its crisis, a writer who had only ten years, from the crisis in 1801 to his death in 1811, to stage the paradigm shift in a compellingly critical way. In his visual poetics of knowledge, language does not merely represent: it enacts and performs the very tension to which it refers.

Before the epistemological disorder came to the breaking point, Kleist defined the implicit problem of language by the intractable distance between, if not the incompatibility of, the means and the subject of representation — in semiotic terms, between signifier and signified. He writes in a letter of 5 February 1801, to his sister Ulrike: "Und gern möchte ich Dir Alles mittheilen, wenn es möglich wäre. Aber es ist nicht möglich, und wenn es auch kein weiteres Hinderniß gäbe, als dieses, daß es uns an einem Mittel zur Mittheilung fehlt. Selbst das einzige, das wir besitzen, die Sprache taugt nicht dazu, sie kann die Seele nicht mahlen, und was sie uns giebt sind nur zerrissene Bruchstücke" (4:196). It is the impossibility of representing in language the feeling of communicative incompetence that tortured Kleist to such a degree that he would like to replace the "Mittel zur Mittheilung" with its referent, that is, the very soul or heart out of which he wants to speak. He tells Ulrike in a letter of 13 March 1803: "Ich weiß nicht, was ich dir über mich *unaussprechlichen* Menschen sagen soll. — Ich wollte ich könnte mir das Herz aus dem Leibe reißen, in diesen Brief packen, und Dir zuschicken. — Dummer Gedanke!" (4:313). In order to put himself, his own "unspeakability," into words, Kleist would have to mail his heart — not the metaphorical heart the rhetoric of love has known for so long but the very organ itself that is the heartbeat of his life. He would have to sacrifice his heart and, thus, his life to attain what is entirely beyond reach. Only in the bloody act of self-mutilation, similar to the cutting off of the eyelids, would it be possible for him to achieve the material identity of word and referent, the complete "Mittheilung" for which he is striving. What Kleist pretends to dismiss as a dumb idea constitutes a rather provocative thought that is central to his entire work, a thought that has become widely appreciated only in our time in postmodern theories of representation.

If language cannot "paint" the soul, neither can a painting — not even a painting as powerful as Friedrich's *Der Mönch am Meer.* To achieve what Kleist so desperately expects from language, the painter would have to make the material substance of the intended subject the medium for representing it: "Ja, wenn man diese Landschaft mit ihrer eignen Kreide und mit ihrem eigenen Wasser malte; so, glaube ich, man könnte die Füchse und Wölfe damit zum Heulen bringen: das Stärkste, was man, ohne allen Zweifel, zum Lobe für diese Art von Landschaftsmalerei beibringen kann."[8] But even Friedrich's painting cannot represent — that is, make present in its material reality — the dune and the sea it invokes. In a backhanded compliment Kleist praises the painting for what it cannot do, only because it makes the viewer wish that it could be done. The desired complete unity of signifier and signified, so it appears, is impossible. Yet, the image Kleist uses to emphasize this impossibility is a mythological allusion, easily overlooked, that just might show the way out of the semiotic dilemma. The image of foxes and wolves howling in case the painting could really *be* what it only purports to represent suggests a creative act of poetic imagination. For it was Orpheus, the archetypal poet in Greek myth and Romantic imagination, who worked magic with songs that could move even wild animals to tears. Legends related in Novalis's *Heinrich von Ofterdingen* tell of mythical poets in ancient Greece, "die durch den seltsamen Klang wunderbarer Werkzeuge . . . grausame Tiere gezähmt . . . und selbst die totesten Steine in regelmäßige tanzende Bewegungen hingerissen haben" (1:211).[9] The Romantic solution to the epistemological disorder that afflicted Kleist rests in the magical power of language, with its wealth of metaphors, images, and mythological allusions, to give the world a musical order.

While Kleist would hardly agree with their harmonizing concept of a poetically enchanted world, he shared with the Romantics the belief in the cognitive value of metaphors. He differed from them, however, by insisting on the sensual materiality of metaphors and by often carrying their creative power to a violent extreme. Characteristically, Kleist's wild animals are not just shedding tears; they would, indeed, be howling if the impossible became possible and the object and the material of signification became one. Thus, cutting off eyelids and tearing out the heart are epistemological images that only anticipate much more violent scenes in which Kleist staged desperation over the impossibility of welding signifier and signified into one. His strongest images of bodily injury are mutilations; they range from a witch cutting off and cooking a child's finger in *Die Familie Schroffenstein* to Thusnelda having a bear tear apart her Roman admirer in *Die Hermannsschlacht* and to Penthesilea eating her lover Achilles' shoulder like a dog. The most shockingly violent image, however, is staged in the drama of national hatred, *Die Hermannsschlacht*. In a biblical allusion to Judges 19:22, the mutilated body of a woman named Hally, who has been raped by Roman soldiers, is cut into ten pieces to represent the ten German tribes and their need to be united again into one whole body. To anticipate German unification, Hally is literally turned into the kind of "zerrissene Bruchstücke" that, according to the earlier reference, symbolize, beyond the plot level, the inability of language fully to convey meaning. Mutilation and fragmentation, the kind of "Zerrissenheit" and "Gebrochenheit" that is symbolized in the material image of the *Zerbrochne Krug,* are the only way "die ungeheure Wahrheit anzuschaun" (*Die Hermannsschlacht* 1.3.349), to grasp the unimaginable truth that there is no representation of truth other than in the image of mutilation. Throughout his life Kleist struggled, eventually ending in disastrous failure, to earn the utopian, even metaphysical forgiveness his narrator granted the Count F. in "Die Marquise von O . . .": "um der gebrechlichen Einrichtung der Welt willen" (3:186). A literary microcosm of the modern world, Kleist's world was forever "broken" — save for a few moments of poetic grace.

The spectator's eyes are heavily involved in the spectacularly dramatic scenes of tearing to pieces any claim to bodily wholeness. The eyes are not spared from this mutilation. Again, as if the eyelids were cut off, the spectator is condemned to see what Aristotle criticized as mere *teras*, horror of the eye.[10] The truth may prove so horrible that when it eventually becomes visible, the eyes are metaphorically separated from the viewer and no longer at his or her full disposal. Time and again Kleist has entrusted the eyes with finding the truth by holding them to their task of overcoming the distance between subject and object, by bringing the truth literally within grasp. Characteristically taking language at face value, Kleist develops striking images and scenes to symbolize corporeal access to truth.

In *Der zerbrochne Krug,* to give the first of two examples, he elaborates on the common phrase "die Augen auf etwas werfen" in an extended metaphor that plays on the presumed materiality of the eyes. In his testimony Ruprecht, the sole eyewitness to Eve's secret encounter with Adam, turns his eyes into messengers he sends out to establish truth, only to scold them when they come back with unwanted sights:

> Und schicke freudig euch, von wo die Ohren
> Mir Kundschaft brachten, meine Augen nach —
> Und schelte sie, da sie mir wiederkommen,
> Für blind, und schicke sie zum zweitenmal, sich besser umzusehen,
> Und schimpfe sie nichtswürdige Verleumder,
> Aufhetzer, niederträcht'ge Ohrenbläser,
> Und schicke sie zum drittenmal, und denke,
> Sie werden, weil sie ihre Pflicht getan,
> Unwillig los sich aus dem Kopf mir reißen,
> Und sich in einen andern Dienst begeben. (7.904–14)

Ruprecht would choose blindness over the truth of what he saw: "So sag' ich zu mir, blind ist auch nicht übel. / Ich hätte meine Augen hingegeben, / Knippkügelchen, wer will, damit zu spielen" (7.1031–33). Because they convey the terrible truth the eyewitness did not want to see, the eyes are denigrated to the status of disobedient servants who betrayed their master's interests. Such supposedly willful eyes, which, on the one hand, take on a life of their own, can, on the other hand, be traded like marbles ("Knippkügelgen") in a child's game — not because they saw nothing (as Frau von Kügelgen would complain in front of Friedrich's painting),[11] but because they saw too much.

In *Penthesilea,* to give also the other, more complex example, eyes are not just messengers reporting back to the mind what they have seen but hunters who chase down the fleeting object until they finally grasp it in a powerful image of defeat. Before Achilles enters the stage for the first time, his image is visually constructed out of its body parts as they become visible, one by one from the top down, when he comes up like the rising sun from behind a hill:

> Seht! Steigt dort über jenes Berges Rücken,
> Ein Haupt nicht, ein bewaffnetes, empor?
> Ein Helm, von Federbüschen überschattet?
> Der Nacken schon, der mächt'ge, der es trägt?
> Die Schultern auch, die Arme, stahlumglänzt?
> Das ganze Brustgebild, o seht doch, Freunde,
> Bis wo den Leib der gold'ne Gurt umschließt?. . .
> Nur noch die Schenkel sind,
> Die Hufen, von der Höhe Rand bedeckt!
> Jetzt, auf dem Horizonte, steht das ganze
> Kriegsfahrzeug da! So geht die Sonne prachtvoll
> An einem heitern Frühlingstage auf! (3.356–62, 365–69)

Even in the cosmological dimension where Achilles is imagined as the sun and Penthesilea as the moon, the body, in whose destruction the failed meeting of the antipodes ends, is first put together from the limited "Sehepunkt" of *teichoscopia,* in a dramatic staging of synthetic perspectivism. Once again seeing and the attempt to grasp literally and metaphorically what appears in sight but out of reach is central to the dramatic development. From the very first moment when Penthesilea's "Aug auf den Peliden trifft" (1.68), the pursuit of Achilles becomes a visual obsession with dissolving the distance to the unattainable: "Mit jedem Hufschlag, / Schlingt sie, wie hungerheiß, ein Stück des Weges, / Der sie von den Peliden trennt, hinunter" (3.405–7). Metaphorically eating up the distance until she almost reaches him in a chaotic tumble, Penthesilea soon loses sight of her victim: "Kaum mehr mit Blicken kann sie ihn erreichen, / Und der Gedanke selbst, der strebende, / Macht ihr im atemlosen Busen: halt!" (3.458–60). When in the end she literally eats up her prey "hungerheiß," as if she were one of her dogs, this most horrendous scene transforms the metaphor of visually consuming what separates her from the object of desire into the paradox of grasping truth (cf.

Chaouli). Losing her mind, she kills the man she loves, believing that she has conquered him at last. In this most devastating moment, when the pursuit of knowledge turns into dehumanizing madness, the power of language reigns supreme, but with a tragic vengeance: Penthesilea kills herself by creating, through sheer willpower, a verbal dagger that she thrusts into her heart. Only in this suicide has the signifier at last become identical with the signified.

If the heart could be mailed, if the eyes could be sent, if the distance between viewing subject and intended object could be reduced if not eliminated, there would be no reason for the maddening despair that pushed both Penthesilea and, eventually, her author to commit suicide. In view of the abyss, whether it is painted by Friedrich or staged by Kleist, there is nothing left to see in terms of mimetic representation, no consoling foregrounding of the fact that truth cannot completely be attained. Frau von Kügelgen's naive expression of irritation "Aber es gibt ja nichts zu sehen" is only the least *conditio sine qua non* of aesthetic imagination taking the place of universal knowledge and epistemological certainty. Even truth is in the eye of the beholder only if we accept the "Gebrechlichkeit der Welt" and take the risk of seeing the unknown. This is the lesson we can learn from Frau Marthe, when she tells the court both the history *of* the pitcher and the history once represented *on* it when it was still whole. Now broken, the "Krug" is nothing but a word whose referent has disappeared:

> *FRAU MARTHE:* Seht ihr den Krug, ihr wertgeschätzten Herren?
> Seht ihr den Krug?
> *ADAM:* O ja, wir sehen ihn.
> *FRAU MARTHE:* Nichts seht ihr, mit Verlaub, die Scherben seht ihr;
> Der Krüge schönster ist entzwei geschlagen.
> Hier grade auf dem Loch, wo jetzo nichts,
> Sind die gesamten niederländischen Provinzen
> Dem span'schen Philipp übergeben worden. . . .
> Hier guckt noch ein Neugier'ger aus dem Fenster:
> Doch was er jetzo sieht, das weiß ich nicht.
>
> $(7.644-50, 673-74)^{12}$

In view (quite literally) of the loss of the historical subject, the process of "sehen" versus "wissen" has become thematic once again. After history has collapsed into the hole of "nichts" we cannot *know* what we do not *see*. We cannot even know what an ideally placed eyewitness once *saw*. We can only *imagine* — not what history was really like but how images of the past, as seen from individual perspectives, can be *told* in stories that are structured according to the rules of poetics. The stories boast poetic truths (in the plural, reflecting the multiplication of perspectives) as mere metaphors for a certain way of ordering reality. *History* has dissolved into multifaceted *stories,* stories that must be narrated if the absent past is to be re-presented in verbal fictions of reality. Epistemological disorder, thus, inspired a poetic order that, however precarious, carries the promise of survival. Rather than pronouncing rules in the abstract, Kleist's visual poetics of knowledge enacts and performs the very "brokenness," the "Gebrechlichkeit der Welt," that is visually represented in the broken pitcher and kept in balance by the utopian hope for a pardon from Adam to Count F.

Notes

[1] Surprisingly, the proverbial "Beauty is in the eye of the beholder" was coined neither by Shakespeare nor by advocates of eighteenth-century perspectivism but by the author of *Ben Hur,* Lew Wallace, in his *The Prince of India* (1893).

[2] Heinrich von Kleist, "Empfindungen vor Friedrichs Seelandschaft," first published in *Berliner Abendblätter* 12–13 November 1810. While Clemens Brentano wrote most of the heavily edited article, the image of the eyelids belongs only to the editor, Kleist. Cf. Begemann 77–79; Traeger.

[3] Foucault 16: "representation undertakes to represent itself here in all its elements, with its images, the eyes to which it is offered, the faces it makes visible, the gestures that call it into being."

[4] Dating from the first century A.D., the Roman copy of a lost Greek original from the fifth century B.C. was on display in Paris in Kleist's time.

[5] The theoretical parallel to Jacques Lacan's famous Zurich lecture of 17 July 1949, "La stade du miroir comme formateur de la fonction de Je, telle qu'elle nous est révélée dans l'expérience psychoanalytique," is obvious; but Lacan placed the "mirror stage" in the development of a child's sense of self much earlier, in the first two years.

[6] Brendecke 201: "Um die Schwellenrhetorik der Jahre um 1800 recht zu verstehen, sollte man die Nähe zum Modell der Krise nicht übersehen." Surprisingly, Brendecke makes no reference to Kleist.

[7] *Robert Guiscard* 6.139; *Amphitryon* 2.3.1042, 2.4.1107, 2.6.1635, 3.11.2154; *Das Käthchen von Heilbronn* 1.2.545, 590, 674; 3.8.1830, 4.7.2289, 5.1.2462; *Penthesilea* 5.664, 8.1116, 23.2605; *Prinz Friedrich von Homburg* 3.5.980, 4.1.1147.

[8] Kleist, *Empfindungen vor Friedrichs Seelandschaft,* 3:543–44.

[9] Cf. Horace, *Carmina* 3.11, v. 13–14.: "tu potes tigris comitesque silvas / ducere et rivos celeres morari."

[10] Aristotle, *Poetics* 78: "Those who employ spectacular means to create a sense not of the terrible but only the monstrous, are strangers to the purpose of Tragedy."

[11] Considering Kleist's frequent playing on names, with the title of *Der zerbrochne Krug* possibly referring to Traugott Krug, Kant's successor in Königsberg and the husband of Kleist's erstwhile fiancée, Wilhelmine von Zenge, one could speculate that Kleist's use of the uncommon term *Knippkügelgen* may not be entirely incidental during his time in Dresden, where he socialized with the Kügelgen family.

[12] On the disappearance of the referent in *Der zerbrochne Krug* cf. Seeba, "Overdragt der Nederlanden in't jaar 1555 . . ."

Works Cited

Aristotle's Poetics. Trans. S. H. Butcher. New York: Hill & Wang, 1961.

Asvarishch, Boris I. "Friedrich's Russian Patrons." In *The Romantic Vision of Caspar David Friedrich: Paintings and Drawings from the U.S.S.R.* Ed. Sabine Rewald. New York: Metropolitan Museum; Chicago: Art Institute, 1990, 19–40.

Begemann, Christian. "Brentano und Kleist vor Friedrichs Mönch am Meer: Aspekte eines Umbruchs in der Geschichte der Wahrnehmung." *Deutsche Vierteljahresschrift* 64 (1990): 54–94.

Börsch-Supan, Helmut. "Bemerkungen zu Caspar David Friedrichs 'Mönch am Meer.'" *Zeitschrift des deutschen Vereins für Kunstwissenschaft* 19 (1965): 63–76.

Brendecke, Arndt. *Die Jahrhundertwenden: Eine Geschichte ihrer Wahrnehmung und Wirkung*. Frankfurt a.M.: Campus, 1999.

Castle, Terry. "Phantasmagoria: Spectral Technology and the Metaphorics of Modern Reverie." *Critical Inquiry* 15:1 (1988): 26–61.

Chaouli, Michel. "Devouring Metaphor: Disgust and Taste in Kleist's *Penthesilea*." *German Quarterly* 69 (1996): 125–43. German version: "Die Verschlingung der Metapher: Geschmack und Ekel in der *Penthesilea*." *Kleist-Jahrbuch* (1998): 127–49.

Chladenius, Johann Martin. *Einleitung zur richtigen Auslegung vernünfftiger Reden und Schrifften*. 1742. Rpt. Düsseldorf: Stern-Verlag Janssen, 1969.

Foucault, Michel. *The Order of Things: An Archeology of the Human Sciences*. New York: Vintage, 1973.

Galerie der Romantik. Ed. Nationalgalerie Berlin. 2nd ed. Berlin: Staatliche Museen Preußischer Kulturbesitz, 1987.

Gebhard, Walter. *"Der Zusammenhang der Dinge": Weltgleichnis und Naturverklärung im Totalitätsbewußtsein des 19. Jahrhunderts*. Tübingen: Niemeyer, 1984.

Goethe, Johann Wolfgang von. *Faust: Erster Teil*. Vol. 3 of his *Werke*. Ed. Erich Trunz. 7th ed. Hamburg: Wegner, 1964, 7–145.

————. "Zur Farbenlehre." In his *Werke*. Vol. 13. Ed. Erich Trunz. 4th ed. Hamburg: Wegner, 1962, 314–523.

Hart, Gail K. "*Anmut*'s Gender: The 'Marionettentheater' and Kleist's Revision of 'Anmut und Würde.'" *Women in German Yearbook* 10 (1994): 83–95.

Hart Nibbrig, Christiaan L. *Die Auferstehung des Körpers im Text*. Frankfurt a.M.: Suhrkamp, 1985.

Herder, Johann Gottfried. *Abhandlung über den Ursprung der Sprache*. 1772. Rpt. Stuttgart: Reclam, 1966.

————. "Aus 'Verstand und Erfahrung': Eine Metakritik zur *Kritik der reinen Vernunft*." 1799. In his *Sprachphilosophie: Ausgewählte Schriften*. Ed. Erich Heintel. Hamburg: Felix Meiner, 1980, 181–227.

————. *Ideen zur Philosophie der Geschichte der Menschheit: 1784–85*. Vol. 13 of his *Sämmtliche Werke*. Ed. Bernhard Suphan. Berlin: Weidmann, 1887.

Jameson, Fredric. *The Prison-House of Language: A Critical Account of Structuralism and Russian Formalism*. Princeton: Princeton UP, 1974.

Jay, Martin. *Downcast Eyes: The Denigration of Vision in Twentieth-Century French Thought*. Berkeley: U of California P, 1993.

Kant, Immanuel. "Rezension zu Johann Gottfried Herders Ideen." In his *Werke*. Vol. 12. Ed. Wilhelm Weischedel. Frankfurt a.M.: Suhrkamp, 1964.

Kleist, Heinrich von. *Sämtliche Werke und Briefe in vier Bänden*. 4 vols. Ed. Ilse-Marie Barth et al. Frankfurt a.M.: Deutscher Klassiker Verlag, 1987–97.

Lacoue-Labarthe, Philippe, and Jean-Luc Nancy. *L'Absolu littéraire*. Paris: Editions du Seuil, 1978; Trans. Philip Barnard and Cheryl Lester as *The Literary Absolute: The Theory of Literature in German Romanticism*. Albany: State U of New York P, 1988.

Langen, August. *Anschauungsformen in der deutschen Dichtung des 18. Jahrhunderts: Rahmenschau und Rationalismus*. 1934. Rpt. Darmstadt: Wissenschaftliche Buchgesellschaft, 1965.

Lessing, Gotthold Ephraim. *Werke*. Vol. 1. Ed. Herbert G. Göpfert. Munich: Hanser, 1970.

Nietzsche, Friedrich. *Werke in drei Bänden*. Vol. 3. Ed. Karl Schlechta. 5th ed. Munich: Hanser, 1966.

Novalis. *Schriften: Die Werke Friedrich von Hardenbergs*. 2 vols. Ed. Paul Kluckhohn and Richard Samuel. 2nd ed. Stuttgart: Kohlhammer Verlag, 1960–65.

Ohlschläger, Claudia, and Birgit Wiens, eds. *Körper — Gedächtnis — Schrift: Der Körper als Medium kultureller Erinnerung*. Berlin: Schmidt, 1997.

Peter, Lawrence J. *The Peter Principle*. New York: Morrow, 1969.

Ranke, Leopold von. *Sämtliche Werke*. Vol. 33. 2nd ed. Leipzig, 1874.

Rilke, Rainer Maria. *Gesammelte Gedichte*. Frankfurt a.M.: Insel, 1962.

Seeba, Hinrich C. "Erscheinung eines Dichters." In Heinrich von Kleist, *Sämtliche Werke und Briefe*. Vol. 1: *Dramen 1802–1808*. Ed. Ilse-Marie Barth et al. Frankfurt a.M.: Deutscher Klassiker Verlag, 1991, 465–78.

———. "Overdragt der Nederlanden in't jaar 1555: Das historische Faktum und das Loch im Bild der Geschichte bei Kleist." In *Barocker Lust-Spiegel: Studien zur Literatur des Barock. Festschrift für Blake Lee Spahr*. Ed. Martin Bircher et al. Amsterdam: Rodopi, 1984, 409–43.

———. "'Der wahre Standort einer jeden Person': Lessings Beitrag zum historischen Perspektivismus." In *Nation und Gelehrtenrepublik: Lessing im europäischen Zusammenhang*. Special issue of *Lessing Yearbook*. Ed. Wilfried Barner and Albert M. Reh. Detroit: Wayne State UP.; Munich: edition text + kritik, 1984, 193–214.

Traeger, Jörg. "'. . . als ob einem die Augenlider weggeschnitten wären': Bildtheoretische Betrachtungen zu einer Metapher bei Kleist." *Kleist-Jahrbuch* (1980): 86–106.

Utz, Peter. *Das Auge und das Ohr im Text: Literarische Sinneswahrnehmung in der Goethezeit*. Munich: Fink, 1990.

The Performative Turn of the Beautiful: "Free Play" of Language and the "Unspeakable Person"

Bernhard Greiner

KLEIST'S EXPERIENCE AND CONCEPTION of language and speech, as well as those of his characters, are ambiguous. They vacillate between a secure faith that language can achieve everything through speech and a deep skepticism of language — a belief that what is to be communicated fails in principle through language. The stagnation of language (Neumann 1994) that befalls Kleist's figures over and over is an expression of this ambivalence. This situation is hardly surprising for an artist whose medium is language. But the areas in which Kleist, nevertheless, postulates positively or *ex negativo* a successful type of speech are quite notable. Determining these moments in their linguistic environment promises insights into Kleist's reflections on language[1] and will help us recognize the models on which they are based.

Kleist drafted his oft-discussed paradigm of successful speech in the essay "Über die allmählige Verfertigung der Gedanken beim Reden." Speech in situations such as an oral examination or the delivery of ideas conceived beforehand in a non-communicative manner are offered as examples of unsuccessful speech. At the same time, the success of the essay itself as a speech act proves to be doubly limited. At the end of the essay Kleist promises a further installment that, however, never appeared and thus categorizes his essay as unfinished. Furthermore, the essay, with its dedication to a friend, Rühle von Lilienstern, is an unsent message; it is placed in a communicative context that was likewise never realized because it was never published. A paradigm of unsuccessful speech emerges in the confessional letters, in which Kleist declares himself to be an "unspeakable person" (see letters of 5 February 1801 and 13–14 March 1803 to Ulrike and of 4 August 1806 to von Stein). As a counterexample of successful speech, which remains, however, purely hypothetical, Kleist envisions a type of speech that would be sovereign in its use of all rhetorical means. It would do so in a way that is capable of fully silencing the inherent meanings of the rhetorical devices — that is, those that are not intended by the author and are not controllable ("Brief eines Dichters an einen anderen"; an inverse form of this is the desire for an immediacy devoid of signs: for example, in the letter to Ulrike of 13–14 March 1803).

Both paradigms of speech determine in three ways what mode of speech occurs. Language is used with regard to a specific listener or reader; it has a specific topic; and it is associated with a specific self-awareness. The essay "Über die allmählige Verfertigung der Gedanken beim Reden" explains the thesis formulated in the title through three examples. First, the speaker reports from his own experiences. Next, the essay cites the historical example of Mirabeau's "Donnerwort," which marked the beginning of the French Revolution. Finally, it gives a literary example: the fable of Lafontaine. Although the thoroughly explained personal example finds evidence in the literary and historical examples, it is here that the paradigm is actually formulated. As regards the relationship of speaker and listener, which is sketched here, it is conspicuous that the position of the listener — here, the sister — has a double function. On the one hand, through her mere existence and listening she will ensure that the speaker will clarify his muddled thoughts into a specific thought:

> Es liegt ein sonderbarer Quell der Begeisterung für denjenigen, der spricht, in einem menschlichen Antlitz, das ihm gegenübersteht; und ein Blick, der uns einen halbausgedrückten Gedanken schon als begriffenen ankündigt, schenkt uns oft den Ausdruck für die ganze andere Hälfte desselben. (3:536)

On the other hand, the listening sister assumes the role of a virtual interrupter. She holds the position of a potential inquirer, one who demands differentiations or specifications. The will to preempt such demands for definitions and differentiations puts the speaker, according to the essay's argument, into such an intense state of mind that he is now able to develop what previously was only a muddled idea into complete clarity (cf. 3:535).

> Dabei ist mir nichts heilsamer, als eine Bewegung meiner Schwester, als ob sie mich unterbrechen wollte; denn mein ohnehin schon angestrengtes Gemüt wird durch diesen Versuch von außen, ihm die Rede, in deren Besitz es sich befindet, zu entreißen, nur noch mehr erregt, und in seiner Fähigkeit, wie ein großer General, wenn die Umstände drängen, noch um einen Grad höher gespannt. (3:536–37)

What kind of relationship exists here? The "you" guarantees that the muddled idea can be formed into a fully developed thought. At the same time, preventing the intervention of the "you" safeguards the thought from being defined and limited from the outside (outside the Ego as a thinking speaker and a speaking thinker). This relationship corresponds in a remarkable manner to the aesthetic judgment as one of a "free play of imagination and reason" (cf. Kant 1974, 28). If the predicate "beautiful" is attributed to an object of our experience, then the representation that is produced by our imagination is, in principle, recognized as adequate to conceptualization, without, however, becoming the precedence of a rule through the application of a specific concept. The ability to understand corresponds in the treatment of language in the essay to the approving look of the "you," which proclaims the half-expressed thought already comprehended. The part of reason in aesthetic judgment that wants to subsume the given representation under a concept but experiences every attempt at doing so as unsatisfactory and thus sees its capacity for conceptualization challenged is congruent with the questioning look of the "you." Through its questions — if any were, indeed, to be posed — the "you" would limit and guide the speaking thinker until reason would have filtered out an appropriate concept for the muddled thought. In rejecting such a prescription, the speaker keeps his capacity for "cognition in general" (Kant 1951, 52) alive — "free" (in the sense that it is not limited by the listener's faculty of reason) — until it has produced the new thought simultaneously with the expression that apparently could not be attained through deduction. The mysterious fabrication of thought while speaking thus appears to be grounded on the premise that speech occurs in a speaker/listener configuration that opens up the realm of beauty or — to put it in a philosophically more accurate way — the realm of "aesthetic judgment." Successful speech — speech that not only allows the speaker to communicate his thoughts but lets them first emerge through speech — is, thus, beauty turned into performance. This type of speaking enacts the structure of aesthetic judgment as Kant defines it. This interpretation is further reinforced by the fact that the other definitions of aesthetic judgment that Kant makes in his analysis of beauty are also accentuated in Kleist's paradigm of successful speech.

Insofar as aesthetic judgment is not concerned with the object but only with the "feeling in the subject as it is affected by the representation" (Kant 1951, 38), Kant has introduced a subjective turn into the discourse of aesthetics. This turn is manifested in Kleist's description of successful speech in that it is explicitly limited to an instance where the speaker intends to instruct himself and not others. "Disinterested satisfaction" (Kant 1951, 38) is a further, fundamental redefinition of beauty, which Kant had undertaken (i.e., the indifference of the aesthetic judgment with regard to moral as well as culinary aspects). This is accentuated by the historical and literary examples of the fabrication of thoughts while speaking. Just as, according to Kant's definition, something can receive the predicate *beautiful* even if it is morally problematic, and just as this judgment is not limited to the subject that is isolated in its pleasurable consumption but, instead, lays claim to universal validity, Kleist's historical and literary examples design problematic speeches and speakers. In one example, the fox produces his thoughts while speaking and, in order to save himself, convinces the other animals that the donkey is the most bloodthirsty animal, upon which the donkey is promptly torn to pieces by the others. In hindsight, this example casts doubt on another, the great speaker Mirabeau, in whose rhetorical wake the *terreur* was enforced as the revolution progressed (even though Mirabeau's grave was removed from the Pantheon in 1794 and replaced with Marat's, because the count's connection to the court and the court's financial contributions to him were revealed to the public.)[2] Successful speech as the transfiguration of a muddled idea into a clear thought (in a performative turn of the beautiful) must, like beauty itself, be seen as indifferent to moral aspects. Furthermore, with its prompt effect, successful speech is not limited to the individual speaker but is understood at once by the entire audience.

Kant's "freedom" of the aesthetic judgment, the "free play of imagination and reason" that provides the judging subject with a pleasing self-awareness of the self-perpetuating activity of its cognitive faculties, which are not subjected to any restrictions (i.e., the intuitive diversity refuses to be subsumed under one concept), is accentuated in several ways in Kleist's theory of successful speech. First, it is accentuated in that the "you" — insofar as it virtually contains the force of reason that is intended to act as an agent of restraint — does not stand in a hierarchical relationship to the "ego" (the intimately known sister or the friend, neither of whom pressures the "ego"). Conversely, such a hierarchical relationship is characteristic of those instances that are cited as examples of unsuccessful speech. During an examination or an interrogation, for example, the "you" has power, and through its use of its speaking privileges it circumscribes the thought processes of the speaker. During an expression of a thought that was conceived non-communicatively, the only position remaining for the listener is that of judge, in whose power the speaker has thereby placed himself. In both cases the listener — in a manner analogous to the conceptualizing potentiality of beauty — does not guarantee that the muddled thought can be formulated into a finely contoured thought. Rather, the speaker must prove this through the success or failure of his actions. In successful speech, however, the speaker is not only not subjected to a hierarchical relationship with regard to the "you," but speech itself does not proceed hierarchically: it does not rule over its own thought. This idea is expressed in the essay's often quoted formulation: "denn nicht wir wissen, es ist allererst ein gewisser Zustand unsrer, welcher weiß" (3:450). Kleist's theory of successful speech thus allows for a pleasing self-awareness in the activity of its own cognitive faculties, which are subjected neither to any external limitations nor to any limitations from within the self. At the same time, these cognitive faculties are stimulated by — or, rather, receive encouragement from — the "you," who confirms the thought in advance. Caught in such a flux of constant give-and-take between the "ego" and the "you" (in the "condition that knows"), however, the self cannot be clearly defined — that is, it cannot be clearly distinguished from the "you." The pleasing self-experience refers, therefore, to an uncertain self. If the "ego" were to attempt to prove itself through speech, it would once again be in a hierarchical relationship with the "you." Correspondingly, although the object of speech in the constellation that provides thought is, to be sure, not explicitly limited in any manner, it is implicitly limited insofar as its most personal elements, those in which the self distinguishes itself from all others, cannot be brought into question as an object of speech in the constellation as it is sketched out here. The paradigm of unsuccessful speech — or, rather, impossible speech — will then refer precisely to this case: that is, the case in which the speaker wants to speak about himself, to communicate his innermost self.

Successful speech as a successful fabrication of thoughts while speaking, whereby the speech constellation concretizes and carries out the structure of the aesthetic judgment — and is, thus, a performative turn of the beautiful — is not an unfounded metaphoricization of beauty as a result of Kant's conceptualization of beauty. Kleist only picks up on the "linguisticality" of beauty, which Kant had already accentuated and which was of special interest to the discourse of aesthetics in the twentieth century (in the context of the general "linguistic turn" of philosophy). Kleist's paradigm of successful speech makes this aspect of the linguisticality of the beautiful doubly productive. First, the aesthetic judgment, which has been conceived as an internal process among the emotive faculties, is now, so to speak, turned to the outside and concretized as a specific speech formation. Next, this medially inflected beauty is then itself thought of as productive, that is, it produces thoughts whereby speech must retreat behind the limits of language as a differentiated structure: be it a retreat into speechlessness as an unstructured expression of sounds or a retreat into the use of language particles (phrases, filler words) that fail to convey meaning:

> Ich mische unartikulierte Töne ein, ziehe die Verbindungswörter in die Länge, gebrauche auch wohl eine Apposition, wo sie nicht nötig wäre, und bediene mich anderer, die Rede ausdehnender Kunstgriffe. (3:535)

Here we are considering a type of speech that is not restricted by rules (they would appear with the "you" if it were allowed to introduce questions and differentiation) and that produces something new by delving into the unstructured: the thought and, at the same time, its expression. The conception of such a productive form of speech is clearly oriented to the model of the "genius." Successful speech as productive speech is the province of "genial" creativity. Just as with the creation of the genius, something is created that must obey rules and the order of concepts (because only then can that which is created be a "thought"), without the condition that these rules and concepts would have to exist already in the process of creation. They can thus only be produced through the act of creation itself. Kant describes such a capacity as a — not further justifiable — gift of nature: "Genius is the talent (or natural gift) . . . the innate mental disposition (ingenium) through which nature gives the rule to art" (Kant 1951, 150). Kleist delineates this capacity from a specific speech constellation that is also a field of transition from the "beautiful in nature," which Kant primarily has in mind, to the "beautiful in art," which is, of course, of central importance for Kleist.

In Kleist's theory the paradigm of successful speech reveals the "linguisticality" of beauty as transformed into the material. An analogous material transformation of speech also characterizes the paradigm of unsuccessful or, rather, unachievable speech, which Kleist depicts in his self-characterizations as an "unspeakable person" (letters of 13–14 March 1803 and 4 August 1806), which must be complemented by the contrasting background of the essay "Brief eines Dichters an einen anderen," published in the *Berliner Abendblätter* on 5 January 1811. The shift to the material takes place, however, not on the pragmatic level of language (speech as an act between communicative participants) but, rather, on the semantic level.

In the "Brief eines Dichters an einen anderen" the letter writer complains to his poet friend that the latter reads "falsely." The friend apparently places emphasis on the external aspects of the writings, on the style of the texts, on their "expression" (Kleist 1982, 236) — that is, on their means of expression, rather than on what is expressed. Through many variations, the letter writer bases his arguments on the familiar opposition between spirit and letter:

Nur weil der Gedanke, um zu erscheinen, wie jene flüchtigen, undar-
stellbaren, chemischen Stoffe, mit etwas Gröberem, Körperlichen, ver-
bunden sein muß; nur darum bediene ich mich, wenn ich mich Dir
mitteilen will, und nur darum bedarfst Du, um mich zu verstehen, der
Rede, Sprache, des Rhythmus, Wohlklangs usw. und so reizend diese
Dinge auch, in sofern sie den Geist enthüllen, sein mögen, so sind sie
doch an und für sich, aus diesem höheren Gesichtspunkt betrachtet,
nichts, als ein wahrer, obschon natürlicher und notwendiger Übelstand;
und die Kunst kann, in Bezug auf sie, auf nichts gehen, als sie mög-
lichst verschwinden zu machen. (3:565–66)

Other oppositions appear as well: spirit and form; thought and clothing;
fruit and peel; the essence of poesy and its arbitrary quality, that is, its
form. If the artist is supposed to silence this undeniable formal presence,
if he must prohibit it from achieving its own intrinsic value, if he must
thus treat the form in such a manner "that the essence momentarily and
directly emerges from it" (Kleist 1982, 236), then the ideal becomes
perfect transparency and, therefore, a self-revocation of the sign — which
is, thus, the paradox of a signless sign. Poets have complained again and
again that this is an impossibility, that the opposition between spirit and
letter, as long as one recognizes it, cannot be resolved. Schiller's famous
distich deserves mention here:

Sprache
Warum kann der lebendige Geist dem Geist nicht erscheinen!
Spricht die Seele, so spricht ach! schon die Seele nicht mehr. (313)

With his ideal of a signless sign, does the poet of Kleist's essay retreat
behind this realization? He reprimands his poet friend, who, however,
does not allow the letter writer to dissuade him from paying attention to
the signs themselves and to their order, instead of immediately attending
to what is denoted through them. The oppositions spirit/letter and
thought/linguistic dressing become highly questionable, however, when
the letter writer ponders the conditions under which the oppositions that
he names would fall apart:

Wenn ich beim Dichten in meinen Busen fassen, meinen Gedanken er-
greifen, und mit Händen, ohne weitere Zutat, in den Deinigen legen
könnte: so wäre die Wahrheit zu gestehen, die ganze innere Forderung
meiner Seele erfüllt. Und auch Dir, Freund, dünkt mich, bliebe nichts
zu wünschen übrig. (3:565)

Analogously, Kleist writes to Ulrike on 13–14 March 1803: "Ich weiß
nicht, was ich Dir über mich unaussprechlichen Menschen sagen soll. —

Ich wollte ich könnte mir das Herz aus dem Leibe reißen, in diesen Brief packen, und Dir zuschicken" (4:313).

Kleist, however, concludes this mental game with the remark "Dummer Gedanke!" (4:313). Does the stupidity consist only in the factual contradiction that what is alive and is to be conveyed would then just be killed? Or does it refer to the logical contradiction that the "innermost being," which should preclude any comprehension by being presented in signs, must, however, be comprehended as a "heart" and has thus already been demoted to a metaphor? The latter bears an implication for the signified that the signifiers — as a necessary evil and, thus, ideally in the manner of a signless sign — are to conceive: that this signified itself has the status of a signifier. The letter writer of the "Brief eines Dichters an einen anderen" remains trapped in this dilemma: to "take hold of my thought" without transposing it into a sign system is conceived of as to "reach into my heart" — which is, thus, equally metaphorical. The attempt to take the metaphors (of the innermost being as a "heart" and of one's own thought as one's "own breast") not metaphorically but concretely, materially, only reveals that it is caught in the space of metaphor. Thus, the problem is not the question of resolving the dichotomy between spirit and letter, which would lead to the paradox of a signless sign, but, rather, that this dichotomy is no longer tenable; that is, each signified, in order to be one, must have the status of a signifier and must, further, maintain it. What is at stake here is, thus, not the highest possible degree of transparency of the signifier for the signified but, rather, the authentication of the references between the signs. (In the alternate ending of *Der zerbrochne Krug* this is known as "Wahrheit-geben": so that the words of the assessor correspond to the document of the conscription.) The popular binary oppositions we find in Kleist scholarship — immediacy and mediation (Schulte), oversight and recognition (Müller-Seidel), language and the unspeakable (Kommerell), the language of law and the language of love (Neumann 1986), etc. — fail to show that Kleist's texts are concerned not with mediating or resolving such oppositions but, rather, with showing that they do not function. An apt illustration of his treatment of the dichotomy "spirit/letter" can be found in the semiological drama that unfolds in *Das Käthchen von Heilbronn*. Seemingly, the picture and its protective case are contrasted — for example, in Kunigunde's rhymed verse: "Das Bild mit dem Futteral, Herr Graf vom Strahl" (3.12.1880). With Kleist, however, the images are not in their protective cases, nor are letters to be found in the right envelopes (cf. 3.4.1675–76). Thus, Kunigunde, who has been assembled from many artificial pieces, must immediately admit which of the pieces she meant. The "naive" (in Schiller's sense) and innocently loving Käthchen rescues the image of the count with the aid of a cherub, which Kleist was daring enough to place on the stage quite unironically at the beginning of the nineteenth century, and is being chastened by Kunigunde:

KUNIGUNDE:	Die dumme Trine!
	Hatt' ich ihr nicht gesagt, das Futteral?
GRAF VOM STRAHL:	Nun beim gerechten Gott, das muß ich sagen —!
	— Ihr wolltet das Futtral?
KUNIGUNDE:	Ja und nichts Anders! (3.15.1972–75)

Kunigunde wants the protective case because it has its own independent signification. It does not protect the image of her "Schatz" but, rather, that of a quite different "treasure": the count's documents that transfer the contentious lands to her. The opposition that appears to be emerging here between a "pure" gesture toward the image and a false insistence on the protective case, however, is misleading. This is so because here we do not have the original image and the copy in opposition to each other but, rather, two types of signification. What is at issue is if and how the two signifiers authenticate each other in their referential capability (if image and case were together, the signature of the person represented on the case would authenticate the image, which itself would authenticate the signature). We are confronted with a field of relations with which signifiers can engage or refuse to engage, a field that produces various effects of meaning independent of the intended meanings or those that are privileged by interpreters because the possibility of establishing or perceiving relations between signifiers is open and arbitrary. It is precisely this arbitrariness ("Zufällige," 3:566) that the poet of the essay wants to exclude when he reprimands his friend for directing his attention to the signs and their order and interrelationships, rather than to what is represented by them. But is it even conceivable that one can escape from the coincidental and never fully controllable production of meaning in the field of signification? In his texts Kleist develops three mental images to transcend the "inverse nature" of signs.[3]

The first mental image has already been discussed: the practice of radical "literalness," which completely eschews any figurative speech. Word and object are taken as identical: for example, to write tears, rather than to write *about* tears, as we see in a letter to Baron von Stein of 4 August 1806: "Wie soll ich es möglich machen, in einem Briefe etwas so

Zartes, als ein Gedanke ist, auszuprägen? Ja, wenn man Thränen schreiben könnte" (4:359). Another example is the heart that has been torn from the body to be sent like a letter, as the most intimate form of expression. A third example can be found in Penthesilea's speech about loving a friend so much that one could devour him. Penthesilea's "speech" performs this act literally, "word for word" (24.2998). Precisely this rude concretion, however, has the effect that the word, which has thus become reality, means something else and that this realization is again merely another metaphorization. The severed heart differs from the innermost being of the "ego." The handwriting that was written with tears differs from the state of mind of the one who wrote it. The dismemberment of Achilles was not a speech of love, as Penthesilea claims after the fact. In all of these cases, the signifier is formed out of the material substrate of the signified. This is not a literalness resulting from the convergence of word and object but, rather, a strategy that is familiar to us from Kleist's essay on Caspar David Friedrich: the strategy of guaranteeing the sign reference from the materiality of the signified.

A second mental image referring to the transcendence of the "inverse nature" of signs is sketched out in the essay "Über das Marionettentheater" in the anecdote about the fencing bear. What is important for us is his bewildering skill not only in parrying all of the earnestly intended blows (cf. 3:562) but also in refusing to succumb to the feints (cf. Greiner 2000, 197–218). Because it is a blow that is not earnestly intended — or, to be precise, it is a movement in one specific direction yet is targeted toward a goal that actually lies in an entirely different direction — the feint conceals and embodies the movement in this direction and, thus, represents movement in the realm of signs. The bear's ability to distinguish earnestly intended blows from feints is described as a type of reading: "Aug' in Auge, als ob er darin meine Seele lesen könnte, stand er" (3:562). Paul de Man has interpreted this as a super-reading, by which he means a complete mastery of the production of meaning (cf. 223). This mastery includes the ability to distinguish the intended from the unintended production of meaning, as well as to know the produced meaning. This mastery is not possible, however, for a finite speaker. For such a speaker, language is always a feint, because the speaker is also always producing meanings that he does not intend and because the speaker must always remain uncertain whether the intended meaning reaches its goal. The skill of not being fooled at all by feints/signs and the ability to steer the movement in the realm of signs to a state of bewilderment, as is done to "Herrn C." in the bear story, is a skill that is attributed to the ideal-hermeneutic bear and does not imply that the realm of signs has been transcended. What it does mean is that absolute mastery in the realm of signs can be attained; that is, *all* possibilities of the production of meaning can be kept in view, and thus it would always be possible to distinguish authentic from inauthentic meaning (from the viewpoint of both the producer as well as the receiver of signs). Only an infinite consciousness (as a contradiction *in adjecto,* since consciousness assumes differentiation and is, thus, relegated to the space of finiteness) can maintain such absolute control over a speech or text. The bear, who can apparently read the soul, can also only be a finite, and thus false, sign for such a "consciousness." Seen together, these two mental images of the transcendence of the inverse nature of signs reveal themselves to be two sides of a return to an "absolutism of reality" (cf. Blumenberg, especially the chapter "Nach dem Absolutismus der Wirklichkeit"). Either this "absolutism" does not realize any distancing through representation (that is, there is not a "mere word" that could stand for an object), or this absolutism is a realm that oversees the totality of all representations and thereby fully controls the possible meanings, which thus likewise opens up a space outside of all representation.

Several times in Kleist's texts we find a third mental image that is conceived to transcend the "inverse nature" of signs. We find this image in stories in which a type of ray from the heavens joins together existing signs and thus exposes a divine, that is, "true" meaning. An example can be found in an anecdote published in the *Berliner Abendblätter* on 5 October 1810:

Der Griffel Gottes

In Pohlen war eine Gräfin von P. . . ., eine bejahrte Dame, die ein sehr bösartiges Leben führte, und besonders ihre Untergebenen durch ihren Geiz und ihre Grausamkeit, bis auf das Blut quälte. Diese Dame, als sie starb, vermachte einem Kloster, das ihr die Absolution erteilt hatte, ihr Vermögen; wofür ihr das Kloster, auf dem Gottesacker, einen kostbaren, aus Erz gegossenen, Leichenstein setzen ließ, auf welchem dieses Umstandes, mit vielem Gepränge, Erwähnung geschehen war. Tags darauf schlug der Blitz, das Erz schmelzend, über den Leichenstein ein, und ließ nichts, als eine Anzahl von Buchstaben stehen, die, zusammen gelesen, also lauteten: sie ist gerichtet! — Der Vorfall (die Schriftgelehrten mögen ihn erklären) ist gegründet; der Leichenstein existiert noch, und es leben Männer in dieser Stadt, die ihn samt der besagten Inschrift gesehen. (3:355)

Such an overcoming of the "inverse nature" of signs, in that its ever contingent combinational possibilities are transformed into providence, is already an object of suspicion for the narrator, since he charges the scribes with the authority of passing judgment on them. These are the professional interpreters of God's proclamations, but this is meant, at least within the horizon of the New Testament, in a pejorative sense. These interpreters will surely use this incident for an edifying sermon and will know how to dismiss the latent critique of the church, which granted absolution to one who has been judged in such a way. At the same time, however, this heavenly script is mediated in a most earthly — or, rather, literary — way: it is a quotation from the conclusion of Goethe's *Faust I*. The "voice from above" in Kleist's anecdote, however, judges rather than saves — unless, of course, we presume Mephisto to be the writer. In that case, the quote would be literal, whereby the anecdote would thus be in search of a new theory — be it one of God, the devil, or the script. The story "Der Zweikampf," in a similarly questionable way, treats God's judgment as another example of divine providence (and as a contemporary means of legal action). This narrative concludes with the skeptical postulation that it is not possible to decide between contingency and providence in the classification of the signs, so that the legal means can only prove the truth of divine judgment: "wenn es Gottes Wille ist" (3:349). In "Das Erdbeben in Chili" the all too rushed, all too hasty reinterpretation of contingency as a form of providence is further criticized.

By orienting it to the parameters of successful speech, which we outlined at the beginning of this paper, one can evaluate the constellation in which the paradigm of unsuccessful speech — or, rather, unspeakableness — is developed as follows: speech, as well as writing, is directed toward a listener or reader, and this reader/listener is aware that he cannot escape from the signifiers' arbitrary production of meaning (because of their unlimited possibility for variable associations) and thus must direct his attention toward them. Different things appear to have arisen as a specific object of the type of speech we are discussing here. For one, we are dealing with self-expression, an expression of the innermost being of the speaking "ego." Next, we can generally say that the object of speech is apparently in a relationship of difference with regard to its linguistic expression (only then can the deceptive dichotomy between spirit and letter emerge; or rather, only then can the rhetorical model be put to use, according to which the thought is positioned first so that one can then ask for means to express it most effectively). The common denominator that stands out among these different objects of speech is that we have a type of speech that is intentional and produces meaning. It is a type of speech that must be denoted by others, a skill that can never be fully mastered by sign producers or receivers. If freedom was the specific self-awareness for the paradigm of successful speech (in a performative turn of the "free play" that Kant takes into account for aesthetic judgment), then it is a lack of freedom that is the specific self-awareness for the speaker in the paradigm of unsuccessful speech — that is, it is the awareness of being bound to the rules of others, of a structural negation that, as a principle of differentiation, is needed to constitute the realm of the signs.

The paradigm of successful speech establishes on a linguistically pragmatic level the speech formation of aesthetic judgment. In contrast, on a semantic level the paradigm of unsuccessful speech accentuates the uncontrollable rhetoricization of speech. The reflection on language reveals itself to be implicitly a part of the discourse on grace that Kleist, in a striking break with tradition, develops theoretically and practically in his essay "Über das Marionettentheater." In this essay the constellation of successful speech with regard to a "you" that, without intervening, simultaneously provides the speaker with both expression and thought is described as the grace of the puppet. This grace is determined not as an inherent quality but, rather, as a relationship between the puppet and the operator. In the field of linguistic reflection the discourse of grace touches on the discourse of beauty in Kant's conception, and thus the discourse of grace also touches on that of the "Kunstperiode" to the extent that the constellation of speech that is decisive here could be interpreted as a performative turn of the aesthetic judgment.

The provenance of the principle of differentiation proved to be constitutive for unsuccessful speech (in the sense that the production of meaning cannot be controlled), and it is also constitutive for the impossibility of the individual's speaking his innermost being. The principle of differentiation ruptures the dyadic constellation of grace and opens up the realm of infinite signification. Unsuccessful speech thus reveals itself as belonging to the stage of lost grace within the idealist philosophy of history, a stage in which all movements remain only signs (such as the movements in front of the mirror of the youth, who has been robbed of his identity as the graceful remover of the thorn by the narrator's interdiction) that point to what has been removed and can never be regained, precisely because it is being represented. The mental images that aim to transcend the "inverse nature" of the signs refer — as absolute mastery of the production of meaning in language (analogous to the bear as absolute reader) — to the grace of the infinite consciousness (cf. 3:563). This complete disposal of all the effects of meaning and combinational possibilities of a conglomeration of signs can be regarded as the "coming together again" of the "two lines intersecting at a point," which occurs after a "passing through infinity" (Kleist *Writings*, 416). Its first instance can then be recognized as the union of word and object. The process of doing things "word for word" no longer recognizes any mere word. This capacity for transparency in Kleist's reflection on language with regard to his discourse on grace is not of interest to us for its own sake but, rather, because it promises insights into peculiar discursive strategies that he employs in his own writings. If Kleist's turn to art and the subsequent artistic production that results from it can be understood as a constant and rigorous self-interrogation of precisely this turn (the questioning of the promise of the beautiful, as well as of the sublime and of the founding of a teleological system of interpretation) and, thus, as an abysmal questioning of the discourse of the beautiful that Kant initiated, then a second discourse, one fundamentally different from the first, reveals itself to be simultaneously at work in the field of reflection on language, as well as in its own practice of literary speech. This is the discourse of grace, which Kleist separates from the idea of bridging the physical and the ideal. The discourse of beauty, the entire discourse that is obligated to Kant's Third Critique, is manifestly present in Kleist's texts. The discourse of grace, however, is at work — implicitly — in both the reflection on language and in Kleist's poetic practice as a type of "geometric vanishing point" of speech. The fact that Kleist fuses two fundamentally different discourses and thus exposes ever new moments of interference between them at each point of observation contributes significantly to the elasticity and inexhaustibility that we still find in the works of this author.

Translated by Nikhil Sathe

Notes

[1] In contrast, Bettina Schulte's study of Kleist, which centers on the problem of language, remains limited in its perspective. A fundamental study in this regard is Max Kommerell's article of 1940. For newer studies on the problem of language in Kleist, see Zeeb.

[2] In misjudging the indifference that is an analogue to the sublime, Gernot Müller (82–83) uses these two examples as an occasion for subsuming this essay under his central motif of misrepresentation. Regarding the shift in the public estimation of Mirabeau as a revolutionary cf. Etienne Charavay.

[3] Cf. Novalis's Poem "Wenn nicht mehr Zahlen und Figuren . . ." in the continuation of the novel *Heinrich von Ofterdingen* (*Schriften* 360).

Works Cited

Blumenberg, Hans. *Arbeit am Mythos.* 2nd ed. Frankfurt a.M.: Suhrkamp, 1979.

Charavay, Etienne. "Mirabeau." In *La grande encyclopédie: Inventaire raisonné des sciences, des lettres et des arts par une société de savants et gens de lettre.* Vol. 23. Ed. André Berthelot et al. Paris: Société Anonyme de la Grande Encyclopédie, 1886–1902, 1088–94.

De Man, Paul. *Allegorien des Lesens*. Frankfurt a.M.: Suhrkamp, 1988.

Greiner, Bernhard. *Kleists Dramen und Erzählungen: Experimente zum "Fall" der Kunst*. Tübingen: Franke, 2000.

Kant, Immanuel. *Critique of Judgment*. Ed. and tr. J. H. Bernard. New York: Hafner, 1951.

———. *Kritik der Urteilskraft*. Ed. Karl Vorländer. Hamburg: Meiner, 1974 (pagination corresponds to 2nd ed., 1793).

Kleist, Heinrich von. *An Abyss Deep Enough: Letters of Heinrich von Kleist with a Selection of Essays and Anecdotes*. Ed. and tr. Philipp B. Miller. New York: Dutton, 1982.

———. *Sämtliche Werke und Briefe in vier Bänden*. 4 vols. Ed. Ilse-Marie Barth et al. Frankfurt a.M.: Deutscher Klassiker Verlag, 1987–1997.

———. *Selected Writings*. Ed. and tr. David Constantine. London: Dent, 1997.

Kommerell, Max. "Die Sprache und das Unaussprechliche: Eine Betrachtung über Heinrich von Kleist." In his *Geist und Buchstabe der Dichtung*. Frankfurt a.M.: Klostermann, 1944, 243–317.

Müller, Gernot. *"Man müßte auf dem Gemälde selbst stehen": Kleist und die bildende Kunst*. Tübingen: Francke, 1995.

Müller-Seidel, Walter. *Versehen und Erkennen: Eine Studie über Heinrich von Kleist*. Cologne: Böhlau, 1961.

Neumann, Gerhard. "Hexenküche und Abendmahl. Die Sprache der Liebe im Werk Heinrich von Kleists." *Freiburger Universitätsblätter* 91 (1986): 9–31.

———. "Das Stocken der Sprache und das Straucheln des Körpers. Umrisse von Kleists kultureller Anthropologie." In *Heinrich von Kleist: Kriegsfall. Rechtsfall. Sündenfall*. Ed. Gerhard Neumann. Freiburg: Rombach, 1994, 13–29.

Novalis. *Schriften: Die Werke Friedrich von Hardenbergs*. Vol. 1. Ed. Paul Kluckhohn and Richard Samuel. Stuttgart: Kohlhammer, 1977.

Schiller, Friedrich. *Sämtliche Werke*. Vol. 1. Ed. Gerhard Fricke and Herbert G. Göpfert. Munich: Hanser, 1967.

Schulte, Bettine. *Unmittelbarkeit und Vermittlung im Werk Heinrich von Kleists*. Göttingen: Vandenhoeck & Ruprecht, 1988.

Zeeb, Ekkehard. *Die Unlesbarkeit der Welt und die Lesbarkeit der Texte: Ausschreitungen des Rahmens der Literatur in den Schriften Heinrich von Kleists*. Würzburg: Königshausen & Neumann, 1995.

Intellectual Paradigms

The Facts of Life: Kleist's Challenge to Enlightenment Humanism (Lessing)

Helmut J. Schneider

IT IS ALMOST a commonplace that the most basic "facts of life" — intercourse, conception, and pregnancy or birth — form the center of Kleist's prose and drama. Take his two comedies, *Der Zerbrochne Krug* and *Amphitryon,* or stories such as "Die Marquise von O . . .," "Die Verlobung in St. Domingo," "Der Findling," and "Der Zweikampf": common to all of them is a sexual encounter that precipitates a narrative conflict that, even as it unfolds, bears a strangely hidden, enigmatic quality. More often than not, then, the famous Kleistian "event" disrupting the status quo with such ineluctable force is traceable to the most prosaic of human experiences.

Nowhere did Kleist make his point with greater economy than with the notorious dash in the "Marquise von O . . .": a horizontal mark filling, or bridging, the narrative void in which the untold, and untellable, rape occurs. But more than an act is embedded in the dash; it signals the rupture that the naked fact of human physical reproduction represents within the cultural order, as well as within language. This rupture is not just the opposite or the other of culture but its prerequisite, as well. The story of rape and impregnation ends with the perpetrator being granted universal forgiveness "um der gebrechlichen Einrichtung der Welt willen" (2:143). The phrase "die gebrechliche Einrichtung" may capture the paradox of an order the very constitution of which rests on the condition that it be broken apart. The fires of war and sexuality die down once the count has penetrated both fortress and female body; the only erection left is of a social edifice in which a legal father (and all that comes with it: name, paperwork, and inheritance) is installed.

Similarly, though with less felicitous consequences for the protagonists, "Das Erdbeben in Chili" revolves around a moment of natural upheaval that effects at once society's annihilation and its reconstitution. This story of an earthquake is one of birth on a cosmic scale. Precisely at the midpoint of the text we are told, via the anecdote of an awestruck survivor, "wie die Stadt gleich nach der ersten Haupterschütterung von Weibern ganz voll gewesen, die vor den Augen aller Männer niederge-kommen seien" (2:151). The most basic corporeal event normally occur-ring behind closed doors, hence shielded from the public gaze, becomes here an outrageously physical public spectacle, one uniting destruction and rejuvenation, much as the fortuitous fissure in the jailhouse wall had earlier permitted its inmate to escape and be reborn.[1]

In both "Die Marquise von O . . ." and "Das Erdbeben in Chili" a child conceived out of wedlock is ultimately legitimized and thus ac-cepted as part of the societal order that had been provoked, if not threat-ened, by its existence, its "coming about." Neither story, however, is concerned primarily with the law's affirmation of its own violation but, rather, with the tension between the biological reproduction that grounds human culture and that culture's need to exorcise such crude physicality from its representational order. Hence the obsessive search within Kleistian narratives for a cultural father to supplant the natural progenitor (represented a fortiori by the mother). Regardless of whether the paternal representative of societal legitimacy is identical with the biological father, as in "Die Marquise von O . . .," or not, as in "Das Erdbeben in Chili," he functions to remove the (in eighteenth-century parlance) "child of nature" from its origin and place it firmly into the symbolic order of culture. The concluding line of the "Erdbeben" no-vella captures this transfer from nature to culture with characteristic Kleistian irony, even brutality. Don Fernando, who replaces the son he has lost to the bloodthirsty mob with the child of the couple whose illicit love had provoked the carnage in the first place, draws an unlikely con-clusion when weighing recent events: "wenn Don Fernando Philippen mit Juan verglich, und wie er beide erworben hatte, so war es ihm fast, als müßt er sich freuen" (2:159). The statement stretches credibility, however, only if taken on the level of character psychology. Read on a more abstract plane, it articulates the wound inflicted by all culture on the natural and physical; moreover, its ironic tone suggests that Don Fernando's rationalization of his loss is a kind of retrospective teleology.

Unlike "Die Marquise von O . . .," however, the "Erdbeben" no-vella does not focus exclusively on an erotic relationship; the illicit love affair is secondary to the enormity of the natural catastrophe and its consequences for the community. But precisely the story's more abstract and even philosophical character underlines the significance of physical reproduction for the conception of human culture and history. The text takes up the premises of an Enlightenment philosophy of history pre-cisely to deconstruct them (cf. Schneider 1984). One of these is what might be called the enlightened myth of adoption. The adoptive father Don Fernando, a Kleistian "göttlicher Held" (2:158), who acquires his (second) child through a moral rather than sexual act, harks back to an Enlightenment tradition of cultural fathers whose most prominent exemplar is the protagonist of Lessing's drama *Nathan der Weise* (1779). To be sure, Don Fernando is not a pedagogue like Lessing's wise Jew; nevertheless, the novella's final sentence, evoking the opposition between natural birth and cultural adoption or, more principally, the precedence of the qualities of *achievement* over those of *ascription* (to use a well-known opposition from sociology), remains clear enough.

"Die Marquise von O . . ." embodies the same opposition within a single, albeit split, individual, the Count F., at once rapist and noble officer, whose subdued chivalrous behavior, culminating in his transference of a major inheritance to his newborn son, earns him first the legal title of husband and eventually the conjugal affection of his wife. Despite this story's outrageousness, playful tone, and seemingly happy outcome, it is hard to overlook its almost nihilistic implications. Underneath the veneer of societal convention lurks a primeval — in the final analysis uncheckable — physical violence that is always poised to erupt. "Der Findling," the dark counterpart to "Die Marquise von O . . .," drives this notion to an uncompromising extreme. As the title suggests, the text centers on the theme of adoption. This story of a foundling whose rescue from a plague-infested town indirectly causes the death of his benefactor's son, and who repays the affections showered upon him with the cold-blooded usurpation of his new parents' possessions, utterly voids the Enlightenment adoption myth of its humanistic substance. In Lessing's *Nathan der Weise* adoption had symbolized the triumph of reason and culture over the forces of blood, descent, and tradition — ultimately, the forces of the body. Nature's loss (symbolized in the loss of the natural parents) was culture's and humanity's gain. In Kleist's "Der Findling" Nicolo, the son of nature — or, as the text names him, "Gottes Sohn," whom "niemand . . . vermissen würde" (2:200) — when embraced as a surrogate son by the tradesman ("Güterhändler"), ends up attempting to rape his adoptive mother and driving the father out of his own house. When the old father takes revenge on the monster by crushing his brains against the wall and stuffing into his mouth the very court decree that confirmed the Tartuffian usurper's ownership of the house (cf. 2:214), he ironically converts the symbolic medium of the adoptive bond — the written document — into a physical weapon against the child. The inversion of the rationalist act of adoption into a kind of negative birth could scarcely be more explicit: in place of the mother nourishing the son with milk is a father choking him with a legal document; Nicolo's position "between the knees" of his father perverts the scene of physical birth (cf. 2:214). The moral story of adoption is aborted by an eruption of violence redolent of the sexual and procreative force that, in Enlightenment discourse, it was designed to replace.

Most readers of Kleist today would likely agree that the typical blend of passion with violence in his works resists as much as it invites psychological explanations. In Kleist explicit sexual violence constitutes some surplus, some residue that cannot be assimilated by any civilizing, "humanizing" effort; it likewise manifests the texts' resistance to efforts of hermeneutical mastery, including psychoanalysis. But I believe that we can access the nature of this resistance more precisely by placing the texts in the context of late Enlightenment rationalism. As *Spätaufklärung* grappled with the problem of how reason could be put to work in a world governed by the instincts and bodily drives, fiction did more to shed light on the aporetic nature of reason's claim to autonomy than did tomes of philosophical reflection. It is to the credit of Enlightenment thinkers such as Lessing that their narratives work through a problematic issue only later articulated in philosophical discourse: that the rational progress so fervently aspired to came at the price of the body and its physicality, whose sacrifice was demanded by that progress.

One can make this claim most cogently with respect to Lessing's *Nathan der Weise*. Arguably the most important work of German Enlightenment, the play sums up the philosophical aspirations and humanistic optimism of the period before the French Revolution. It offers a singular foil to Kleist, by means of which I hope to elucidate the Kleistian theme developed above. Indeed, Kleist himself makes references to this seminal text that predated his own work by some thirty years. My concern in scrutinizing this intertextual relationship is not one of literary influence but of Kleist's relationship to a rationalist discourse he at once shared and shattered. If Enlightenment can be defined broadly as the demand for human emancipation through reason from everything that is merely "natural" (including the second nature of an unquestioned tradition), in other words, from everything that is just given to and not achieved by us, then the crude fact of our physical origin, to which we owe our existence but to which we have contributed nothing, poses a threat, if not an insurmountable obstacle, to the emancipatory endeavor. The otherness of nature and the body flies in the face of the postulate for human autonomy. The Enlightenment project is thus stymied by an essential contradiction that Lessing, lacking a clear theoretical resolution, expressed in the self-reflective playfulness of his philosophical comedy.

Kleist pushed Lessing's articulation to a radical and hopeless extreme by inverting a key discursive opposition of Enlightenment thinking (in which the first term is privileged): adoption versus birth became, in the Kleistian paradigm, birth versus adoption.

This is not to say that Kleist revoked the Enlightenment notion of emancipation but that he relentlessly exposed its underlying paradox, one Lessing had only been able to resolve in an ultimate leap of optimistic faith. Indeed, the obsessiveness of Kleist's fixation on the naked facts of human procreation suggests his own brand of patricide; it smacks of revenge for the Enlightenment's broken promise that autonomy could be achieved through reason. The poignant heteronomy of our biological origin, the "accident of birth," apes the utopia of the subject's rational self-grounding, which through Kleist's lens appears as the vain presumption of human autogenesis, as reason's delusion about its power to generate itself.

It is well known how deeply Kleist was immersed in his formative years in the Weltanschauung of the late Enlightenment. His early biographical project of the "Lebensplan" famously or infamously documents this adherence to a rigid rationalist creed. In a letter to his half sister Ulrike from the year 1799 Kleist quotes from *Nathan der Weise* (without referring to it) to underline his argument for the indispensable duty of any "thinking" subject to create and legitimate himself: "Ein freier, denkender Mensch bleibt da nicht stehen, wo der Zufall ihn hinstößt; oder wenn er bleibt, so bleibt er aus Gründen, aus Wahl des Bessern" (2:488). Kleist's remark is a variation on the sultan's line in the third act of Lessing's drama, in which — as a lead-in to his famous question to Nathan about the one true religion — he argues that inner conviction cannot be grounded merely in accident of birth: "Ein Mann, wie du, bleibt da / Nicht stehen, wo der Zufall der Geburt / Ihn hingeworfen: oder wenn er bleibt, / Bleibt er aus Einsicht, Gründen, Wahl des Bessern" (3.5.1845–48). The remark formulates concisely the Enlightenment call for man to emancipate himself from the blind determinations of his descent, *Herkunft*. Nathan, however, is too wise to answer the monarch's imposing question directly. Instead, he narrates the parable of the three rings, suggesting that the historical religions are equally legitimate and that each individual has the right to remain loyal to the belief of his fathers. Neither Lessing's enlightened protagonist nor the play as whole support the rigid demand for a clear-cut rationalist choice implied by the young Kleist's use of the quotation; rather, they aim at a precarious balance between the universalist demands of reason and the particularist forces of blood and tradition. Far from extolling rationalist uniformity, *Nathan der Weise* strives to set free the realm of difference in the light of a "modest" or "humble"[2] reason aware of its own limits. Nevertheless, the drama does establish the priority of this liberal, broad-minded, tolerant reason over the bare factuality of birth, the "Zufall der Geburt," representing all of the unchangeable natural or quasi-natural factors of gender, race, family, or tradition that are merely given to us — literally "fall upon us." This factuality must be reckoned with and respected in its otherness, but it also has to be transformed and sublimated in order to enter the free play of enlightened tolerance.

As a philosophical drama about birth, *Nathan der Weise* will stay with Kleist beyond the breakdown of his rationalist creed and will even serve as a catalyst for his poetic work, writings that bear a debt to the very discourse of the historical Enlightenment they implode.

In the following section I will, thus, take Lessing's drama as the reference point for the discussion of Kleist's poetic treatment of the contingency of the body, focusing on a motif that Kleist took from Lessing and integrated into several of his works: that of rescue. In the third section I will concentrate on the "Findling" novella as the text that inverts and revokes the Lessing model most drastically. The concluding section attempts to open the perspective to the broader issue of the place and function of the aesthetic in the Enlightenment's treatment of the problem of contingency, using *Der zerbrochne Krug* as the primary reference text.

In "Die Marquise von O . . ." Graf F. rescues a young widow from fierce assailants in a burning castle; she feels deep gratitude and devotion to him before recognizing that it was none other than he who had violated her when she lay unconscious. Now she abhors as "devil" the same man who, when he came to her protection, had appeared to her "wie ein Engel" (2:143). Only by recognizing her own psychological extremism will the woman find her way to a normal marital (sexual) life. In "Der Findling" the adoptive mother Elvire, at the age of thirteen, had been saved from the flames of her father's house by a young knight on whom she remains strangely fixated for the rest of her life. And, finally, in "Die Verlobung in St. Domingo" it is the male hero, a Swiss mercenary in the service of France, who, in a reversal of gender roles, expects to be rescued by a mestizo girl from black island revolutionaries determined to kill all the whites. Although the plot constellation in this novella differs considerably from the other two, the prominence of the rescue theme invites comparison to "Die Marquise von O . . ." and "Der Findling."

The degree of Kleist's fascination with rescue — specifically, rescue from fire — is likewise suggested by its reappearance in two dramas: in the romantic melodrama *Das Käthchen von Heilbronn* the heroine is assisted by an angel as she foolhardily retrieves a picture from a burning house, and in the early tragedy *Die Familie Schroffenstein* a young man is saved from death by an Amazon-like girl. In these two cases the rescuer is again, as in "Die Verlobung in St. Domingo," a woman. Setting aside the issue of gender, the question remains what attracted Kleist to this motif. A closer look at the analogous constellation in Lessing's *Nathan der Weise* may help us to find an answer.[3]

The plot of *Nathan der Weise* is built around several life-saving interventions through which the main persons are already unknowingly connected when the play begins. The action on stage consists of a gradual process in which the various characters consciously appropriate the good deeds they have either carried out or have benefited from more or less instinctively. They have to come to grasp the moral potential of their own good deeds, come to see and accept past actions as the basis of an ongoing obligation. This progression from spontaneous to conscious moral action constitutes, then, the symbolic dimension of the dramatic plot. But the play also harbors a regression, a reaching backward even behind the spontaneous or quasi-natural origin of ethical action to the biological origin of human life. On the most fundamental level, Lessing's heroic acts of rescue signify a moral recuperation and spiritual transformation of the physical acts of conception and birth. It is here, at the intersection both of the origin of life and of humanity (*Humanität*), that the libidinal energies of the body and the symbolic universalism of *Geschichtsphilosophie* meet.

The crucial impetus setting off the dramatic chain (or, more graphically, the "ring") of rescues (cf. Saße 216–17), which will eventually reveal the protagonists of divergent ethnic and religious backgrounds to each other as members of one family, is the rescue of Nathan's adoptive daughter Recha from her burning house by an unknown Templar knight. Nathan learns of the event in the first scene, when he returns home from an extended journey. He wants to thank the man in person, but the Templar had already refused to accept displays of gratitude and has since mysteriously disappeared. Nathan seeks him out and persuades him to meet Recha, with whom the knight instantly falls in love. The later revelation that his newly discovered love object is not the Jew he took her to be but his own sister calls for some serious rethinking of his erotic passion. Seen retrospectively from this ending, the gratuitous act by which the Christian soldier saved the Jewish girl only renewed — or, rather, *realized* — the preexisting blood bond. In the play's value system it is this kind of compassionate action toward one's fellow human being, *Mitmenschlichkeit*, that establishes the true fraternal or sisterly union for which the actual family relationship is but the external sign; the blood family, in fact, becomes the dramatic symbol for a moral brotherhood, or *Geschwisterlichkeit*, of mankind across the divide of race, nationality, and creed. In other words, if the Christian knight heeded the "voice of blood" by following the screams of his unknown sister in a state of mortal danger, this voice was nothing but the inner appeal of a general human disposition. In Lessing the physical and the particular become the symbol of the universal. Hence, the inner plot of the play can be described as a process of symbolization, which is at the same time a process of spiritualization. When, in the final scene, the dispersed family reunites in an all-encompassing embrace, the theater spectators have witnessed nothing less than the production of Enlightenment humanity as the symbolic body of mankind (cf. Schneider 1995).

Kleist reverses this process in favor of the physical and particular; and Lessing's own text provides the point of departure for this reversal, for his reliance on the blood bond as the symbolic basis of a universal humanitarianism exacts a price. If, on the one hand, on the moral and spiritual plane the young knight's action recovers the physical act of birth, on the other hand, the same action carries a dangerous erotic — indeed, incestuous — implication. The fire threatening Recha's life is also that of sexual passion. Symbolic birth and erotic-incestuous encounter fuse in this scene of rescue, which precedes the play's opening scene but is subjected to a process of reflection in the course of the dramatic action and dialogue. It is, we may properly say, the off-scene par excellence, the unrepresentable event, which has already happened before the curtain is drawn. What we witness after the curtain rises is its cultural integration through language as the medium of dialogic-rational interaction. The young woman is still under the impact of the event when she first meets her returning father; she is reveling in feverish enthusiasm ("Schwärmerei") about her "angel," as she calls her rescuer, who has since withdrawn into miraculous invisibility (cf. 1.2.195–97). Nathan sets out to cure his daughter of this adolescent fantasy, the erotic and religious elements of which he resents equally, by confronting her with the possibility of the "angel's" sickness, which would call for active help instead of idle adoration. The scene is a superb pedagogical example of Enlightenment *Religionskritik;* by giving back to the idolized person his truly human shape as a needy being, Nathan replaces idolatrous worship with ethical humanism. But another, easily overlooked effect is that he also eventually cures his daughter of the passion of erotic love. *Eros* is to become *agape.*

The completion of this therapeutic transformation — the final demystification of the erotic-religious idol — only comes about when Recha meets her rescuer face to face. Only in and through the physical presence of her alleged "angel" is the woman's enflamed imagination brought back to reason and her desire "gestillt" (3.3.1717). Only then has her emotional energy been shifted from the vertical dimension of passive contemplation into the active horizontal communication between equal human beings. Before her now is a physical presence much different from the blind corporeality of the rescuing scene in the midst of flames, smoke, and screams. Now she is confronted with, above all, a visible presence marked by corporeal distantiation, the sight of the other's face and the mutual look into each other's eyes. Exposed to her savior's "voller Anblick, sein Gespräch, sein Tun" (3.3.1717), Recha overcomes her passionate daydreaming, filling the primordial absence of birth and sex and transforming father (procreator) qua lover into brother (even before she learns the truth of their sibling relationship). Thus, Recha brings to a conclusion what her father had initiated with his pedagogical enlightenment; for Nathan's cure of his fever-stricken daughter passionately addicted to her angel-rescuer can also be read as the enactment of a "true" birth against the superstitious mystification of the "erste unbegreifliche Ursache unserer Rettung" (1.2.291–92) — the always ungraspable origin of our life. The adoptive father, the father of reason, becomes reason as father; Recha will later speak of the "Samen der Vernunft, / Den er [Nathan] so rein in meine Seele streute" (3.1.1564–65).

The insemination of the female body by paternal reason: this is what the adoptive daughter in *Nathan der Weise* stands for. Obviously, this process constitutes a male appropriation of the female power of natural reproduction, and it is no accident that Lessing's drama is dominated by male figures (except for Recha and the sultan's unmarried sister, there is only the former's old nurse, who embodies both religious prejudice and the advocacy of the blood bond, in addition to her — not insignificant — narrative role as erotic matchmaker). Female sexuality is all but obliterated for the realization of enlightened humanity. With the male counterpart, however, it is a somewhat different story. The play devotes more energy to demonstrating the sublimation of the male hero's desire in favor of familial affection, its redirection from the female to the *sister*. Here the dramatic action also manifests the indissoluble entanglement of erotic desire with familial relationships. At the sight of Recha, the Templar regresses into an unconscious recollection of his mother (whom he never consciously knew) and falls captive to this incestuous image — an implication clearly spelled out in Lessing's first sketch of the play, although the completed version eliminates the explicit reference to the mother (Lessing 2:737–38). But whether explicit or implicit, Lessing's son and lover has a long way to go before reaching the universalist stance of the play's ending; he undergoes an educational process in which he must abstract from the female body, as both the locus of physical origin and the object of sexual desire, the noncorporeal, ideal *Mitmensch*.

Such, then, is Lessing's Enlightenment model that Kleist takes up and subverts. Where Lessing spiritualizes and humanizes the physical-sexual moment of absence into a mode of human ethics, Kleist insists on that blank moment, subjecting it to torturing interrogations and self-interrogations or filling it with idolatric or fetishistic substitutions. The integration of sexuality and procreation into culture happens either in a highly violent or ironic way, as both "Das Erdbeben in Chili" and "Die Marquise von O . . ." illustrate; it can hardly even be called integration. Never is the rupture healed in the mode of idealistic reconciliation. The blind spot will always remain, be it as black hole or as an unenlightened, idolatrous, or mythological image.

Before returning definitively to Kleist, I would like to emphasize one point underlying the preceding discussion. The fact that birth, in the sense of the pure givenness of the natural and contingent factors of human life, represented an insurmountable resistance to the enlightened quest for rational autonomy is only one side of the problem. The other is the fact that Enlightenment humanism appealed to the values of emotional intimacy bred by the new, close-knit family, with its characteristic close relationship between parents and children. Familial relations furnished the *image* and the *source* of enlightened universalism — and there is no more significant expression of this connection than the concluding scenic image of *Nathan der Weise*. To draw on this wellspring of humanistic emotionalism, therefore, also meant the risk of regressing to the bodily closeness of our earliest childhood, of becoming fixed to that very origin from which it was civilization's task to remove man. The deepest reason for the impossibility of the blind spot of birth ever being totally "enlightened" and made compatible with the universalist aspiration lay in the fact that this aspiration itself fed on its energy.

The Kleistian text most closely approximating the constellation described in Lessing's drama is "Der Findling." I discussed earlier the novella's simultaneous indebtedness to and subversion of the Enlightenment adoption theme; we will find a similar dynamic in its rendition of the rescue motif of *Nathan der Weise*, the incestuous character of which "Der Findling" drives to a logical extreme. The plot conjoins two stories: the adopted son who grows into a monster, and the young woman whose devotion to the memory of her rescuer (he had died of wounds received in the course of his brave action) takes on a fetishistic, addictive character. The life-size portrait of the handsome knight, Colino, which she keeps hidden in a niche of her bedroom "hinter einem rotseidenen

Vorhang, von einem besondern Lichte bestrahlt" (2:207) and before which she kneels every day, is not simply the idealized representation of a revered person. Colino's enshrinement paradoxically *repeats* the trauma of danger and rescue by bringing it into the house and *domesticates* the event, framing and containing it in a remote space of intimacy. The details of the "rührender Vorfall" (2:202) that inspired Elvire's deep devotion are given in a flashback account after the adoptive son Nicolo discovers the picture and its strong resemblance to himself. For a time, Nicolo believes the portrait to be of him and flatters himself that his stepmother carries a secret passion for him. Frustrated on learning the true identity of the figure in the painting, he decides to dress up in the costume worn by the knight in the portrait and to stand before the painting (which he has covered) as his perfect revenant. The narrator characterizes the scheme with typical Kleistian hyperbole: "Beschämung, Wollust und Rache vereinigten sich jetzt, um die abscheulichste Tat, die je verübt worden ist, auszubrüten" (2:212). We will see how the word *ausbrüten* assumes a literal ring in this context.

It is at the point of this "most abominable deed" that the two storylines intersect, bringing the novella's symbolic plot to a climax. The foundling whose name (like that of Colino) reads anagrammatically as "in loco," Latin for "in place of," finally takes action to find a place for himself, to compensate for his lack of a past, for being made to occupy positions meant for others, like the adoptive parents' biological child (cf. Miller 120). The place he covets is a distinguished one, indeed, the one place whose occupant, in blatant contrast to Nicolo, is always and unconditionally "meant" (cf. 2:207) — meant as the recipient of an unquestioned, unprejudiced love. It is the place archetypically marked by the child's relation to the mother, in which the child always *is* and *has been* and where s/he does not, and cannot, "place" him- or herself. But this is exactly what Nicolo attempts to do: he paradoxically positions himself in a frame where he would like to think he already was, but that he can only come to occupy by staging the appearance of another. By framing himself in another's place, Nicolo repeats, in an act of conscious and willful fraud, what had been done to him before — "originally" — when he was "taken home," taken, that is, to another home, the home of another, of Piachi and his dead son, in whose role he was placed. The "son of God" who "belonged to nobody" when he was picked up by the tradesman — who had, the text reads, "den Jungen in dem Maße liebgewonnen, als er ihm teuer zu stehen gekommen war," in other words, with his own son's death (2:201) — attempts to arrogate to himself the position of the primordial love object of his mother.

Of course, this position, which extends into a past predating the child's conscious existence, is also the position of the father. Nicolo's self-framing as the one and only beloved of the mother is more than reminiscent of an oedipal wish fulfillment. The son assumes the place of the father as lover of the mother, in whom he revives the erotic feelings experienced earlier. To complete the classical Freudian scenario, he even dislodges the father as head of the house. Kleist's adoptive father is a weak father unable to perform the role assigned to him in the conflict, which is to subject the son to his power and to inscribe the paternal law within him. He is clearly impotent (cf. 2:101), and he forfeits his legal right to his own property. Only at the very end does he live up to his cultural task — and then, as we have seen, through an atrocious physical act that reverses (externalizes) the Freudian internalization of paternal force.

Within the symbolic structure of the novella's plot, the portrait of the Genoese knight embodies the phantasmagoria of the ideal father. Nicolo's identification with him can be read in terms of yet another Freudian fantasy, the "family romance," whereby the child imagines for him- or herself a higher and nobler family background, usually aided by the knowledge that biological fatherhood is uncertain. Colino's patrician background is well suited for such a dream, just as Nicolo's foundling status invites it. There have, in fact, been critical speculations that Colino might be Nicolo's natural father (cf. Ryder). As Nicolo steps into the frame of his stepmother's idol, expecting to become the object of her "Vergötterung" (2:212), he displaces a devalued paternal authority and replaces it with an idealized counterpart.

And even more than that: by projecting himself as the lover and beloved of the mother, Nicolo literally renders himself his own (real, true) father. The foundling who has no origin invents one for himself; reaching beyond the Freudian fiction of a higher descent, he stages his status of *no descent* as *self-descent*. The invention of an origin becomes self-invention in the plain sense of self-generation. The play of substitutions has run amok and been arrested at the same time; by collapsing the roles of son, father, and mother's lover, Nicolo establishes a closed circuit defining his existence, a circuit that at once compensates for the open wound of his unknown origin and armors him against the contingency of his existence. Separated from his origin, the foundling almost literally reaches back behind the beginning of his life (he was always there for the mother) and places himself in the originating position, the position of self-engenderment.

Keeping in mind that the Kleistian narrator rarely accords the reader insight into his characters' psyche, one can draw, nevertheless, on yet another — the third — Freudian model to illustrate the idea of self-engenderment suggested by the text: the primal scene or *Urszene*, the child observing parental intercourse. Nicolo accidentally stumbles on his stepmother's secret quasi-erotic activity when he stands before her closed bedroom door. He "beugte . . . sich mit Augen und Ohren gegen das Schloß nieder, und," — here the narrator interrupts himself with a dash:

> — Himmel! was erblickte er? Da lag sie, in der Stellung der Verzük-kung, zu jemandes Füßen, und ob er gleich die Person nicht erkennen konnte, so vernahm er doch ganz deutlich, recht mit dem Akzent der Liebe ausgesprochen, das geflüsterte Wort: Colino. (2:207)

By being exposed to the secret of sexuality via the primal scene, the child symbolically confronts the blind spot of his own procreation; the *Urszene* is an *Ursprungsszene*. In this passage, which continues with the account of the picture's discovery (and which, incidentally, again is placed at the precise center of the text), the foundling discovers himself as his own father. Nicolo's later sexual assault on the mother drives this scenario of autogenesis to its logical extreme.

The regression into the abyss of origin and self-birth remained occluded in Lessing's *Nathan der Weise* because of the strong position of the cultural father. Seen from the vantage point of Kleist's "Der Findling," the precariousness of Lessing's humanist utopia and its basis, Enlightenment pedagogy, emerges with even greater clarity. The adoptive bond, as realized in Nathan's relation to Recha and quasi-instinctively reinitiated in the rescue scene between Recha and the Templar, was a bond of active love representing not a *replacement* but a *redemption* of the blood bond. In its redeemed status at the end of the play the blood bond could, therefore, become a symbol of the primordial nature of universal human bonding. Like Kleist, Lessing removed the biological father but accorded its adoptive surrogate the same quasi-naturalness of biological parental authority, which children accept as natural and beneficial.

Kleist's story subverts the firm anchor of paternal authority, be it biological or cultural, and renders the father figure a receptacle for fantasies of self-generation, as is underscored by a closer look at Elvire's history. Much like Lessing's Recha, the adolescent girl becomes enraptured by the man who has saved her life at the risk of his own. In sharp deviance from Lessing, however, Elvire is never cured of her erotic-religious enrapture; she remains, rather, chained to the traumatic event and elevates her rescuer to savior. Again as in *Nathan der Weise*, this past event carries all the associations of a scene of passion and birth (symbolized by the elements of fire and water); the rescuer represents simultaneously the figures of father and lover, the one becoming (con)fused with the other. But Kleist's male rescuer gives life in more than a symbolic and spiritual sense; Kleist literalizes the life-giving symbolism of the act of rescue. When the rescuer undergoes surgery for head wounds, the removal of "mehrere Knochen aus dem Gehirn" (2:203) may allude to the male "cerebral birth" and its mythological model, Athene leaping to life from the forehead of Zeus (it recalls, moreover, the biblical creation of Eve from a rib of Adam). The crude motif appears as a parodistic literalization of Lessing's metaphor of the "Samen der Vernunft." Corresponding to Nicolo's wish to put himself in the place of absolute origin, Elvire's devotion to the memorial of her rescuer is an attempt to hold onto the reified origin of her existence. In both cases the blind spot of birth is negated and filled at the same time.

As we have seen in the discussion of Lessing's play, this blind spot needed to be transformed into a symbol in order to enter the life of cultural exchange and become productive for the ethics of *Mitmenschlichkeit*. Such a transformation does not, of course, occur in Kleist. Lacking a cultural father able to mediate between nature and culture, Elvire, qua unreformed Recha, is held captive by the mythicized stand-in for nature's blind force. Kleist's revocation of Lessing goes even further if we consider that the young girl actually follows the moral imperative implied by Nathan's (albeit playful) hypothesis that the rescuing angel might have "fallen sick." Elvire's hero *has* fallen gravely ill, and the young woman cares for him for three years. The futility of her humanitarian engagement contradicts Nathan's humanistic confidence that "Dem Menschen ist / Ein Mensch noch immer lieber, als ein Engel" (1.1.164–65). Elvire's selfless overinvestment only helps to launch her rescuer precisely into that superhuman sphere that, in Lessing, it was destined to humanize.

With this explicit reversal of Lessing's model, Kleist delivers the unwelcome message to the Enlightenment that no human compassion can erase the blind corporeal moments of procreation, birth, and passion. The accident of birth does not transmute into the ethics of human interaction; no continuity exists between physical contingency and cultural values, between natural and moral bonds. What we get in Kleist are just the facts — the facts of coming there and being there, happening and being found, of random physical existence and cultural adoption, the latter signifying the always precarious moments of exchange and substitution. While in Lessing the cultural bond feeds on the natural one that it attempts — paradoxically and, to be sure, never quite successfully — to absorb, for Kleist a sharp caesura divides the natural from the cultural, one deepened by the cultural acts, such as adoption, that would close the gap with ever new substitutions. What remains is a festering wound.

In reading Kleist and Lessing against each other, I have concentrated up to this point on narrative constellations, motifs, and philosophical or ideological "messages." I would like to conclude by exploring in broader terms what the narrative configuration of birth and adoption means for the nature of poetic fiction and its function for the project of philosophy of history in (Lessingian) Enlightenment and (Kleistian) post-Enlightenment discourse, respectively. Another close look at *Nathan der Weise* — specifically, a comparison of its ring parable with Kleist's comedy *Der zerbrochne Krug*, arguably the most "historico-philosophical" of his plays, and its title "hero" — will provide my focus.

The redemption of the blood bond, or, as I put it earlier, the spiritualization of the contingent factors of birth and descent in *Nathan der Weise* corresponds to the classical definition of the aesthetic symbol as a reconciliation of the particular and the sensual (intuitive) with the universal and abstract. At the same time, the emergence of the blood family as the "family of mankind" discloses a temporal dynamism between the origin and the goal in which the latter represents the complete unfolding of the former, just as the former carries the promise of this fulfillment. This closed circle of teleology — the origin is the goal, the *telos* — underlay the structure of both Enlightenment *Geschichtsphilosophie* and the classical work of art.

Lessing's play fits this circular model only to a degree; the circle does not completely close on itself but remains marked by an opening, a fracture (most significantly in the fact that the Jewish hero does not belong to the blood family and is excluded from the final familial embrace). To the extent, however, that *Nathan der Weise* realizes the teleological model, it does so with a high degree of aesthetic self-reflection; more crucially, the drama makes its own aesthetic constructedness a central theme of its stage action. In this self-reflexivity lies the significance of the scene with the famous ring parable (3.7.1911–65), which the young Kleist had quoted and which contains in miniature Lessing's aesthetics of symbolic representation.

Apart from its obvious philosophical implications, the parable has a pivotal function within the play's action. Through its narration the Jew, who had entered the sultan's palace as a potential victim, succeeds in winning the monarch over as a trusting friend, which proves crucial for the drama's happy ending. This bonding *through* the fictional parable corresponds to another bond forged *within* it. Nathan's story of the three brothers fighting over the possession of the father's ring likewise introduces a piece of fiction as means of arbitration and equalization. Each of the brothers believes that he has received the one and only ring from the father, and, indeed, each believes correctly but for one detail: the father had secretly ordered the genuine ring duplicated by an artist or artisan ("Künstler"), because he loved all three sons equally and found all to be worthy of succeeding him. Paternal love breaks with the "tyranny of the [one] ring"; emotional and pedagogical adoption replaces the feudal right of primogeniture. The break with tradition creates the realm of human diversity, while also providing a common ground for it. For the different and yet seemingly identical rings still relate back to the original that is now unlocatable or even, as the presiding judge suggests, "lost." Once the judge decrees that the brothers emulate their father's loving example and *earn* the distinction symbolized (promised) by the ring — whereby its genuineness will be proved through open competition and moral achievement — the question of the "true" factual origin cedes to another: how a future origin may be created.

The transformation of a single ring into many rings that remain equal yet singular can only be achieved through the medium of the aesthetic. Fiction sets in motion the transition from the law of blood and body to the spirit of ethics. It should not be overlooked that the judge subverts the uniqueness of the "real" ring by speculatively reconstructing the case; moreover, by interpreting the biological father's legacy, the judge serves as yet another adoptive father. As he assumes und infers, he picks up the storytelling craft that had allowed Nathan to evade the sultan's question by offering in place of an answer a fairy tale ("Märchen" or "Geschichtchen") that is at once *about* the lost one faith and compensates *for* its loss. What is the adoptive father if not the ideal narrator, in that both do away with the contingency of the beginning and project a teleological origin, instead? We may say that narration is adoption. The skill of the parable's narrator, Nathan, had already contrived the original object such as to anticipate its aim, for the primordial ring exerted its magical power only in conjunction with the subjective confidence of its owner. With the help of the artful narrative, nature and substance had prescribed their own transformation into reason and function. The artifact of the ring, then, symbolizes nothing less than poetic fiction itself, which, in order to come into its own, that is, into its teleological (circular) structure, has to remove the crude facticity represented. by birth and body. Finally, does not the play as a whole revolve around the parable as not only its literal but also its epistemological center, replacing the unfathomable and unrepresentable source of life with the inexhaustible source of meaning? The circle of the plot, which extends from the (biological) origin of the family in a dark and never quite enlightened past to its final spiritual recognition, recognizes in the parable its own aesthetic structure. The plot *is* the ring that mounts the shining opal of sense and meaning ("der hundert schöne Farben spielte"), as the promise of an infinite creativity in the perspective of an imaginary unity.

The *continuity* that the aesthetic symbol postulates between the particular and the universal, the corporeal and the spiritual, thus relies on a fictional subversion of the very particularity and corporeality of nature. But this subversion stands in the service of a moral postulate, the truth of which is proven by its pedagogical necessity and its effectiveness. *Nathan der Weise* weaves into its plot another example for this subversion, one more concrete but no less striking than the ring parable, with all its philosophical overtones. In a long monologue (5.3.3227–86) the Templar knight reconciles himself with Nathan's adoptive paternity of a Christian girl by imagining his beloved as a beautiful statue crafted by the hands of her adoptive father. Thus, while the *father qua artist* gains legitimacy beyond, and even against, the right of birth, the *woman qua statue* becomes decorporealized, desexualized. The "true" erotic appeal of the desired body can only be the work of (aesthetic) culture, and not of (physical) nature; hence, the young man re-creates his love object and prepares himself for the role of brother.

A far cry from Elvire's transformation of her dearly departed rescuer into an erotic fetish! Moreover, Kleist's novella ascribes no authorship to the painting, makes no reference to an artist capable of authorizing or "fathering" a mediation between the event the painting conjures and its recipient. There is, in other words, no cultural accommodation — no "humanization" — of the incommensurate through the aesthetic medium. Instead, the aesthetic representation repeats the traumatic event and perpetuates its spellbinding force. In Kleist, the aesthetic participates in, rather than sublating or mitigating, the violence of physical contingency; it thus sustains the latter's mystification and authority. The cultural artifact functions as an *idol* rather than as a *symbol*. Correspondingly, the Kleistian text does not reflect on the harmonizing potential of its own aesthetic character — or, if it does, only to ironize itself as a merely aesthetic device devoid of truth. Instead, it mimics at once the primordial violence of nature and of a culture separating itself from nature.

No where does Kleist outline this double mimicry more sharply than in his comedy *Der zerbrochene Krug*. In this work a broken object represents the destruction of the aesthetic symbol; its extensive description in the middle scene of the play is Kleist's reply to Lessing's ring parable. The jug that shatters when a male sneaks into a woman's bedroom and that subsequently becomes the key evidence in the trial of the alleged assailant is, of course, a traditional symbol of violated virginity; Frau Marthe's speech lamenting the irreparability of the damage to her jug underscores the connection. But the jug's brokenness suggests far more: that symbolic representation itself has gone to pieces. As witnesses to the action, we are in on the secret: it is none other than the presiding judge who is guilty of the crime he is trying. Wounded and bereft of his signifier of authority, the wig, which was lost in the course of his adventure, Adam confronts Eve; the culprit ensconced on the seat of justice silences the witness/victim. But Adam stumbles, as well, over the gaping hole that once was the jug's center: "Hier in der Mitte, mit der heilgen Mütze, / Sah man den Erzbischof von Arras stehn; / Den hat der Teufel ganz und gar geholt" (1:200). Adam's gaze into the empty center of authority — the "true" place of origin — presupposes a physical, as opposed to spiritual, concept of truth. The broken jug is the exploding body of passion and birth. Kleist's comedy about the first couple, Adam and Eve, and about man's first fall is itself the trial of this incomplete and needy body — a body that incorporates and intrudes, encompasses and splits, begets and gives birth — against all the phantasmata of wholeness and integrity underlying the myths of authority, including, ultimately, the authority of symbolic representation.

The real object of the dramatic action is the physical origin of life. The events of the preceding night that are now on trial are those facts that can never be enlightened. The guilty judge pitted against himself wreaks havoc with the Enlightenment endeavor to rationalize the unrationalizable. Indeed, the play's opening words consist of a question put by the scribe Licht, whose name ironizes the Enlightenment project: "Ei, was zum Henker, sagt, Gevatter Adam! / Was ist mit Euch geschehn? Wie seht Ihr aus?" (1:177) *What has happened to you?* — "in the beginning," of creation and of Kleist's drama, there was not paradise and unity but fall and discord. The one and only true accident happens to man and makes him into an object before he can begin making sense of himself, before he becomes a subject — before, that is, he can start inventing stories and project a wholeness covering up the wound of his unaccountable origin: the accident of birth. When Licht presents the battered Adam the mirror in which he can view and simultaneously re-collect his fractured body, he not only sets the stage for the subsequent action but also encapsulates human history, which is constituted by the futile search for unity and integrity against the primordial split or *Entzweiung* (whereby it is no coincidence that Adam's head wounds are reminiscent of a newborn infant's).

The desire for wholeness und fullness, which owes itself to the pre-ceding and always prevailing split, comes to the fore when Frau Marthe — not accidentally, a midwife — describes the rich pictorial ornamentation that decorated the jug before the nighttime accident "happened to it" (a phrase reiterating the formulation of Licht's opening question to Adam). It is only through this accident, which, crucially, precedes order and integrity, and the shards it leaves behind that the "original" image appears — or, rather, does not appear. For Frau Marthe, as many critics have remarked, does not evoke the illustration that adorned the jar in its former status of integrity but presents the pieces as fragments of a forever lost representation. Given the circumstances, her attempt to reconstitute the jug's picture verbally can only come across as its ultimate shattering. By confusing the two planes of signifier and signified, Frau Marthe unknowingly does justice to the nature of signification: the historical event that is — rather, was   depicted on the jug is now removed into that absence that the undamaged signifier had only masked through its illusionary presence. The plaintiff points at the rupture of the sign, which is also a rupture of tradition, of history, and of authority.

The scene painted on the jug had depicted a significant moment in modern history: the transfer of power over the Spanish and Dutch provinces from the emperor Charles V to his son, the later Philipp II of Spain, which constituted an initial step toward the independence of the Netherlands and a decisive step toward the emergence of modern Europe — of modernity itself. The power transfer constituted an act of succession but also one of splitting: it divided the huge Hapsburg empire, which, it should be recalled, had grown as a patchwork of territories acquired through marriage and tied together by the dynasty. Once the jug has broken, the historical moment of legitimate succession from father to son takes place literally in a void. But more is at stake here than a shattered representation; for was not the original act a substitute male birth, an act of political and legal procreation within a patriarchal world that the present tense of the drama finds severely damaged? Does not the description by the old woman, widow and midwife, shatter this world of male dignitaries — "die Schwerter unten jetzt sind weggeschlagen" (1:200) — as decisively as Adam's fall decimated the vessel the night before? Before the courtroom authorities Frau Marthe lays bare the one inerasable trace of our origin that precedes and exceeds all other political and cultural origins. Adam, who knows only too well what he is talking about, interrupts her lengthy (and enthusiastic) harangue: "Uns geht das Loch — nichts die Provinzen an, die / Darauf übergeben worden sind" (1:201; note the sequence of three nulls: hole, dash, nothing). Indeed, this hole, this void, this "Mitte, wo jetzo nichts," is no longer the origin of a meaningful history created for all time; it is the gap of the unforeseen, unseen, and unseeable, the random occurrence, the contingency of the sheer event that happens to be our existence.

It is this void that marks the place of fiction in Kleist's work, the place for the representation of a reality that has escaped the confines of Enlightened philosophical reassurance and ceded to its enigmatic character. Instead of a conclusion, I wish at least to hint at a further important feature of Kleist's inversion of the Enlightenment model: the replacement of *seeing* by *reading* as the dominant mode of aesthetic perception. Of course, Lessing was the theoretician who established the primacy of language and literature against the pictorial arts; but he did so precisely in the name of aesthetic intuitiveness ("Anschaulichkeit"), an ideal hence likewise indebted to pictorial representation. Fiction in the form of teleological narrative was to realize this ideal more fully (cf. Wellbery 1984). Again, the Templar's statue monologue offers a good example; it is by imagining the (female) body *in speech* that the man frees himself of its seductive power, whereas the direct sight of Recha had ensnared him. Likewise, only the ring narrative was able to persuade the sultan to drop his desire for the one truth as the one, touchable substance.

In contrast, we have seen how Frau Marthe laments the blinded and shattered pictorial representation without replacing it with an integral recollection of its lost unity. By insisting on the materiality of the signifier, the shards, and refusing to restore the signified whole, the premodern midwife *reads* and teaches the court to read, after the auratic presence of the representation has been irretrievably lost. Reading replaces or fills the void left behind by vision at many other points in Kleist's oeuvre. One is the anagrammatic play with the names Colino and Nicolo in "Der Findling," which also warns against any assurance that reading approximates truth more closely than does seeing (which here suggests the deceptive similarity of Colino's picture to Nicolo's appearance). Kleist reminds the reader that even the name, that most iconic of linguistic signs, is arbitrary and naturalized only through the force of habit (the letters the foundling shifts around are left over from his playful childhood reading; 2:209–10). On the other hand, in *Amphitryon* the initial "J" engraved on the diadem given to the heroine seems unmistakably to prove the identity of her nighttime bedfellow, while the loving and faithful wife is deceived by Jupiter's godly appearance precisely because her husband is a god in her eyes. Kleist plays reading off against seeing and seeing against reading in a game of vexation lacking an anchor; nor is the reader left out of this play. The advertisement opening

"Die Marquise von O . . .," in which the woman seeks the father of her unborn child, thus seemingly inviting the inscription of patriarchal authority, is, at the same time, a facetious offer to the reader to inscribe meaning into the void of the text — an activity by no means devoid of libidinal satisfaction, as is evident when the perpetrator himself finally reads, blushing heavily, the newspaper ad, "indessen er mit ganzer Seele über dem Papier lag, und den Sinn desselben gierig verschlang" (2:130). It is hard to overlook the parallel between this act of reading and the earlier act that led to the ad's appearance in the first place. Similarly, the wanton judge had entered Eve's chamber under the pretext that he must fill in the name of her fiancé on the fake document releasing him from military service; the blank space left for writing substitutes for another place to be filled ("den Platz erfüllen"; 1:847), that of the lover.

Writing and reading, then, can displace the void but never ultimately replace or fill it. In "Die Verlobung in St. Domingo" the white colonial soldier and the mestizo girl supporting the black revolution find each other across racial lines and amid threats. Their (delusive, as it soon turns out) union is encouraged by the images that each shapes of the other, images of a past into which they adopt their partner. The narrator interrupts the love scene with the comment: "Was weiter erfolgte, brauchen wir nicht zu melden, weil es jeder, der an diese Stelle kommt, von selbst liest" (2:175).

This moment — rather, this place, this "Stelle" — mocks the true moment of Enlightenment humanity: the union across all differences of body and culture in which even the signs of language are to dissolve into a spiritual universality. The narrator's suggestion that language can be dispensed with is left hanging as a sentence yet to be read, a sentence that insists on its necessity at the very moment in which it concedes its superfluousness. The blind moment of the body is not encompassed by the full presence of humanist ethics but repeats itself in the blind moment of language.

Notes

[1] This is strongly suggested by the description of the collapse of the jail building: "alle Wände des Gefängnisses rissen, der ganze Bau neigte sich, nach der Straße zu einzustürzen, und nur der, seinem langsamen Fall begegnende, Fall des gegenüberstehen den Gebäudes verhinderte, durch eine zufällige Wölbung, die gänzliche Zubodenstreckung desselben. Zitternd, mit sträubenden Haaren, und Knieen, die unter ihm brechen wollten, glitt Jeronimo über den schiefgesenkten Fußboden hinweg, der Öffnung zu, die der Zusammenschlag beider Häuser in die vordere Wand des Gefängnisses eingerissen hatte" (2:145–46). The similarity of this passage

to the famous image of the arch being held upright by the simultaneous falling of its single stones has often been noted; the image is used by Kleist also as a metaphor for birth (cf. letter to Wilhelmine of 18 November 1800; 2:593).

[2] The word *bescheiden* is used several times in the text with reference to Nathan and his "reasonable" attitude; for instance, in this scene the sultan uses the significant oxymoron "so stolz bescheiden" for the Jew's refusal of a direct metaphysical answer (3.7.394).

[3] Ruth Klüger was, as far as I can see, the first to draw attention to this connection.

Works Cited

Kleist, Heinrich von. *Sämtliche Werke und Briefe*. 2 Vols. 7th edition. Ed. Helmut Semdner. Munich: Hanser, 1984.

Lessing, Gotthold Ephraim. *Werke*. 8 Vols. Ed. Herbert G. Göpfert. Munich: Hanser, 1970–79.

Freud, Sigmund. *Studienausgabe*. Vol. 4. Ed. Alexander Mitscherlich et al. Frankfurt a.M.: Fischer, 1970.

Klüger, Ruth. "Tellheims Neffe: Kleists Abkehr von der Aufklärung." In her *Katastrophen: Über deutsche Literatur*. Göttingen: Wallstein, 1994, 163–88.

Miller, J. Hillis. "Just Reading: Kleist's 'Der Findling.'" In his *Versions of Pygmalion*. Cambridge, Mass.: Harvard UP, 1990, 82–140.

Neumann, Gerhard: "Das Stocken der Sprache und das Straucheln des Körpers. Umrisse von Kleists kultureller Anthropologie." In *Heinrich von Kleist: Kriegsfall-Rechtsfall-Sündenfall*. Ed. Gerhard Neumann. Freiburg im Breisgau: Rombach, 1994, 13–30.

Oesterle, Günter. "Der Findling." In *Kleists Erzählungen*. Ed. Walter Hinderer. Stuttgart: Reclam, 1998, 157–80.

Ryder, Frank G. "Kleist's 'Findling': Oedipus manqué?" *Modern Language Notes* 92 (1977): 509–24.

Sasse, Günther. *Die aufgeklärte Familie: Untersuchungen zur Genese, Funktion und Realitätsbezogenheit des familialen Wertsystems im Drama der Aufklärung*. Tübingen: Niemeyer, 1988.

Schneider, Helmut J. "Die Blindheit der Bilder: Kleists Ursprungsszenarien." In *Bildersturm und Bilderflut um 1800*. Ed. Schneider et al. Bielefeld: Aisthesis, 2001, 289–306.

———. "Lessing's *Nathan der Weise*." In *Deutsche Dramen des 17. und 18. Jahrhunderts*. Stuttgart: Reclam, 2000, 295–332.

———. "Der Zufall der Geburt: Lessing's *Nathan der Weise* und der imaginäre Körper der Geschichtsphilosophie." In *Körper/Kultur: Kalifornische Studien zur deutschen Moderne*. Ed. Thomas W. Kniesche. Würzburg: Königshausen & Neumann, 1995, 100–124.

————. "Der Zusammensturz des Allgemeinen." In *Positionen der Literaturwissenschaft: Acht Modellanalysen am Beispiel von Kleists "Das Erdbeben in Chili."* Ed. David E. Wellbery. Munich: Beck, 1984, 110–29.

Schröder, Jürgen "Kleists Novelle 'Der Findling': Ein Plädoyer für Nicolo." *Kleist-Jahrbuch* (1985): 109–27.

Soboczynski, Adam. "Die Impotenz des Händlers und das Geheimnis einer trefflichen Frau: Ökonomie und Verstellung in Kleists Novelle Der Findling.'" *Kleist-Jahrbuch* (2000): 118–35.

Vinken, Barbara, and Anselm Haverkamp. "Die zurechtgelegte Frau: Gottesbegehren und transzendentale Familie in Kleists Marquise von O. . . ." In *Heinrich von Kleist: Kriegsfall-Rechtsfall-Sündenfall.* Ed. Gerhard Neumann. Freiburg im Breisgau: Rombach, 1994, 127–48.

Wellbery, David E. "Das Gesetz der Schönheit: Lessings Ästhetik der Repräsentation." *Was heißt "Darstellen"?* Ed. Christian L. Hart Nibbrig. Frankfurt a.M.. Suhrkamp, 1994, 175–204.

————. *Lessing's Laocoon: Semiotics and Aesthetics in the Age of Reason.* Cambridge: Cambridge UP, 1984.

————. "Der zerbrochne Krug." In *Kleists Dramen.* Ed. Walter Hinderer. Stuttgart: Reclam, 1997, 11–32.

"Betwixt a false reason and none at all": Kleist, Hume, Kant, and the "Thing in Itself"

Tim Mehigan

THE QUESTION "What is Enlightenment?" — the subject of a famous debate in the *Berlinische Monatsschrift* — has been asked again in our own time. In the late eighteenth century the question elicited a variety of responses, most notably from the philosopher Immanuel Kant, who used the question as an opportunity to sum up the thought of his own time and to inspire it in new directions. To the idea of a rationally lived life based on the reasoning human being as the measure of all things, Kant added the crucial notion of "maturity," a special quality that implied that certain limitations attend the operation of reason in practice. These limitations partly had to do with practical considerations, such as the responsibilities incumbent on government officeholders and civil servants when speaking publicly. But they also arose as a condition of the use of reason generally. Kant thought that there was no choice about these limitations. His philosophy was built on the insight that the use of reason is limited because human beings' categories of understanding are limited, so that the invocation to use reason in a mature manner was nothing more than a call to use reason within limits found within human beings themselves. In deriving these categories of understanding in his other works, Kant developed a "critical philosophy" based on the differences between theoretical understanding, experimental reasoning based on proofs, and the more open category of judgment — the type of reasoning typical of aesthetic responses to the world.

The return of the question "What is Enlightenment?" to center stage in the humanities in recent times has focused attention on the rational content of technological modernism — an issue first raised by philosophers of the Frankfurt School of social research before and immediately after the Second World War. Specifically, the question that has been asked of the highly technology-reliant democracies of the Western world is what rationally based societies achieve for their citizens. Do they add to the sum of the citizens' happiness, or does the form of technological rationalism that these societies follow decrease the prospects for happiness in ways that run counter to the utilitarian principles that underlie them? Literary scholarship, following a similar interest in the rational content of life under the conditions of modernity, has retraced the origin of rational ways of thinking to literature that emerged in the late Enlightenment. Scholars have turned to the question of the early encounter with Kant of Heinrich von Kleist, a key author of this period, in order to understand the ways in which Enlightenment philosophy was originally received and how it influenced thought at the end of the eighteenth century. Although consideration of the impact of Kant's philosophy on Kleist from the 1920s to the 1950s was primarily concerned with which of Kant's texts and what parts of Kant's philosophy led to Kleist's "Kant crisis,"[1] recent critical interest seems generally to have taken the issue a step further. Scholars have lately begun to see Kleist's entire literary oeuvre in terms of a reckoning with the Enlightenment in general and with Kant in particular (cf. Greiner 1994; Mehigan). They see a parallel between the questions that occupied Kleist during his early Kant-inspired existential crisis and the literary experiments he throws up in his dramas and stories. It is apparent that Kleist tries to move beyond Kant's thinking in his literary works but finds himself caught again and again between the need for a rational response to the world and the position that rationality provides no final answer to the problem of how to live. Accordingly, the view has gained ground that Kleist remained under the sway of the rationality propagated by Kant without ever being entirely in agreement with it.

A study of Kleist's dramas and stories lends much support to the notion that a profound skepticism about knowledge pervades Kleist's worldview generally, along with a specific sense of skepticism with respect to the claims of reason. At the same time, it is not clear how Kleist could have derived such deep skepticism about reason and knowledge simply from reading Kant, especially as Kant's moral philosophy ultimately seeks to offer a positive account of community and the role that reason plays in structuring it. While antirationalist philosophy was gaining influence in Kleist's day — notably through the work of Friedrich Jacobi, a contemporary of Kant and opponent of Kant's idealism (cf. Frank 67–90, 662–89) — there is no record of its impact on Kleist's thinking. Jacobi is never mentioned in Kleist's letters or essays, and there is no evidence that Kleist devoted time to appraising the differences between Kant's and Jacobi's philosophies, much less to considering the related claims about knowledge of the emerging skeptical tradition. The question of the source of Kleist's skepticism, therefore, either remains open or leads back, in the final analysis, to the openly acknowledged influence of the philosophy of Kant in Kleist's letters written in the latter part of 1800 and in early 1801.

Those who have investigated the question of the skeptical turn in Kleist's thinking, which is indicated by Kleist's nebulous references to Kantian philosophy in these early letters but not explained by them, have often made some reference to the singular nature of Kleist's personality. Kleist is presumed to have cast his encounter with Kant in highly dramatic — if not melodramatic — terms for the benefit of Wilhelmine von Zenge, a woman he was wooing in 1800 and 1801 (Kleist 1991, 549). But this explanation downplays the significance of the intellectual encounter with Kant and does not answer how most of Kleist's literary output takes on the appearance — if some recent scholarship (Greiner 1998) can be believed — of a highly differentiated reaction to Kantianism. What is more, there now seems to be broad agreement in Kleist scholarship about Kleist's fundamental outlook,[2] so that even if the encounter with Kant is overlooked, the deep skepticism of Kleist's intellectual position remains.

There is a remarkable consistency to this skepticism throughout his works. Where Kleist concedes happiness to his characters, it is invariably hard-won. Happiness results only after the characters have undergone a thorough acquaintance with the "gebrechliche Einrichtung der Welt" — a programmatic term encountered in Kleist's works[3] that underscores the persistent struggle between order and chaos in the world. This concession to happiness is of such a nature that commentators have wondered whether the happy outcomes described in these cases amount to true happiness at all. Of such a type is the happiness granted to the Marquise of O . . . and her Russian suitor, the Count F., in the story "Die Marquise von O. . . ." Here the price for the positive turn of events at the end of the story is a financial settlement under the terms of which the count must renounce all his fortune to the marquise and her child and give up all conjugal rights to his spouse for an unspecified period. Out of such unlikely circumstances Kleist still manages to construe a happy ending of sorts, but, I would argue, only if we follow the line of argument suggested by Dorrit Cohn (1975) that the marquise was secretly in love with the defiler of her virtue all along.

Skepticism and Enlightenment are related traditions of thought. As R. H. Popkin (1997) has shown, a major early work on skepticism was undertaken as early as the end of the eighteenth century by Carl Friedrich Stäudlin in his *Geschichte und Geist des Skeptizismus*. Stäudlin traced the influence of the seventeenth-century skeptics, among them Bayle and Huet, on such thinkers as Locke, Berkeley, and the English deists (Popkin 2). The final part of the study, which dealt with the eighteenth century, sought to estimate the impact of skepticism on the author's own day, a period that culminated in the late or "Prussian" Enlightenment. Stäudlin's study gives grounds for the view that skepticism was not fundamentally in conflict with the Enlightenment but, in fact, grew out of the general debate about reason occurring over several centuries and, thus, must be considered one of the central features of thought that went together to make up Enlightenment thinking.

The significance of this seventeenth- and eighteenth-century dialogue between skepticism and rationality within Enlightenment thought (which centered on, but was not confined to, the question of belief) has largely been overlooked, at least until recently. The discovery that certain inconsistencies, if not paradoxes, attach to the idea of rationality — a discovery that has won fame under the rubric of the "dialectic of the Enlightenment" — was introduced to the world by the Frankfurt School philosophers Horkheimer and Adorno in their treatise of the same name in 1944. But this tension within Enlightenment thinking uncovered by Horkheimer and Adorno was not new. The tendency for reason to make more extravagant claims about its capacity to organize life and secure happiness for citizens than can be sustained by its own categories in practice was already acknowledged in the early eighteenth century, particularly in the work of the Scottish philosopher David Hume — himself an heir to a line of thought reaching back a further century or more.

Hume's *A Treatise of Human Nature* unleashed fierce debate immediately after its appearance in print in 1739. Its principal arguments, however, were quickly rejected by most of his contemporaries in England, and Hume soon acquired a reputation as one of Britain's most infamous men of letters. Even in Germany, where translations of the treatise appeared in the 1750s, its early reception was decidedly cool. It was not until the latter part of the eighteenth century that its reception both in England and in Germany improved, partly owing to related developments in thinking that had occurred over the course of the century (see Kulenkampff 162–63). By the 1770s in Germany, for example, Jacobi had begun to voice opposition to the idea of rationality in a prominent debate with Moses Mendelssohn, and elsewhere the propagation of Rousseau's ideas outlined the case in favor of natural instincts and the passions in deciding questions about how rationality related to the organization of human affairs. While such changes in the intellectual climate prepared the ground for a more favorable reception of skeptical ideas in Germany, Kant himself brought about the real breakthrough by attributing to Hume's philosophy no less than the end of his own "dogmatic slumber."[4]

The extent of Kant's debt of gratitude to Hume becomes obvious when the early *A Treatise of Human Nature* (the first part of which was revised in 1748 as *Philosophical Essays Concerning Human Understanding* and republished in 1758 as *An Enquiry Concerning Human Understanding*) is considered against Kant's first major work, the *Kritik der reinen Vernunft* (1781), which appeared nearly fifty years later. For one thing, the idea of a "Copernican" revolution in thought, famously announced by Kant in the introduction to the second edition of the *Kritik der reinen Vernunft* in 1787, first gained expression in the introductory section of Hume's treatise. More importantly, several points of contact in the two philosophies make it clear that Kant derived many of his basic ideas from a study of his predecessor's work. One of these ideas is the logical position that it is not objects that we should take seriously when apprehending the outside world but, rather, the manner in which they appear to perception, that is, the manner in which they are apprehended by human subjects. The conclusion that Hume draws from this insight — one of the basic tenets of his skeptical philosophy — is that perceptions of the world and the world perceived remain forever separate:

> The uniting principle among our internal perceptions is as unintelligible as that among external objects, and is not known to us any other way than by experience. . . . [But experience] never gives us any insight into the internal structure or operating principle of objects, but only accustoms the mind to pass from one to another. (Hume 1739, 219)

All effort we expend in closing the gap between appearances and the objects that appear to us must ultimately fail: not because we do not wish the gap closed, but because perception, by its very nature, does not permit us to close it. The result, as Hume points out, is the humbling of the claims of reason about the world. If reason is a conceptual category that makes known to us the quality and type of our experience, it can tell us nothing about the "internal structure or operating principle of objects." Compare this insight to a similar passage from the introduction to the *Kritik der reinen Vernunft,* where Kant outlines the subjective focus of knowledge:

> die Gegenstände an sich [sind] gar nicht bekannt . . . und, was wir äußere Gegenstände nennen, [sind] nichts anderes als bloße Vorstellungen unserer Sinnlichkeit . . . deren Form der Raum ist, deren wahres Korrelatum, d.i. das Ding an sich selbst, dadurch gar nicht erkannt wird, noch erkannt werden kann, nach welchem aber auch in der Erfahrung niemals gefragt wird. (Kant 1789, 73)

When we apprehend objects, therefore, we perceive that external part of them that suggests itself to human perception. We do not perceive any necessary connection between cause and effect in objects; we merely perceive the appearance of such a connection, as Hume makes clear: "if we go any farther, and ascribe a power or necessary connection to these objects; this is what we can never observe in them, but must draw the idea of it from what we feel internally in contemplating them" (Hume 1739, 219). It follows, furthermore, that perception is subject-bound and limited to the particular type of perception of which a given subject is capable. Moreover, perception owes its particular disposition not to the cognitive potential of human beings but to their sensitive qualities, which are regulated by habit and custom: "all our reasoning concerning causes and effects are deriv'd from nothing but custom; and that belief is more properly an act of the sensitive, than the cognitive part of our natures" (234). Instead of a rational human being who uncovers the constitution of the world and the trajectory of its objects through cognitive understanding alone, Hume thus describes the way in which thinking and feeling human beings are conditioned and *limited* by their senses. Sense perceptions are ordered — Hume does not wish to do away with rationality per se — but they are ordered inductively, which is to say, provisionally, subject to the emergence of new customs and habits with which they might be seen to be associated: "Reason can never satisfy us that the existence of any one object does ever imply that of another; so that when we pass from the impression of one to the idea or belief of another, we are not determin'd by reason, but by custom or a principle of association" (145). The conclusion is: "That reason alone can never give rise to any original idea, and . . . that reason, as distinguish'd from experience, can never make us conclude, that a cause or productive quality is absolutely requisite to every beginning of existence" (207). Under these conditions, reason loses its capacity to distill knowledge of the inner constitution of matter, the shape and structure of the universe. Reason has no necessary connection with objects, except as a regulative force that organizes the impressions of the mind and enables us to transfer our attention from one object to another. The conclusion that Hume reaches from this analysis of the appearance of objects is startling and, indeed, revolutionary: "Upon the whole, necessity is something, that exists in the mind, not in objects" (216). Kant also takes this position in the *Kritik der reinen Vernunt*, but as a starting point rather than as a conclusion. Nevertheless, the underlying skepticism about reason that it implies is another strong link to Hume's thought: "Die Vernunftbegriffe sind . . . bloße Ideen, und haben freilich keinen Gegenstand in irgendeiner Erfahrung, aber bezeichnen

dadurch darum doch gedichtete und zugleich dabei für möglich ange-
nommene Gegenstände" (Kant 1789, 703).

So Hume's basic insight is: If it is not the object world that should
absorb our attention, it is the way the object world appears to our senses.
This being so, a study of the types of understanding human beings have
of appearances will tell us a lot about human beings themselves. Understanding can then be defined as the susceptibility of thought to follow
"general rules," which "regulate our judgment." These rules prescribe
immutable boundaries for understanding. According to Hume, human
reason is always one of three kinds, "*viz.* that from knowledge, from
proofs, and from probabilities" (Hume 1739, 175). He then expands
these categories of understanding in a definition that again leads directly
to Kant: "By knowledge, I mean the assurance arising from the comparison of ideas. By proofs, those arguments, which are deriv'd from the
relation of cause and effect, and which are entirely free from doubt and
uncertainty. By probability, that evidence, which is still attended with
uncertainty" (175). This tripartite division of understanding directly
anticipates Kant's own classification of reason into "pure" and "practical"
operative categories and into the less rule-bound category of aesthetic
judgment. This view of the limitations that attend the categories of
understanding, in fact, constitutes a decisive shift in the history of philosophy. It moves philosophy beyond the grand claims of speculative and
metaphysical thinking to the more circumscribed, but grounded, areas
of so-called critical philosophy — the philosophical project of Kant.

It is clear, then, that Kant's philosophical debt to Hume is significant. Equally significant is Kant's attempt to go beyond Hume and the
basic skepticism in which, according to Hume's philosophy, the world
must be seen to be cast. Kant's project was to construct a philosophy that
would reconcile the insights of skepticism with the need to provide an
alternative to what skepticism would seem to disqualify: both dogmatic
belief and the speculative statements of metaphysical philosophers that
fall outside the bounds of what can be said logically about the world. It
proved enormously influential in Kant's own day and brought about the
rise of movements in literature and philosophy that, following Kant's
lead, sought to close the gap established by skeptical philosophy between
the subjective appearances and the world of objects. The most influential
of these movements — Romanticism in the literary sphere, idealism in
that of philosophy — were essentially "transcendental" in outlook. Romanticism was transcendental in that it sought to overcome the duality
of the world through the inspiration of an intervening force: nature.
Philosophical idealism was transcendental in outlook because it sought

to work out a system of thought by which the tendency of the subject to be given to thought became the very object of thought itself. Both Romanticism and transcendental idealism, properly considered, can be traced back to Kant's critical appropriation of Hume and to Kant's desire to substitute rationality for dogma, speculation, and belief. Kant argued that there must be some reason why human beings come together and build life in common with others and, therefore, ultimately some morally necessary basis to community.[5] Kant's achievement was to find this basis in reason, but a reason squared with the limitations prescribed by skepticism in the philosophy of Hume before him.

While Kleist scholarship has been unsuccessful in determining which of Kant's texts led to the skeptical turn in Kleist's thinking, there may be some grounds for the view that Kleist discovered such skepticism in the very assumptions that Kant used to construct his philosophy. Accordingly, it is argued that Kleist's skepticism — notwithstanding the fact that it arises from the encounter with Kant's thinking — is not to be thought of as issuing from an understanding or misunderstanding[6] of Kant's philosophy so much as from a reaction to the initial positions in which Kantian philosophy is anchored. In this sense, it could be argued that Kleist reads beyond Kant to Hume.[7] Kleist approaches Kant initially both to broaden his understanding of truth and morality in the world and to learn more about the pivotal role of reason in communicating truth and morality. Instead of finding enlightenment through reason, he encounters for the first time the skeptical arguments that Kant outlines and endeavors to transcend. The encounter with Kant's thinking does not provide instruction through the agency of sovereign reason so much as tuition in the "regulative of reason" and its limitations. Kleist, who had hoped to gain certainty about his orientation in the world, instead discovers the uncertainty that attends the full compass of both regulative and contingent events in life.

> Seit diese Überzeugung, nämlich, daß hienieden keine Wahrheit zu finden ist, vor meine Seele trat, habe ich nicht wieder ein Buch angerührt. Ich bin untätig in meinem Zimmer umhergegangen, ich habe mich an das offne Fenster gesetzt, ich bin hinausgelaufen ins Freie, eine innerliche Unruhe trieb mich zuletzt in Tabagien und Kaffeehäuser, ich habe Schauspiele und Konzerte besucht, um mich zu zerstreuen . . .; und dennoch war der einzige Gedanke, den meine Seele in diesem äußeren Tumulte mit glühender Angst bearbeitete, immer nur dieser: dein einziges, dein höchstes Ziel ist gesunken. (Kleist 1983, 2:634)

The "loss" of truth in the world must be understood as the first casualty of the encounter with skepticism. According to skeptical thinking, truth is not a reliable measuring stick underlying all moral action but, at best, a relative concept that foregrounds the importance of context and position in establishing what is meant by truth statements about the world. Hume locates truth not in unchanging structures of veracity but in habit-induced forms of behavior that stabilize our reactions to the world. Truth is, therefore, what we take to be true at a given moment, or it is belief, "an act of the mind arising from custom" (Hume 1739, 163). This redefinition of truth as the truth statements, to which we have become habituated, is, for the young Kleist, tantamount to the loss of truth per se.

While the letter of March 1801 excerpted above does not constitute the first encounter with Kant — a study of the early letters allows us to date this encounter to August 1800 or slightly before — it does indicate a conscious understanding of skeptical arguments. Accordingly, it is the cognitive aspect of reason that absorbs Kleist's attention. Kleist casts the encounter with skeptical positions as a cognitive loss, a crisis of reason. Kleist does not respond to what Kant's philosophy sets out to make possible, the grounding of perception in the sensitive categories of human awareness. Instead, it is the loss of the cognitive aspect of truth that Kleist outlines in his letter to his fiancée, Wilhelmine von Zenge, of 22 March 1801: "Wir können nicht entscheiden, ob das, was wir Wahrheit nennen, wahrhaft Wahrheit ist, oder ob es uns nur so scheint. Ist das letzte, so *ist* die Wahrheit, die wir hier sammeln, nach dem Tode nicht mehr — und alles Bestreben, ein Eigentum sich zu erwerben, das uns auch in das Grab folgt, ist vergeblich — " (Kleist 1983, 2:634). Looking through the lens of human perception, we are unable to decide if truth actually exists, or whether it only *appears* to exist. If it is the latter, as Kleist remarks, then the prospect of attaining unchanging, absolute truth within the context of earthbound categories of knowledge is in vain. Compare this realization with the position Kleist had adopted in a letter to Wilhelmine of 10 and 11 October 1800: "*Liebe und Bildung,* das ist alles, was ich begehre, und wie froh bin ich, daß die Erfüllung dieser beiden unerlaßlichen [*sic*] Bedürfnisse, ohne die ich *jetzt* nicht mehr glücklich sein könnte, nicht von dem Himmel abhangt [*sic*], der, wie bekannt, die Wünsche der armen Menschen so oft unerfüllt läßt, sondern *einzig und allein von Dir*" (574).

Love and education connect earthbound life to reliable categories of growth and development. Already in this letter there is the sense of skepticism about belief, and, correspondingly, the metaphysical sphere appears decidedly remote. Yet, Kleist invests trust in the here and now, appearing to content himself with the pursuit of happiness in the material world. This is reinforced in a passage from another letter (to Wilhelmine von Zenge of 13–18 September 1800) that predates the "Kant crisis":

> Über den Zweck unseres ganzen *ewigen* Daseins nachzudenken, auszu-
> forschen, ob der Genuß der Glückseligkeit, wie *Epikur* meinte, oder die
> Erreichung der Vollkommenheit, wie *Leibniz* glaubte, oder die Erfüllung
> der trocknen Pflicht, wie *Kant* versichert, der letzte Zweck des Menschen
> sei, das ist selbst für Männer unfruchtbar und oft verderblich. Wie kön-
> nen wir uns getrauen in den Plan einzugreifen, den die Natur für die
> Ewigkeit entworfen hat, da wir nur ein so unendlich kleines Stück von
> ihm, unser Erdenleben, übersehen? Also wage Dich mit Deinem Ver-
> stande nie über die Grenzen Deines Lebens hinaus. (565)

We may deduce from a reading of Kleist's letters that the encounter with Kant's thinking occurs in two distinct stages.[8] In the first instance Kleist responds to the basic teaching of Kant with a little glumness (note here the reference to Kant's "dry" moral philosophy) yet, certainly, with some understanding. Kleist accepts that limitations attend the human position, and that we should not look for instruction about the divine plan by applying sensory data from our material lives to the metaphysical sphere beyond our lives. The letters of late 1800 are cheerful enough in tone, and Kleist seems ready to accept an accommodation with the essential unknowability of the supersensible, as long as the human hope for happiness remains intact. The later letter of October 1800 confirms this position, anchoring happiness to the concrete categories of self-instruction and love for another person. In this sense Kleist's fiancée is not just a spectator before whom a crisis about knowledge is played out[9] but a participant in the project Kleist constructs. In fact, her role in Kleist's thinking becomes more significant after the first encounter with Kant's philosophy, precisely because she is to collude on the project of happiness in *defiance* of the divine, which is not only unknowable but possibly also indifferent to the plight of human beings.

There are grounds for the view that this first encounter with Kant in the period around August 1800 or slightly before occurs not through a direct reading of Kant's philosophy but in distilled form through a secondary source or through lectures Kleist attended as a student in Berlin. In the absence of concrete information about Kleist's reading of Kant in the letters, however, it is probably not possible to make a more informed judgment on the matter. A second encounter with Kant's philosophy seems to have occurred in early 1801. A change in the tone of the letters is the first sign of a renewed contact with Kant's thought. The note of resignation apparent in the letters of September and October 1800, in which Kleist focuses on what is achievable within the limits of earthbound existence, gives way to a sudden sense of despair at the loss of certainty even within these limitations. The immediacy of the tone of three letters written at this time — the letters to Ulrike of 5 February and 23 March 1801 and the letter to Wilhelmine of 22 March 1801 — suggests a period of direct study of Kant's philosophy in the early weeks of 1801. But even here it is not possible to make a definitive pronouncement about which text or texts Kleist actually read. Of Kant's works, only the *Kritik der Urteilskraft* (1790) is referred to by Kleist by name — once, in a short review written in late 1810 of a play by Voß. Yet none of the references to Kant in late 1800 or early 1801 in Kleist's letters — the period from which we date Kleist's so-called Kant crisis — refer to a particular work of Kant's as such.

Nevertheless, the result of the second encounter with Kant is clear enough. It is not the invocation to live life modestly within earthly confines that concerns Kleist in these letters, for that is already something, as we have seen, with which he has reached some accommodation. The second encounter with Kant brings Kleist in contact with skeptical positions concerning knowledge and perception, and it is this that is recorded in the letter to Wilhelmine of 22 March 1801:

> Vor kurzem ward ich mit der neueren sogenannten Kantischen Philosophie bekannt — und Dir muß ich jetzt daraus einen Gedanken mitteilen, indem ich nicht fürchten darf, daß er Dich so tief, so schmerzhaft erschüttern wird, als mich . . . . Wenn alle Menschen statt der Augen grüne Gläser hätten, so würden sie urteilen müssen, die Gegenstände, welche sie dadurch erblicken, sind grün — und nie würden sie entscheiden können, ob ihr Auge ihnen die Dinge zeigt, wie sie sind, oder ob es nicht etwas zu ihnen hinzutut, was nicht ihnen, sondern dem Auge gehört. So ist es mit dem Verstande. (Kleist 1983, 2:634)

This passage records nothing less than the loss of the "thing in itself." Objects disjoin from the subject, as perception is no longer able to provide secure knowledge of things as they are. Instead, Kleist must concede that perception is circumscribed by the limitations of the subjective position, which is to say, that it is error prone. And errors are clearly that with which the cognitive aspect of reason is meant to dispense. According to the skeptical argument, there is no way out of this dilemma. Human perception communicates a world of objects to the subject, but there is no way of knowing if these objects have any reality or are just appearances that meet the eye — in the most extreme case, mere apparitions that have no necessary relation to the real objects. If the latter is the case — this is the essence of Kleist's crisis — then human beings are restricted by imperfect sensory organs and the inability ever to leave the confines of subjectivity and make contact with the world "out there." As Kleist puts it so touchingly in a letter to his half sister Ulrike: "Mein *einziges* und *höchstes* Ziel ist gesunken, ich habe keines mehr" (Kleist 1983, 2:636).

Hume deals with the question of the reality of the external world in an important section of the *Treatise of Human Nature;* the later *Enquiry Concerning Human Understanding* also deals with the knowability of the external world and will also be referred to in the analysis below. Hume asks what entitles us to believe in the existence of external bodies and considers, in turn, the claims of reason, the senses, and the imagination in evincing proof of the existence of external reality. An argument that denies that we can have any certainty about the existence of reality is advanced in each case.

The claims of rationality are denied by an argument that runs counter to Leibniz's principle of sufficient reason. Hume concedes that it might be appropriate under certain circumstances to assume the existence of a world "out there" and to construct rational working models of it. But these working models say nothing about how the world actually is. A similar argument can be lodged with reference to cause and effect. While we can *imagine* how an effect arises from a cause, our experience of things does not reveal any actual causes. Causes do not appear to the senses, no matter how uniform our experiments or how much similarity we find among objects. The argument Hume uses to demonstrate this point is particularly devastating:

> Let the course of things be allowed hitherto ever so regular; that alone, without some new argument or inference, proves not that, for the future, it will continue so. In vain do you pretend to have learned the nature of bodies from your past experience. Their secret nature, and consequently all their effects and influence, may change, without any change in their sensible qualities. This happens sometimes, and with regard to some objects: Why may it not happen always, and with regard to all objects? (Hume 1964, 33)

In other words, the rational interrogation of our experience does not elicit the shape of reality, no matter how regular the conjunction we find in it. It is custom or habit that gives shape to our experience, not reason. Hume is compelled therefore to conclude: "in all reasonings from experience, there is a step taken by the mind which is not supported by an argument or process of understanding" (Hume 1964, 36). This reference to the limits of reason — though it was not understood in its entirety until much later, in the work of Kant — actually marks the end of the first stage of the rational project of the Enlightenment.

A similar argument is advanced to deny the claim of the senses. Perception supplies us with data about an external reality. Accordingly, the external world is considered real only as long as data corresponding to such a world are received. Yet, if this world is to be considered independent of the senses, an argument would have to be advanced that maintains the independent reality of this world beyond the point where we continue to have information about it. Hume points out the essential absurdity of this position. It is untenable, he says, to assume that a world that exists because we have perception of it might continue to exist though we cease to have evidence about it.

A slightly different picture presents itself with respect to the imagination. Hume concedes that the imagination is a powerful tool in suggesting to us the existence of objects in an external world. Imagination creates a world of forms and shapes by copying the images it receives about the world onto memory. Memory, in turn, though it may vary this information in particular ways (i.e., by imagining events and objects that do not occur in reality), operates to stabilize these images over time and to confer on them the appearance of constancy. Such constancy in memory, in turn, enables us to act, as it gives us the impression that our memories of past perceptions correspond to actual perceptions (and, therefore, real past events). Yet, Hume says, this is an illusion, albeit a useful one. For though the succession of our ideas resembles the outside world, custom is the principle by which the appearance of correspondence has been effected (Hume 1964, 46). In other words, nothing entitles us to assume that our memories — copies of past perceptions held alive for us with varying degrees of intensity by our emotions — are anything more than *fictional* accounts of the existence of an outside world. And yet, action in the world would not be possible without the belief that such memories were "true," that is, identical with those perceived occurrences of which we have memory.

Once these arguments against, respectively, reason, the senses, and the imagination are put forward, we are again left with skeptical propositions about the world. The world of objects and outside bodies lies beyond our capacity to have direct knowledge of it. As Kant, who follows Hume's reasoning closely on this point, puts it: we can apprehend objects and have knowledge of the appearances, but we can have no direct access to the "thing in itself." The world we perceive "out there" is a world entirely of our own making. It takes shape because of our ability to have perception of it, but nothing can guarantee that our perception of the external world actually coincides with that world. Instead, Hume indicates how habit or custom enlivens the world for us in relatively consistent ways, yet without any capacity to overcome the gap between ourselves and the objects we perceive to be around us:

> And how must we be disappointed, when we learn, that this connection, tie, or energy lies merely in ourselves, and is nothing but that determination of the mind, which is acquir'd by custom, and causes us to make a transition from an object to its usual attendant, and from the impression of one to the lively idea of another? Such a discovery not only cuts off all hope of ever attaining satisfaction, but even prevents our very wishes; since it appears, that when we say we desire to know the ultimate and operating principle, as something, which resides in the external object, we either contradict ourselves, or talk without a meaning. . . . For I have already shewn, that the understanding, when it acts alone, and according to its most general principles, entirely subverts itself, and leaves not the lowest degree of evidence in any proposition, either in philosophy or common life. . . . What party, then, shall we choose among these difficulties? If we embrace this principle, and condemn all refin'd reasoning, we run into the most manifest absurdities. If we reject it in favour of these reasonings, we subvert entirely the human understanding. We have, therefore, no choice left but betwixt a false reason and none at all. (Hume 1739, 314–15)

The encounter with skeptical propositions on the threshold of maturity propels Kleist into a writing career. Writing becomes for Kleist a vehicle to evaluate the claims of reason about the world. The project of Enlightenment reason, as propounded by Kant, is tested again and again in Kleist's works against the underlying skepticism, which it both implicitly and explicitly opposes. Kleist asks whether the conduct of human life is truly informed by the general principles of understanding laid down by Kant's philosophy, or whether, as Hume suggests, understanding, on its own, "leaves not the lowest degree of evidence in any proposition, either in philosophy or common life." The traumatic second encounter with Kant's philosophy, therefore, leads Kleist to address what is arguably the most pressing issue of the late Enlightenment period: whether reason, properly considered, has the capacity to say anything at all about the world.

This question is explored from various points of view in Kleist's stories. Particularly enlightening is the treatment it receives in "Der Findling," a story long held to be no more than a simple tale about the taking in of a foundling who erupts in unpredictable ways upon the settled family life of the Italian trader Piachi.[10] Yet, the collapse of Piachi's world is attributable less to malevolent qualities in the foundling Nicolo's character than to Piachi's dogged allegiance to rational ideals. Nothing but the belief in a rationally ordered universe motivates him to take in the stray boy Nicolo in place of his son Paolo, who falls victim to the plague while Piachi is on a business trip. The initial exchange of the adoptive son for the natural one provides the experimental conditions for a proposition that is tested in the narrative: can the adoptive son take the place of the natural son; can social education compensate for natural identity or, indeed, create it ex nihilo? Can, in short, a rational order inspired by the Enlightenment ideal of education stand for a natural order or take its place?

Consider Piachi's attempts to reform Nicolo and make him into a suitable replacement for the lost son, Paolo. On returning from Ragusa, Nicolo is sent off to school. As he quickly masters the basic skills in reading, writing, and arithmetic, Piachi's fondness for him grows. In fact, it is Nicolo's response to this early schooling, rather than any spontaneous act of generosity, that leads Piachi formally to adopt Nicolo after just a few weeks: "Piachi schickte ihn in die Schule . . . und da er, auf eine leicht begreifliche Weise, den Jungen in dem Maße lieb gewonnen, als er ihm teuer zu stehen gekommen war, so adoptierte er ihn" (Kleist 1983, 2:201). Nicolo is then quickly installed in the family business. Again, the point is made that Piachi was displeased with the boy he had previously engaged in the business and had good reason to look for a replacement. Nicolo — now a stand-in for both the dead Paolo and the unsatisfactory office boy — repays this faith by dealing with the affairs that are entrusted to him "auf das tätigste und vorteilhafteste" (201). Nicolo soon encounters the monks of the local Carmelite monastery. They see in him a future benefactor, as he is clearly destined to inherit the old man's fortune. At this point Nicolo is led astray by the lascivious Xaviera Tartini, the "Beischläferin ihres Bischofs" (210). Piachi admonishes the fifteen-year-old Nicolo to break off contact with her. When, a few years later, Nicolo agrees to a match with the socially suitable Constanza Parquet, Piachi believes Nicolo to have reformed and rewards him with money and formal installation as his heir. Little more than a year later, however, Constanza dies in childbirth. Consoling himself in the company of the Carmelite monks and with the attentions of the seductive Tartini, Nicolo does not demonstrate the Catholic piety expected of him on the eve of Constanza's interment. Piachi's punishment of him is severe. He stages a funeral procession in which not the dead Constanza but Xaviera Tartini, the woman with whom Nicolo has arranged a rendezvous, is said to be laid to rest. Such punishment is designed to effect a cure for Nicolo's "Hange zu den Weibern" (205). Instead, it tutors him in psychological abuse. Later, Nicolo uses this schooling against his presumed tormentor, Piachi's wife, Elvire. But it is not Elvire, but Piachi, who cajoles, disciplines, and punishes Nicolo in order to turn him into both compliant heir and "enlightened" citizen free from the weaknesses of the flesh.

So Kleist's narrative maneuvers the foundling Nicolo into circumstances in which a new family order is countenanced. None of the elements in the family order, which is the subject of Kleist's experiment, can be considered natural. The foundling Nicolo enters the new family structure to take the place of the natural son Paolo. Equally, Elvire takes the place of Piachi's unnamed first wife, after Piachi's respectful two-year courtship of her. The age difference between Piachi and Elvire is significant — so significant, in fact, that Piachi is no longer considered able to father a child with her. Elvire, for her part, nurses a silent passion for the Genoese knight who saved her from a burning house when she was thirteen but died in effecting the rescue. She regularly pays homage to her rescuer in a secret part of her bedroom. Piachi, who understands the reverence in which Elvire holds her now long dead rescuer, "hütete sich sehr, seinen Namen vor ihr zu nennen, oder sie sonst an ihn zu erinnern" (203).

Nicolo, therefore, becomes the third element in a thoroughly "unnatural" family structure. Kleist's point is not to commend the value of intact natural families but to consider whether an artificial family can be established by rationality and social education alone. Piachi is the key element in this calculation. Having lost both a wife and a child from a previous marriage, he attempts to assemble a new family along nonnatural but socially enlightened lines. It is for this reason that he is attentive to the social needs of the substitute son, Nicolo, and the psychological needs of the substitute wife, Elvire. Moreover, Piachi appreciates the functional nature of substitutions, as his cunning deception of Nicolo shows. When Piachi arranges the funeral procession for the "deceased" Xaviera Tartini, Nicolo is skillfully brought to heel — at least temporarily.

The name of the dead Genoese knight, which is never uttered for fear of plunging the poor Elvire into a renewed fever, stands — much as it does in other works of Kleist's — for a lost and unrecoverable "nature." The diadem that bears not the initial of Alkmene's revered husband but that of the god Jupiter in *Amphitryon* and the scrap of paper that presages the fate of the Saxon dynasty in "Michael Kohlhaas," which Kohlhaas reads and swallows just before his execution, are but two examples that speak of the loss of presence, the loss of the "Ding an sich." In "Der Findling," however, Kleist views this loss with some irony (in general, the use of irony marks off the stories from the plays). Kleist radicalizes the loss of presence in "Der Findling" in two important ways. First, he introduces the idea of a substitute referential to test the claims of rational, which is to say artificial, orders. This substitute order, the new family structure in "Der Findling," let it be said, fails. Second, he disjoins the name from its "natural" point of reference and provides for a free play of substitutions on the level of signification — the level that constitutes narrative discourse. This goal is achieved in "Der Findling" most obviously when Nicolo realizes that the letters of his own name can be rearranged to give the name of Elvire's savior, the Genoese knight Colino. Kleist constructs this scene with conscious reference to the Enlightenment project of education, for the ivory letters that give Nicolo the key to his "satanic plan" are the same letters that were used to instruct him as a boy:

> Da nun Nicolo die Lettern . . . in die Hand nahm, und . . . damit spielte, fand er — zufällig, in der Tat, selbst, denn er erstaunte darüber, wie er noch in seinem Leben nicht getan — die Verbindung heraus, welche den Namen: *Colino* bildet. Nicolo, dem diese logographische Eigenschaft seines Namens fremd war, warf, von rasenden Hoffnungen von neuem getroffen, einen ungewissen und scheuen Blick auf die ihm zur Seite sitzende Elvire. Die Übereinstimmung, die sich zwischen beiden Wörtern angeordnet fand, schien ihm mehr als ein bloßer Zufall. (210)

The means that are meant to realize Enlightenment rationality set up the very conditions that commit it to failure. The letters of the alphabet, whose arrangement provides the textual material that underpins the rationalist project of education, are nonreferential, which is to say, nonnatural. They have no necessary reference to objects in the outside world. These letters can, therefore, serve quite unnatural ends, such as the manipulation of identity that provides the key to the suffering of the pining Elvire. The point, again, is not that Nicolo is "satanic." Far from being evil incarnate, he is, in fact, nothing more than an opportunist, albeit a cunning one, who applies the logic of substitutions learned from his foster father to devastating effect. Nicolo understands that names are codes that can provide a key[11] to the deepest subconscious. Yet the code is also a simulacrum, which is to say, a non-thing. Codes are to be cracked like nuts and consumed with equal relish.[12]

At the end, of course, Nicolo shows no fidelity to his educator. If there is an expectation that he should, Kleist wishes to expose it for what it is — a habit of mind, no more. This result is entirely in keeping with the view of the skeptic about the world, as exemplified by Hume's insight about promises: "there is naturally no inclination to observe promises, distinct from a sense of their obligation; it follows, that fidelity is no natural virtue, and that promises have no force, antecedent to human conventions" (Hume 1739, 571).

If there is a sense at the start of "Der Findling" that the foundling should repay the loyalty shown to him, Kleist reveals that this expectation has "no force, antecedent to human conventions." Therefore, nothing can ensure that the project of education on which Piachi embarks will bring any result. We may hope to instill a sense of fidelity in those we favor, but this remains only a hope. As Hume observes, fidelity has "no natural virtue"; it does not exist as a condition of nature.

This insight on its own provides a key to the treatment of nature in Kleist's works. The fact that there is no natural virtue underlying human life explains why Kleist — unlike his direct contemporaries, the Romantics — is unable to see any instruction in nature for human affairs. This inability is most apparent in the story "Das Erdbeben in Chili," where a spectacular earthquake liberates the lovers Josephe and Jeronimo just as the former is being escorted to his execution. Out of the confusion of fleeing people and collapsing buildings, which perpetrate their own summary justice — mostly on the tormentors of Josephe and Jeronimo — Kleist creates an idyll of sorts outside the city as the lovers are reunited. But the Rousseau-like[13] idyll in the bosom of nature beyond the walls of corrupted civilization is short lived, and Kleist soon returns the lovers, along with a small band of like-minded souls, to a city church, where they fall victim to the repressed fury of a mob. Kleist's point is that nature can provide no palliative for those in search of natural virtue. Instead, nature is a blind and, therefore, morally neutral force that in no sense precedes or underlies the organization of human affairs. Because it is not antecedent to human affairs, it exercises no force in sanctioning them.

"Betwixt a false reason and none at all" — that is the position in which the young Kleist finds himself as a result of his contact with the skepticism underlying Kant's philosophy. It is neither the schematism of the rational categories of understanding, nor the inherent restrictiveness of moral positions worked out in Kant's philosophy that disturbs Kleist. Instead, it is the realization that subjective knowledge and the objective world around us remain forever separate that precipitates crisis. Kleist's despair, in other words, is directed at the loss of reality, at the loss of the "thing in itself."

In a fateful second encounter with Kant's philosophy, Kleist becomes acquainted with the Humean skepticism that divorces appearances from their objects and takes the human being, in a certain sense, out of nature. To this extent Kleist sees *beyond* Kant to Hume. Instead of rejoicing in the new possibilities open to rational subjects who choose to exercise reason in a mature manner, Kleist sees the paradoxes on which the Kantian project is forged. In "Der Findling" he reenacts the Enlightenment project of education, only to describe its spectacular failure. Instead of regularity between ideas and reality, there is only accident and contingency. This situation is particularly evident in the idea of the name, which is revealed as an accidental conjunction of letters with no necessary connection to identity. It is partly for this reason that the project of education can have no guarantee of success. That the well-meaning and rational Piachi, who takes in the foundling Nicolo in place of his dead son and attempts to educate him, can metamorphose into an irrational and unrepentant murderer indicates Kleist's skepticism about all such rational projects.

We are left with the admonition to accept that our habits of mind are just this — habits only. Human existence is, accordingly, material rather than essential, artificial rather than natural, conventional rather than real. In a way that anticipates the philosophy of Friedrich Nietzsche, we could even say that existence is not even moral. Morality, as Hume teaches, is not discoverable by applying reason to human affairs; it can only be known as a powerful effect of sentiment. As such, it lies outside the realm of what can be considered necessary about life, even as it would appear to be the only thing that can give life meaning. Equally, there would appear to be nothing at all necessary about the operation of rationality in the world. Rationality provides working models for human affairs, to be applied regulatively. Yet, these working models say nothing at all about the full compass of contingent events in life, just as they tell us nothing about its "real" content. The mature use of reason that Kant advocates in his essay "Beantwortung der Frage: Was ist Aufklärung?" sets out guidelines for applying reason in special cases, but this does not mean that reason can be used beyond these special cases or that reason reflects the way human beings really live their lives. If Kant's project was the insight that reason functions best when its limits are properly understood, Kleist's was to point out the limits of these limits when applied to life situations. His deepest insight lies close to the teaching of the Scottish skeptic David Hume, who remarked: "In all the incidents of life we ought still to preserve our skepticism" (Hume 1739, 317).

Notes

[1] Representative of this trend is Ludwig Muth (1954), who supports the view that it was Kant's third critique, the *Kritik der Urteilskraft*, that brought about Kleist's crisis. Contrast this view with that of Ernst Cassirer (1919), who held that it was Fichte's *Die Bestimmung des Menschen* (1800) that precipitated the crisis. The move away from seeing Kleist's crisis as resulting from a particular text of Kant's was signaled by Müller-Seidel (1961), who urged caution in dealing with the question

of philosophical influence: "der Ursprung aller Erkenntnisnot ist . . . nicht in irgend-
einem rätselhaften Faktum, in einem Zufall oder Schicksal zu suchen, sondern im
Menschen selbst, im Typischen seiner Denkweise, im Verhältnis zu der Welt, die ihn
umgibt und von der aus er selbst sich versteht" (218).

[2] Despite the vast amount of scholarship devoted to Kleist in recent years, there are
broad areas of agreement about Kleist's intellectual position. A great many scholars,
for example, while emphasizing particular aspects of Kleist's narrative and/or dramatic work, accept that Kleist was anchored in the idealistic positions of his own time
and never went beyond them. Cf. Bernd Fischer: "Kleists Erzählungen [können]
durchaus historisch als Auseinandersetzung mit dem herrschenden Paradigma seiner
Zeit (das vielleicht immer noch am treffendsten mit dem epochalen Schlagwort
Idealismus gefaßt wird) begriffen werden, dessen Grenzen er im ironischen Experiment aufzuzeigen vermag, ohne sie freilich . . . grundsätzlich überschreiten zu
können" (12). A similar, although less strictly historical, line of argument, has been
followed by Anthony Stephens (1994) and Gerhard Neumann (1994), both of
whom underscore that Kleist is ultimately skeptical about the prospects for knowledge in the world. Where they see "scenarios of truth" at work in Kleist's fictional
world, these inevitably unfold in ambiguous ways that see truth as counterintuitive
or, at any rate, rationally improbable for Kleist's characters. Neumann, therefore,
speaks of "Experimentalordnungen, in denen das ungeschützte und gleichsam
hautlose, seiner Körperlichkeit ausgelieferte Subjekt — 'als ob ihm die Augenlider
abgeschnitten wären' — sich den Redeordnungen und Zeichensystemen einer durch
Bürokratie und Verwaltung, durch Wissenschaft und Mächtespiel der Politik be-
stimmten Gesellschaft aussetzt" (9). The result of this fateful openness to the world
is that there can be no reliable access to truth in the human world. Two other views
of Kleist have emerged in recent times. One view, advanced by Wolf Kittler (1987),
moves away from the literary content of Kleist's work in order to foreground the
question of Kleist's political aspirations in the period following the French Revolution. Here it is argued that Kleist's *Hermannsschlacht,* in particular, expresses a desire
to realize an "insurrection of the German people" (342) and that his essay "Über das
Marionettentheater" represents Kleist's response to the question of the failure of the
Prussian generals to secure a victory over the French in the war of 1792–93 (345).
Only a reinvigoration of the ideal of man, Kittler argues, could, in Kleist's eyes, revive
the fortunes of the Prussian army: "Kleists Position in der Debatte um die Reorgani-
sation des preußischen Heeres ist insofern einzigartig, als er den Widerspruch zwischen Drill und Freiheit, der in offiziellen Dokumenten wie dem Infanterie-
Reglement von 1812 eher verhüllt zur Sprache kommt, in paradoxer Überspitzung
formuliert" (362). In the most recent scholarship on Kleist, Günter Blamberger
(1999) has stressed a more aristocratic, though still trenchantly skeptical, strain in
Kleist's thinking. In his view, Kleist moves between aristocratic concepts of behavior
rooted in (especially) sixteenth-century Italian moralism, on the one hand, and
bourgeois emotiveness, on the other hand. The result: "Zur heiteren Distanz sind
Kleists Figuren nicht fähig. Sie changieren hoffnungslos zwischen der bürgerlichen
Idee der Herzensprache, die Richard Sennett treffend 'Tyrannei der Intimität' ge-
nannt hat, und den nicht weniger gewaltsam aristokratischen Verhaltenslehren der

Kälte in Notsituationen. Der Kleistsche Zwiespalt ist, daß die Moralistik bei ihm aus enttäuschtem Idealismus hervorgeht" (39).

[3] See, for example, "Michael Kohlhaas": "Denn ein richtiges, mit der gebrechlichen Einrichtung der Welt schon bekanntes Gefühl machte ihn . . . geneigt . . ., den Verlust der Pferde, als eine gerechte Folge davon, zu verschmerzen" (Kleist 1983, 2:16).

[4] As Kant said in the preface to the *Prolegomena:* "Ich gestehe frei: die Erinnerung des David Hume war eben dasjenige, was mir vor vielen Jahren zuerst den dogmatischen Schlummer unterbrach und meinen Untersuchungen auf dem Felde der spekulativen Philosophie eine andere Richtung gab" (Akademie-Textausgabe 4:260).

[5] Communicating a judgment to others about something that is felt to be true is for Kant the very source of community ("sensus communis"). Kant develops this idea under the heading "Vom Geschmacke als einer Art von sensus communis" in the *Kritik der Urteilskraft.* Cf. *Werke* 5:388–92.

[6] That Kleist misunderstood Kant's philosophy is a popularly held view in Kleist scholarship. For a recent restatement of this view, cf. Peter Ensberg (1999).

[7] Kleist's tendency to push Kantianism beyond the boundaries within which Kant himself wished to be understood has already been remarked on, particularly in early Kleist criticism. Blöcker, for example, said: "Für Kleist . . ., dem es um eben das geht, was Kant ausklammert, wird . . . die menschliche Erkenntnisfähigkeit überhaupt fragwürdig. . . . Kleist treibt Kant, *seinen* Kant, bereits in Schopenhauerische Bezirke vor, in das Reich des sinnlos waltenden Willens" (22). In similar vein, cf. Friedrich Gundolf (1922): "[Kleist] treibt Kant als eine Gewaltkur und ohne philosophischen Sinn bis zur Verwirrung des Geistes" (10).

[8] Blöcker's analysis also implies a contact with Kant's philosophy in two distinct stages: "Damals [August 1800: TM], als Zweiundzwanzigjähriger, stand Kleist positiv zu Kant. . . . Dann aber begegnet er Kant als dem Kritiker der Erkenntnis, und der schreckt ihn aus der naiven Sicherheit seines Rationalismus auf, nimmt ihm den fröhlichen Glauben an die All-Einsicht der Vernunft, an die Einsehbarkeit des göttlichen Grundplans überhaupt" (20).

[9] Cf. Ensberg (77): "Kleist verfolgt in den Briefen an seine Verlobte Wilhelmine von Zenge eine Strategie der Selbstdarstellung und Selbstinszenierung, die sich rhetorischer Stilmittel bedient."

[10] Cf. Günter Blöcker: "Nicolo richtet Elvire zugrunde und jagt Piachi aus dem eigenen Hause. Aber das Böse schafft nicht nur Opfer, sondern auch Mittäter. Piachi wird von ihm angesteckt wie einst sein Sohn von der Pest" (136). This popular view, which endorsed uncritically certain statements of the narrator about the character Nicolo while at the same time leaving other, more problematic, aspects aside, held sway, with some reservations, until the mid 1980s. A more even-handed view had been put forward, for example, by Müller-Seidel, who emphasized the tragic edge to events and the perceptive flaws of all three central figures of the story (1967, 69). The new view of the story that emerged in the 1980s pointed to dysfunctional aspects of the family into which Nicolo is introduced (e.g., Jürgen Schröder 1985). This view sees Nicolo's behavior less in terms of inherent failings in his own character and more in terms of the corrupting influence of the "unnatural" family into which

he is introduced. A recent study of the story (Günter Oesterle 1998) has continued to lead attention away from the character of Nicolo. This view has cast the story along the lines of an "Experimentanordnung . . ., in der gezeigt wird, wie die Welthaltung aufklärerisch-bürgerlicher Redlichkeit mit ihrer Kombination aus unmittelbarem Gefühl, kalkulierter Klugheit und risikobereitem Vertrauen in . . . Gefährdung gerät" (167). According to this approach, the story follows the debate inspired by Kant at the end of the eighteenth century on the nature of evil and focuses less on the character of Nicolo than on the question of how, why, and at what point Piachi's altruism turns into its opposite: evil incarnate. The study concludes that Kleist both follows Kant's "ethical revolution" and, at the same time, goes beyond it. Piachi's rejection of absolution in order to pursue the delinquent Nicolo in hell is understood as "ein radikaler, von Kants Autonomieethik ausgehender, sie aber zugleich überschreitender 'Anspruch auf Selbstgesetzgebung'" (179).

[11] This is the word used in the narrative to describe the unlocking of Elvire's identity: "so glaubte Nicolo den Schlüssel zu allen rätselhaften Auftritten dieser Art . . . gefunden zu haben" (Kleist 1983, 2:211).

[12] "Von Zeit zu Zeit holte er sich, mit stillen und geräuschlosen Bewegungen, eine Handvoll Nüsse aus der Tasche, die er bei sich trug, und während Piachi sich die Tränen vom Auge wischte, nahm er sie zwischen die Zähne und knackte sie auf" (Kleist 1983, 2:200–201).

[13] Ezelquiel de Olaso (1997) has pointed out the tensions in Rousseau's view of nature. In the confession by the Savoyard vicar in *Émile ou de l'education* (1762) and also later in *Les Réveries du promeneur solitaire* (1782) Rousseau himself became engulfed in a crisis of doubt owing to an encounter with skeptical thinking.

Works Cited

Blamberger, Günter. "Agonalität und Theatralität. Kleists Gedankenfigur des Duells im Kontext der europäischen Moralistik." *Kleist-Jahrbuch* (1999): 25–40.

Blöcker, Günter. *Heinrich von Kleist oder das absolute Ich.* Berlin: Argon, 1960.

Cassirer, Ernst. *Heinrich von Kleist und die Kantische Philosophie.* Berlin: Reuter & Reichard, 1919.

Cohn, Dorrit. "Kleist's 'Marquise von O . . .': The Problem of Knowledge." *Monatshefte* 67 (1975): 129–44.

Ensberg, Peter. "Das Gefäß des Inhalts: Zum Verhältnis von Philosophie und Literatur am Beispiel der 'Kantkrise' Heinrich von Kleists." In *Beiträge zur Kleist-Forschung.* Ed. Wolfgang Barthel and Hans-Jochen Marquardt. Frankfurt a. d. O.: Kleist-Gedenk- und Forschungsstätte, 1999, 74–75.

Fischer, Bernd. *Ironische Metaphysik: Die Erzählungen Heinrich von Kleists.* Munich: Fink, 1988.

Frank, Manfred. *"Unendliche Annäherung": Die Anfänge der philosophischen Frühromantik.* Frankfurt a.M.: Suhrkamp, 1997.

Greiner, Bernhard. *Eine Art Wahnsinn: Dichtung im Horizonte Kants. Studien zu Goethe und Kleist.* Berlin: Schmidt, 1994.

———. "'Die neueste Philosophie in dieses . . . Land verpflanzen': Kleists literarische Experimente mit Kant," *Kleist-Jahrbuch* (1998): 176–208.

Gundolf, Friedrich. *Heinrich von Kleist.* Berlin: Georg Bondi, 1922.

Horkheimer, Max, and Theodor Adorno. *Dialektik der Aufklärung: Philosophische Fragmente.* 1944. Rpt. Frankfurt a.M.: Fischer, 1985.

Hume, David. *An Enquiry Concerning Human Understanding. D. H. Essays Moral, Political and Literary.* Ed. T. H. Green and T. H. Grose. Aalen: Scientia, 1964.

———. *A Treatise of Human Nature.* 1739. Rpt. London: Penguin, 1969.

Kant, Immanuel. *Kants Werke: Akademie-Textausgabe.* Vol. 4. Berlin: Walter de Gruyter, 1968.

———. *Kritik der reinen Vernunft.* Ed. Raymund Schmidt. 1789. Rpt. Hamburg: Meiner, 1956.

———. *Werke in sechs Bänden.* Vol. 5. Ed. Wilhelm Weischedel. Frankfurt a.M.: Insel, 1964.

Kittler, Wolf. *Die Geburt des Partisanen aus dem Geist der Poesie: Heinrich von Kleist und die Strategie der Befreiungskriege.* Freiburg i. Br.: Rombach, 1987.

Kleist, Heinrich von. *Briefe von und an Heinrich von Kleist. Vol. 4, Sämtliche Werke und Briefe.* Ed. Ilse-Marie Barth, et al. Frankfurt a.M.: Deutscher Klassiker Verlag, 1991.

———. *Sämtliche Werke und Briefe.* 2 Vols. Ed. Helmut Sembdner. 7th ed. Darmstadt: Wissenschaftliche Buchgesellschaft, 1983.

Kulenkampff, Jens. *David Hume.* Munich: Beck, 1989.

Mehigan, Tim, ed. *Heinrich von Kleist und die Aufklärung.* Columbia, SC: Camden House, 2001.

Müller-Seidel, Walter. *Versehen und Erkennen: Eine Studie über Heinrich von Kleist.* 1961. Cologne: Böhlau, 1967.

Muth, Ludwig. *Kleist und Kant: Versuch einer neuen Interpretation.* Kant-Studien. Vol. 68. Cologne: Universitätsverlag, 1954.

Neumann, Gerhard. *Heinrich von Kleist: Kriegsfall — Rechtsfall — Sündenfall.* Freiburg: Rombach, 1994.

Oesterle, Günter. "'Der Findling.'" In *Kleists Erzählungen.* Ed. Walter Hinderer. Stuttgart: Reclam, 1998, 157–80.

Olaso, Ezelquiel de. "The Two Scepticisms of the Savoyard Vicar." In *Scepticism in the Enlightenment.* Ed. R. H. Popkin et al. Boston: Kluwer, 1997, 131–46.

Popkin, R. H. "Scepticism in the Enlightenment." In *Scepticism in the Enlightenment.* Ed. Popkin et al. Boston: Kluwer, 1997, 1–16.

Schröder, Jürgen. "Kleists Novelle 'Der Findling': Ein Plädoyer für Nicolo." *Kleist-Jahrbuch* (1985): 109–27.

Stephens, Anthony. *Heinrich von Kleist: The Plays and the Stories*. Oxford & Providence, RI: Berg, 1994.

Themes and Motifs

Changing Color: Kleist's "Die Verlobung in St. Domingo" and the Discourses of Miscegenation

Susanne Zantop †

> "Was kann ich, deren Vater aus St. Jago, von der Insel Cuba, war, für den Schimmer von Licht, der auf meinem Antlitz, wenn es Tag wird, erdämmert? Und was kann meine Tochter, die in Europa empfangen und geboren ist, dafür, daß der volle Tag jenes Weltteils von dem ihrigen widerscheint?" —
>
> "Wie?" rief der Fremde. "Ihr, die Ihr nach Eurer ganzen Gesichtsbildung eine Mulattin und mithin afrikanischen Ursprungs seid, Ihr wäret samt der lieblichen jungen Mestize, die mir das Haus aufmachte, mit uns Europäern in einer Verdammnis?"
>
> — Kleist, "Die Verlobung in St. Domingo"

> Mestizen: Mischlinge; Kinder, welche einen weißen europäischen Vater und eine schwarze amerikanische oder ostindische Mutter haben, oder auch umgekehrt. Die Ersten heißen *gelbe,* die Zweyten *rothe* Mestizen.
>
> — *Wörterbuch zur Erklärung fremder, aus andern Sprachen in die Deutsche aufgenommener Wörter und Redensarten.* Ed. Conrad Schweizer, Zurich 1811

SKIN COLOR AND skin coloring, as even the most superficial reader will undoubtedly notice, play a key role in Kleist's novella "Die Verlobung in St. Domingo," published in 1811, six years after the independence of the former French colony Saint-Domingue, now Haiti. Color divides the society on the island, as blacks murder whites in their all-out battle to overturn colonial rule. Shades of color cause confusion and undermine automatic allegiances. Whose side is Toni, with her "ins Gelbliche gehenden Gesichtsfarbe" (161), really on: her white fiancé Gustav's, or her black extended family's, represented by Babekan and Congo Hoango? Why does "yellow" fever not just destroy the European colonial troops but also serve in this story to define the insidious disease (in the eyes of the white narrator) the black woman is transmitting to the white man in the act of lovemaking/revenge? What does the tone red indicate — Gustav's blushing after admitting to his infatuation with Toni's black eyes (168), Toni's reddening after his suggestion that she might prefer a white man to her black suitor (173), and Toni's flushing with anger as Babekan is explaining her perfidious plan to murder whites? And why does Gustav change color when he perceives the mestiza Toni, as she enters the room with a black boy on her arm and hand-in-hand with a white man? Clearly, black, white, yellow, and red are central markers that hold the story together, drive the characters' actions, create unions, and tear them apart. As signs of difference and clues to personality, motivations, and positionality, they guide not only the participants in this colonial drama but also the readers. Yet, more often than not, they are ambiguous signs that invite *and* defy interpretation and cause misunderstanding, extreme suffering, even death. And clearly, the shades of color are indicators of degrees of attachment: products of forced or voluntary unions, unnatural or natural families, violence or love. In other words, they point to a complex history of race relations on the Caribbean island from the advent of Europeans and African slaves to the slave uprisings and decolonization struggles of the late eighteenth and early nineteenth centuries.

It is not surprising that Kleist's story has elicited much debate about the meaning of color and of racial difference — particularly, but not exclusively, among critics in the United States, to whom race relations are of immediate existential concern, and particularly after the civil rights movement and identity politics have increased awareness of the interplay among historical, individual, and structural racism.[1] Roughly speaking, two kinds of critical approaches have been made to the racial politics of "Die Verlobung in St. Domingo": those that concentrate on Kleist's narrative strategies in the text, on the one hand, and, on the other hand, those that situate the text in the context of other personal and literary utterances by Kleist or in the context of a variety of contemporaneous discourses on colonialism, imperialism, race, and gender. Peter Horn of the University of Capetown first raised the issue of Kleist's position on race in his 1975 article "Hatte Kleist Rassenvorurteile?"[2] in which he answered the title question in the negative on the basis of the novella's complex narrative structure. Later attempts to vindicate Kleist resorted to the same strategy, pointing to conflicting, mutually undercutting perspectives (the narrator's, Gustav's, Toni's, Babekan's, etc.) and stories (Babekan's, the sick slave's, Marianne's) that, in the end, defy simple ideological attributions. Thus, Ruth Angress pits the narrator, who "slants [the facts] to suit the oppressor's point of view" (22), against Babekan and Congo Hoango, whose narratives, if we listen closely, betray "smoldering rage" (23) at the treachery and cruelty suffered at the hands of whites. To her, the confrontation of racist accounts with histories of suffering reveals Kleist's sympathies with the oppressed, rather than a conservative agenda. In a similar vein, although with differing emphases, Sander Gilman, Klaus Müller-Salget, Bernd Fischer, Hans Jakob Werlen, and Ray Fleming have found in the black-vs.-white binary, whose epistemological limitations trigger the catastrophe, evidence of Kleist's "political deconstruction" (Fischer 111) of a rigid aesthetic-moral-economic value system based on skin color. Kleist, they argue, presents white characters who are caught in oppositional thinking and in an "aesthetics of blackness" (cf. Gilman) that associates blackness with terror, violence, and depravity and whiteness with light, succor, and goodness. These mental structures disable the characters from properly assessing the historical reality that surrounds them and the lives and thoughts of "the people of color whom they encounter" (Fleming 308). As Werlen suggests in his psychoanalytically informed reading of the novella:

> The story of Toni's seduction and ultimate betrayal *iterates and simultaneously subverts* a discourse of race which contrasts superior white paternal lineage (Europe) with inferior black maternal lineage (Africa). At the same time, *Kleist's text reveals* the aporetic nature of the universalized enlightenment tenet of equality by demonstrating its dependence on the exclusion of people differing from the white norm. (459–60, my emphasis)

While he does not go so far as to impute Kleist the author with an antiracist agenda, his focus on the text's political unconscious leads him to emphasize its subversive over its affirmative potential.

Proponents of a less positive assessment of Kleist's race politics have not failed to see the dialectics at play in the novella. Their analyses, however, focus less on the subversion of the "master" discourse by slaves' narratives *inside* the text than on the support this master discourse has received in Kleist's other works, such as the *Hermannsschlacht,* or in the writings of authors form which his text drew, such as Heinrich Zschokke's, Louis Dubroca's, Marcus Rainsford's, and Jonathan Edwards's accounts of the situation in the Caribbean plantation colonies (Fink 70–71, 74; Uerlings "Preußen," 189–90). Although Herbert Uerlings, for example, acknowledges Kleist's ambiguous language and sharp critique of conditions in the French plantation colony, he concludes that Kleist does not engage in a "sustained, principled rejection of colonialism and slavery as a 'structural power relationship,' nor a justification of the abolition of slavery by revolutionary means" (Uerlings "Preußen," 192, my translation). According to him, Kleist's compassion for the black slaves and their cause fits well within the abolitionist literature of the late eighteenth century, which, while it laments violent excesses, only advocates an end to the slave *trade* and a return to a kinder, gentler paternalist plantation system.

In Uerlings's analysis, the love story of the two "light-skinned" protagonists, Toni and Gustav, and their failed communication take precedence over complications arising from a racist mindset and colonialist power differential (cf. 194 and Uerlings 1997, 25). As he reiterates in his more recent study, *Poetiken der Interkulturalität: Haiti bei Kleist, Seghers, Müller, Buch und Fichte* (1997), "primarily, the 'Verlobung' is not a discourse on the colonization of the far away, but of the nearby, it is not about cultural, but about sexual alterity" (34, my translation). Uerlings's apodictic conclusion is surprising, particularly since he, like Sigrid Weigel before him, places his analysis of the love story in the novella squarely in the context of colonialism, where discourses of race and gender relations intersect, reinforce one another, and determine individual and collective behavior.[3] As all analyses of the novella — Uerlings's included — point out, only the violent colonial traditions and the context of anticolonial insurgence allow us fully to understand Gustav's anxieties about Toni's insufficient whiteness and, hence, about her commitment to their love.[4] Only a tradition of white man's desire for, and power over, the woman of color can explain the oscillation between trust and distrust, attraction and repulsion constitutive of the colonizer's subjectivity (Bhabha) — whether he is part of the plantocracy or a Swiss mercenary in its service. It, therefore, seems more productive not to dwell on teasing out certainties, that is, whether the novella is about colonial relations between whites and blacks *or* about love relations among whites, about the Other *or* the self, about politics *or* feelings, race *or* gender. Instead, I will focus on the moments of intersection between these binaries, what Weigel termed the "Kreuzpunkt," the actual and metaphoric "miscegenation" the text proposes, problematizes, and plays with. I argue that in the figure of the "Kreuzung" (cross-breeding *and* crossroads — one of the German translations of *miscegenation*), the topic of cross-racial love is tied to the violent historical encounter between whites and blacks. Kleist's text evokes the mix of desire and fear, permissiveness and interdiction, "seduction and betrayal" (cf. Werlen) that undergirds the colonial situation. By focusing on miscegenation it raises, again, the question of the meaning of "color." Its extraordinary power resides in the ambiguities, the overlapping of traditions, feelings, perceptions, and expectations, in short, the physical (and metaphorical) mixing that precedes, determines, and eventually undermines the "contract," the betrothal, between Gustav and Toni, the white, not-quite-colonizer and the not-quite-black colonized. If we read Kleist's text not just as an intervention in contemporaneous discourses on race and gender but, much more specifically, as an intervention in the discourses and psychology of miscegenation, we can better assess the degree to which he articulated, recast, or reconfirmed the desires, fears, and traumas of his European readers when it comes to their relationship to "racial" others. Instead of focusing on white and black, I shall, therefore, concentrate on red and yellow as ambiguous signifiers of various kinds of intersections — or, rather, "Kreuzungen" — both in contemporary popular anthropology and in the text itself.

Ever since Immanuel Kant in 1785 declared skin color to be the determinant factor in the formation of the four distinct human races — "Weisse," "gelbe Indianer," "Neger," and "kupferfarbig-rothe Amerikaner" — skin color as distinctive hereditary property has been at the forefront of "scientific" attention.[5] Most late-eighteenth- and early-nineteenth-century European anthropologists seek to find out not only how and into how many categories humanity can be classified by color but also how skin color fares in racial mixing and how it relates to inner — that is, intellectual or moral — qualities; in other words, how it is to be read. Speculations about the effect of miscegenation are fed by two assumptions that emerge in the context of colonialist expansion and the Lavaterian physiognomical craze: that skin color (like other physiognomic properties such as shape of skull, chin, or nose, and amount and consistency of hair)[6] is an outward expression of inner qualities; and that the military defeat of colonized peoples by superior European forces indicates a cultural-intellectual inferiority of which skin color is one, albeit the most prominent, sign. In other words, skin color signals aesthetic, moral, and cultural superiority or inferiority; it inspires trustworthiness or suspicion.

In order to signal, skin has to be transparent, readable. The whiter, and hence the "thinner" the skin, the more it allows one to see what is underneath: the flow of blood, the emotions, the moral responses. As art historian Angela Rosenthal has argued, racially and culturally "superior" whiteness found its emblematic expression in the blushing white women depicted in countless portraits at the end of the eighteenth century. Referring to texts by British intellectuals such as Charles White (1799) and Charles Bell (1806) — to which one could easily add Germans such as Christoph Meiners and Christian Ernst Wünsch — Rosenthal proposes that late-eighteenth-century Europeans anchored the aesthetic and moral superiority of the white race in the ability of white women to turn red (13). Whiteness is thus constituted in opposition to, or "highlighted by," blackness and against the backdrop of redness: Only that skin that can visibly "change" color can betray emotional, moral, and intellectual "movement," hence the capacity for improvement, for progress.[7] Blacks, whose "thick" skin supposedly prevents this reading process, who cannot "change color," it was argued, are unable to attain a higher stage of morality and, hence, civilization.[8]

The tantalizing question in this rigid moral and developmental color scheme was, of course, what would happen upon the mixing of colors. In other words: which faculties would be gained or lost when people of different races engaged in sexual relations and produced offspring — a question that, judging by its obsessive reiteration, was of theoretical as well as practical consequence at a time of violent decolonization battles among plantation owners, slaves, and freed slaves — or, rather, among white, black, and "yellow" people.[9]

All major anthropologists of the time agreed that if persons of different races mated, the offspring would have an equal share of their parents' physical characteristics. Consequently, philosophers and scholars such as Kant, Johann Friedrich Blumenbach, and Christoph Girtanner spent much thought on imagining and classifying the physiological outcome of racial mixing. Girtanner, for example, dedicated over 100 pages of his comments on Kant to elaborating on the "flesh-colored," "dark-yellow," "brown-yellow," and "brown-white" varieties that would emerge if white and black, "olive-yellow," brown, and "cinnamon-colored" humans intermarried. Despite their strong and uniform views on "racial character" — owing to an "astonishing level of what, today, we would call intertextuality" (Eze 1997, 6) — few serious anthropologists offered suggestions as to the moral-cultural consequences of this miscegenation, maybe because these consequences would be too hard to observe or quantify.[10] Among the ones who did venture to speculate, Meiners and Wünsch were arguably the most influential. As professors of philosophy, anthropology, and physical geography at Göttingen and Frankfurt an der Oder, and as prolific writers of middle-brow treatises on "human nature," they summarized scattered observations on racial character read elsewhere, translated them into easily digestible "theories," and distributed these theories widely, thereby modeling and triggering discussions on the consequences of "bastardization."[11] As Kleist's teacher, Wünsch has (for us) the added advantage of having had a direct impact on Kleist's thinking and possibly on his writing.[12]

Meiners revisits the question of miscegenation repeatedly in the context of the recently erupted slave rebellions in a series of articles published in the *Göttingisches Historisches Magazin/Neues Göttingisches Historisches Magazin*, which he founded in 1787: "Ueber die Natur der Afrikanischen Neger, und die davon abhangende Befreyung, oder Einschränkung der Schwarzen" (1790), "Von den Varietäten und Abarten der Neger" (1790), "Historische Nachrichten über die wahre Beschaffenheit des Sclaven-Handels, und der Knechtschaft der Neger in West-Indien" (1790), "Ueber die Ausartung der Europäer in fremden Erdtheilen" (1791), and "Ueber die Farben und Schattierungen verschiedener Völker" (1792). Wünsch addresses miscegenation in his anthropological textbook *Unterhaltungen über den Menschen* (1780; 2nd ed. 1796), which, following the "Socratic" model espoused by Joachim Heinrich Campe in his pedagogical tracts for young people, includes conversations between a teacher, "Philalectes," and two students who occasionally interject a question into the former's expository prose. Despite the difference in format and the time differential, the texts by both anthropologists exhibit an uncanny overlap in wording — and an even uncannier correspondence with utterances of both Kleist's narrator and his protagonist Gustav.

For both Meiners and Wünsch whites and blacks are diametrically opposed races. Their difference is rooted in immutable biological properties, particularly skin color and skull formation (Wünsch 238). For both men these physical characteristics do not just carry aesthetic connotations (beautiful vs. ugly) but signal moral and intellectual differences: Africans are cowards, cannibals, "savage beasts" who practice slavery among themselves (Wünsch 229–32, 371); they have not yet seen the light of reason (232); they are lazy, weak, dumb, promiscuous (cf. Meiners "Ueber die Natur," 422–37), and treacherous:

> As skillful as Negroes are when it comes to stealing and cheating, as skillful they are when it comes to flattering or poisoning, and — as far as the Negresses are concerned — to seducing and ruining their lovers. Even if the Negresses detest their white lovers or betray them daily, they know how to simulate the most passionate love, the most unflinching jealousy with such artfulness, that they deceive the artless whites constantly, and for a long time. Once they have bereft the whites of their whole fortune to the last penny, they abandon them with a contemptuous laughter. (434, my translation)

Blacks, according to Meiners, are masters of disguise, which they employ to take revenge on Europeans: "The Negroes . . . do not know any stirrings of gratefulness, nor of compassion, shared enjoyment, or admiration for good and noble deeds" (439, my translation). Their "lust for revenge" is "immeasurable, irreconcilable, hidden" (443, my translation). Europeans, in turn, are industrious, strong, intelligent, beautiful, and moral (although their greed often keeps them from acting morally [Wünsch 238 and 261–62]). When it comes to racial stereotyping — and despite the occasional abolitionist remark by Wünsch or a critique of abuses in the plantation system voiced by Meiners — both thus follow patterns established by prior anthropologists/natural philosophers and travelers to Africa and the plantation owners themselves (cf. Mielke 249).

Both are at the "scientific" vanguard in developing theories of miscegenation. Earlier climatological explanations of racial difference (Montesquieu, Buffon, Forster, Kant) linger on when they claim that strong sunshine and hot winds account for the differences in color among different peoples that — they surmise — may eventually become genetic properties. While they do not want to reject these explanations outright, however — there is, of course, abundant evidence that sunshine does affect the shade of the skin, at least temporarily — their main focus is on the changes in skin color brought about by the mixing of "blood." As Wünsch states: "Such [genetic] changes occur at a much more rapid pace, when people of different colors marry one another and procreate; because there even the first generations occupy the middle between the darker and lighter shade of father and mother and are called 'mulattoes,' if produced by brown and black, and 'mestizos,' if produced by white and brown parents" (378–79). Likewise, Meiners postulates that

> the mulattos and mulattas, the first descendants of European fathers and Negresses, share at least half of the color, intelligence, abilities, and virtues of their fathers, and, most of the time, the better blood dominates so that the children of white men and black women resemble more their fathers than their mothers. The color of mulattos is yellow, and many resemble Spaniards. (Meiners "Von den Varietäten," 640, my translation)

Miscegenation can, therefore, lead to the improvement or decline of the races, depending on the sides on which one looks. It ennobles (643) the black race but leads to the degeneration of the white: "One loses with the European blood and European sensibility also the European strength and European nobility." Transplanted into colonies, particularly the "Sugar Islands," Europeans become sluggish, promiscuous, diseased, and insensitive to the sufferings of others, in other words, their slaves (cf. Meiners 1791, 221–22, 261).

In view of this dual outcome of miscegenation, it remains unclear what Wünsch or Meiners would actually advocate. Wünsch does not

broach the subject, and Meiners seems to imply that the progressive enno-
bling of the slaves (cf. Meiners "Historische Nachrichten," 664) will, in
the long run, have beneficial effects on the colonies, for it will make the
whip and other forms of punishment obsolete, will allow more and more
blacks to be released into freedom, and will change the plantation system
from within, without a violent overthrow. Meiners's insistence on the
European's degeneration in the colonies, however, to which he repeatedly
returns, might suggest that from a European perspective, he would consider "amalgamation" (Jefferson) a degradation and, hence, reprehensible.

The combination of the simple physiognomic Platonism — that a
few physical characteristics such as skin color or shape of skull signal a
specific abject "racial character" — with the schematic quantitative theory of racial improvement through miscegenation had to generate its
own brand of ambiguities: for if blacks are passionate, promiscuous,
vindictive, lazy, etc., would they shed all of these properties gradually, or
some of them (and which ones?) through racial mixing? As Meiners puts
it, "as much as mulattos and mulattas may want to elevate themselves
above the Negroes, many of the shortcomings of their half-Negro-status
still stick to them, such as a lesser propensity for work, a greater prone-
ness to luxury, vanity, pride, and untrustworthiness" (Meiners "Von den
Varietäten," 641, my translation). In other words, how many generations
would it take to "cleanse" mixed races of their blemishes, particularly
since, as Meiners readily admits, not all Europeans are quite as unblem-
ished as theory would have it? How can one "know" for sure which of
the "father's" positive traits have been inherited by a "yellow" mulatto
or a "yellowish" mestizo? How can one properly read yellow skin and
come to unshakable conclusions?

These are precisely the questions Kleist raises. While he does not
provide any answers, he problematizes the simplistic theories Meiners
and Wünsch proposed by showing that this reading process, while never
granting ultimate certainty, requires at the very least contextual knowledge — that is, a solid understanding of personal histories and collective
history — if it is to yield any insights.

In "Die Verlobung in St. Domingo" it is Gustav who is faced with
the task of "reading" skin color under extreme duress. While he seeks
clarity ("seid ihr eine Negerin?" [162]), his two "texts," the mulatta
Babekan and her "mestiza" daughter Toni,[13] are presented as ambigu-
ously located between black and white and, therefore, as hard to decipher. Finding himself in a life-threatening situation, Gustav needs to
distinguish between friend and foe. Steeped as he is in racist thinking,
according to which skin color provides clues about character and moti-

vations, and under the immediate impact of traumatic political experiences that have pitted "blacks" against "whites," he is bewildered when confronted with a "mixed" reality. His survival seems to hinge on his interpretation of the color of Babekan's face: "aus der Farbe Eures Gesichts schimmert mir ein Strahl von der meinigen entgegen" (164). And yet, at the same time, her color carries a shadow of kinship with *them* (165), the blacks in revolt. Fixated as Gustav (and the whole colonial society) is on the meaning of skin color, "brownness" as indicator of miscegenation supposedly provides the only key to her behavior — a key that opens up no insights, while setting in motion questions provided by the racist context in which he has operated: is she treacherous ("like all blacks") or trustworthy ("like all whites"), vindictive or grateful, scheming or authentic? Which of her "inherited" traits predominate in the mix?

Gustav's blindness to the historical implications of miscegenation, which could have provided him with clues about her *motives,* that is, her inner life, is particularly evident in his response to her personal story: Babekan tells him — carefully avoiding offensive terminology and "mit unterdrückter Empfindlichkeit" (169) — that she, as a slave, accompanied Mme de Villeneuve to Paris; that she conceived Toni by the French merchant Bertrand, who, before a court, formally repudiated the paternity, and that her master ordered her to be lashed, on top of a bilious fever she contracted in response to Bertrand's rejection. We do not know whether her relationship with Bertrand was consensual, but her status as a mulatto slave and the response of the two white men after she had the audacity to claim her right in court indicate that — as in all other sexual master-slave relationships — a consensual relation is out of the question.[14] The bilious fever, the lashes and subsequent consumption, furthermore, suggest to her audience that Babekan responded to the traumatic event with impotent rage, a rage that is still *evident* to those who can hear or see. Gustav, however, responds to this tale of physical and spiritual violence with "Verlegenheit" (169) and changes the subject.

Gustav's inability to read historically grown race constellations is highlighted in a parallel story of miscegenation, his tale of the young girl "vom Stamm der Negern" (170) who takes revenge on her former master by infecting him with yellow fever during sexual intercourse. First, Gustav misrepresents or muddles her status as a slave and, hence, the power differential: His sentence "sie hatte drei Jahre zuvor einem Pflanzer vom Geschlecht der Weißen als Sklavin gedient" indicates that she is no longer a slave, which is belied by the fact that this planter had sold her "an einen kreolischen Pflanzer" (170). Then, in his description of the events Gustav sides with the planter, playing down the monstrosity of the man's actions by highlighting the monstrosity of hers: Gustav circumscribes the master's attempted rape of his slave as "weil sie sich seinen Wünschen nicht willfährig gezeigt hatte" and his violent revenge, his whippings, merely as "hart behandelt," borne out of "Empfindlichkeit," a sense of personal hurt at her rejection of him (170). *Her* act of revenge, in turn (a "Verrat" [171]) typical of blacks, of course), is underscored by the opposition between her "wilder, kalter Wut" and his "Dankbarkeit," and by the pestilence with which she honors his kisses (170). Gustav's tropes mask what is, at heart, a relationship of inequality and violent coercion. After all, the planter had tried to impose his desire on his female slave, whereas when he later accepts her invitation to spend the night with her, he does so out of his free will, in the hope of saving his skin. In fact, the partners "get equal" because the man, displaced from his elevated position by the slave rebellion, is seeking help, whereas the woman transmits to him the germ of death she *herself* carries inside.

Since Gustav is unable to understand the systemic power differential between white and black under colonialism and its impact on any "love relationship" between the races — the meaningful glances exchanged by mother and daughter annoy him — he cannot fathom the depth of their resentment and the driving force behind Babekan's actions. The yellow color of the "bilial" and "yellow" fevers, both results of sexual contact, connect these two stories to the often violent mixing of black and white under colonialism. The diseases point to the traumatic nature of colonial cross-racial sexual encounters. As Tim Dean has recently argued in his study of colonial trauma and disease, "colonial trauma entails sexual trauma, not that one is simply a metaphor for the other" (323). Dean's argument focuses on Conrad's *Heart of Darkness*, the Belgian Congo, and the discussion of the origins of AIDS; yet, his insights apply to other colonial situations, as well. Disease — whether syphilis (as in the case of the First Encounters), AIDS (as in current neocolonial situations), or yellow fever (the disease that defeated European troops during the Saint-Domingue uprisings) — can be seen as a consequence of the "literal intertwining of imperial and subaltern subjects," concretely and metaphorically. It is "the legacy of the trauma of colonialism, the involuntary mixing of populations characterized by an imbalance of power" — a legacy, according to Dean, that comes to the fore during *de*colonization (323). In Babekan's and Gustav's stories, the link between sexual and colonial violence and disease is made explicit: both "produce" the color yellow.

If Gustav is unable to read Babekan's story "through" her skin color, the situation, at first sight, seems to be more clear-cut in Toni's case, and therefore, perhaps, less so: as a daughter of a white man and a mulatta,

202 ◆ SUSANNE ZANTOP

Toni is, by the European standards of the time, white. Her "whiteness," underscored by white clothes and "eine entfernte Ähnlichkeit" (172) to his former love Marianne Congreve, inspires confidence. Yet Gustav never completely transcends his ambivalence because of his fixation on skin as the site of cultural meaning. On the one hand, he claims that looking into Toni's eyes tells him more about her true nature than her complexion (Hätte ich dir . . . ins Auge sehen können, so wie ich es jetzt kann: so hätte ich, auch wenn alles Übrige an dir schwarz gewesen wäre, aus einem vergifteten Becher mit dir trinken wollen" [168]); on the other hand, we learn that her yellowish complexion "ihm anstößig war" (172). Caught between attraction and repulsion and forced by necessity to gain clarity and establish firm allegiances, Gustav draws Toni to his knees, knowing "daß es nur ein Mittel gab, zu erprüfen, ob das Mädchen ein Herz habe oder nicht" (172). When Gustav asks "ob es vielleicht ein Weißer sein müsse, der ihre Gunst davon tragen solle, . . . ein überaus reizende(s) Erröten" spreads over her "verbranntes Gesicht" (173). Redness seems to obliterate once and for all the yellowish hue that had betrayed her mixed heritage: a sunburn is a condition that only affects delicate whiteness. As a sign of emotion the red blush thus assuages all of Gustav's fears that underneath her yellowish skin she might not be as white as the surface suggests. The sexual encounter, the mingling of tears, and the verbal betrothal symbolized by the cross calm the "Taumel wunderbar verwirrter Sinne, eine Mischung aus Begierde und Angst, die sie ihm eingeflößt" (175).

And yet, this seemingly consensual commingling again raises more questions than it answers. The love that drives the two unequal partners is, again, marred by the complexities of race and historical power relations. Gustav is called upon to interpret another story of miscegenation as it unfolds in front of him, and again his exclusive focus on color keeps him from understanding the intricacies of the situation. First, there is the lack of clarity as to his own motivations: is he overcome by his sexual attraction for the beautiful light-skinned woman with dark locks and black eyes, or is this sexual conquest a last, desperate attempt to ensure protection by making her his ally ("inzwischen sah er so viel ein, daß er gerettet, und in dem Hause, in welchem er sich befand, für ihn nichts von dem Mädchen zu befürchten war" [175])? Was the sexual act a form of rape, taking advantage of an inexperienced virgin, even though Toni, overcome by emotion, freely sank into his arms? What explanations do we or does he have for her profuse tears, her laments, her lifelessness or listlessness ("wie eine Leblose" [176]) afterward? What causes her desperate reaction — the violence of the act of defloration, her bad conscience and shame at having crossed a forbidden threshold, her consciousness of sin, or her fear of her mother's wrath? What causes the breakdown of clear-cut boundaries between whites and blacks, bad and good that had marked her previous world? How do we interpret Gustav's protestations, his promises of eternal love, marriage, and emotional and financial amends? As an attempt to placate her to save his (white) skin, as a sign of true love (so suddenly, and under duress?), or as an unwitting attempt to remedy a tradition of one-sided abuse by elevating concubinage — the only accepted relationship between planter and slave woman — to marriage? How can love or consensual love relations flourish at a moment of violent crisis, and when two partners have nothing on which to rely on aside from a few visual impressions of the other?

Not surprisingly, Gustav — whose understanding of race relations is framed by notions of the blacks' infamous treachery (171) and the lasciviousness of black women ("Hure" [192]), to which Meiners and Wünsch allude[15] — is ready to accuse Toni as soon as the situation becomes murky and interpretation difficult. His "Blicke voll Verachtung" (187) follow professions of eternal love instantaneously, that is, unhampered by reflection: they are part of his subconscious. He gives up on Toni's loyalty as soon as present actions seem to contradict former ones, that is, as soon as actions turn ambiguous. When Toni, "den Knaben Seppy auf dem Arm, an der Hand Herrn Strömli" (192), enters the room, he fires a shot straight at her. Her position between colors — literally between the white man, whose hand she holds, and the black "bastard" boy, whom she carries on her arm — makes her into an emblem of miscegenation and, therefore, of ambiguity, ready to be misread. The "colonial family" that the image seemingly reenacts — a kind of holy trinity framed by the door — is, thus, nothing but a short-lived vision of harmony, an illusion to the sentimental mind of the white observer (Gustav). He evokes familial or erotic relations between whites and blacks (for example, love, betrothal, family) but can never fully trust them, because he knows deep down that they are built on violence.

In the context of the unreadability of skin color, it is significant that Gustav changes color as soon as he sees Toni's ambiguous positioning: "wechselte bei diesem Anblick die Farbe" (192). Whether he turns white as a sheet or red with rage we do not know. What we do know is that Gustav's preconceptions about color have made him incapable of understanding that color, or changes of color, in themselves mean nothing. They are only meaningful insofar as particular historical constellations have attributed (or continue to attribute) meaning to shades of color, and they are only meaningful to those able to read these intricate historical constellations and their own position and investments in them. The question whether Kleist was racist, whether he himself believed in the physical, intellectual, or moral superiority of whites to blacks, thus seems irrelevant. Whether Kleist intended it or not, the text he created raises the issue of the "physiognomic readability of skin colors" (Benthien 186) as it places it squarely into the context of colonial-anticolonial violence. The tragic endings of all stories of miscegenation in this failed "betrothal" suggest that love between the "races" is impossible, as long as an exclusive fixation on skin color and historical preconceptions about the meaning of black, yellow, red, *and* white persist.

Notes

[1] The year 1975 seems to mark a paradigmatic change. Papers written before that date, such as Wolfgang Mieder's, stress formal or existential questions ("Doch das Thema der Novelle gilt nicht dem alles aufwühlenden Rassenkonflikt," 397); those written afterward (Gilman, Angress-Klüger, Fischer, Fink, Uerlings, and Zantop 1997) see race and colonial conflicts as the novella's structural center.

[2] To Horn's dismay, pre-1970 discussions analyze Kleist from the perspective of a Nazi-inspired, racist "Blut- und Rassenmystik" (Congo Hoango as the "blutrünstige Neger . . . der Neger überhaupt," 119) or depoliticize him altogether.

[3] Uerlings's insistence that "die Liebe zwischen Toni und Gustav ist — in dieser Sicht — weniger eine zwischen den Rassen als eine zwischen Menschen heller Hautfarbe" (Uerlings "Preußen," 194; 1997, 25) is surprising in view of his own elaboration of Gustav's repeated attempts to "declare" Toni white, to overcome his revulsion at her "yellow" skin color. The statement is even more surprising, since Uerlings places his analysis of the love affair in the context of colonial and race discourse, to which he returns at the end of the chapter: "Die Gewalttätigkeit, die im Kolonialverhältnis steckt, tritt bei Kleist zutage, und zwar, auch dies eine Besonderheit, im Innern des weißen männlichen Subjekts. . . . In Kleists Verlobung begegnen sich ein kolonialer Diskurs, in dem die kulturelle Fremde immer schon nach dem Muster der sexuell Fremden gedacht wurde, und ein Diskurs über Vertrauen und Verrat zwischen den Geschlechtern und unstillbare Kontrollbedürfnisse" (Uerlings 1997, 48–49).

[4] As Werlen correctly states, "Gustav and the narrator will go to great lengths to overcome this obstacle [Toni's threatening yellow skin color], to whiten out the blemish" (462).

[5] On Kant's importance as a theoretician of race, particularly in Germany, see Eze 1997, 2–4 and 1995, 202–4. Before Kant, natural historians Bernier, Buffon, and LeCat in France had already speculated on the reasons for black as opposed to white skin color. For a discussion of theories of blackness in eighteenth- and nineteenth-century Europe, see Benthien 172–74.

[6] See my discussion in *Colonial Fantasies,* chapters 3 and 4, and "Der Indianer."

[7] Contrasting albinos, "blafards" or "white Negroes" with Europeans, Wünsch, for example, writes: "und sie sind nicht etwa angenehm weiß wie die Blondins und Blondinen unter den Europäern, bei welchen das Blut in den größern und kleinen Adern durch die Oberfläche der Haut hervor scheint, folglich stets eine angenehme Schattierung von Blau und Purpur unter das europäische Weiß einmischt, sondern sie haben vielmehr einen wassersüchtigen oder kreidefarbigen und öfters mit kleinen eingesprengten grauen Flecken getiegerten Teint, woran gar keine Spuhr von Röthe und Fleischfarbe zu finden ist" (325). On theories of readability of skin in the eighteenth and nineteenth centuries see also Benthien 119–21.

[8] See Meiners, "Ueber die Natur" 404. The theories about the skin's composition vary. According to Kant, the thin top layer of skin lets the blood shine through; in black Africans, the blood is saturated with "phlogiston," which gives it a blackish appearance, even though, deeper inside the body, it is actually red. Wünsch blames the black skin color on the "Schleimnetz" that underlies the transparent "Oberhäutchen" and that, together with the "darker" blood, gives the skin its distinctive color (379–80). Blumenbach locates blackness in an "excess of carbonaceum elementum," which mixes with "hydrogen" in the human body and settles under the top layer of skin (97).

[9] See, for example, the proliferation of "casta painting" in late eighteenth and early nineteenth centuries. As Ilona Katzew explains, the paintings of mixed races and their offspring were related to "anxiety over loss of control because of race mixing" in the Spanish colonies (8, 13) and the subsequent decline of social status. Within the Spanish-American context, the basic principle was that "Spanish or white blood is redeemable, Black is not. In other words, while the purity of the Spanish blood was inextricably linked to the idea of 'civilization,' Black blood, bearing the stigma of slavery, connoted atavism and degeneracy" (10).

[10] See Kant, "Bestimmung des Begrifs," paragraphs 4–6 (397–417); Blumenbach 107–12; Girtanner 59–143.

[11] For Meiners's long-term influence on popular perceptions, see Rupp-Eisenreich and Zantop, "The Beautiful."

[12] Kleist studied in Frankfurt an der Oder under Wünsch, whose course on experimental physics he attended in 1799–1800. Grathoff, whose information on Wünsch's publication dates contains some errors (according to him, Wünsch published the *Unterhaltungen* in 1791/98, rather than in 1789/1796), concludes that "die Kleistforschung hat dieses wichtige Material sonst durchweg ignoriert" (38).

[13] See the discussion in Müller-Salget, who takes issue with previous attempts to convey a special status to Toni on the basis of an historical reading of the term *mestizo*. Meiners, in his "Ueber die Farben, und Schattierungen verschiedener Völker," provides further evidence that *Mestize* was in use for children of whites and mulattos: "Children of white fathers and mulatto women are called 'Mastisen' and 'Mastisinnen' in some places . . .; in other places, they are called 'Tercerons.' As a rule, the skin of Mastisen or Tercerons is somewhere in the middle between the white of Europeans and the yellow of mulattoes" (638–39). See also Blumenbach: "Die Europäer [zeugen] mit den Mulatten Terceronen, welche einige aber Quarteronen, andere Moriscen, ja selbst Mestizen nennen" (109).

[14] Speaking about Jefferson's long-term relationship with his slave Sally Hemmings, Peter S. Onuf reminds us that the power differential between white and black, man and woman precluded consensuality: "Sexual attraction does not necessarily lead to romantic love; masters did force their slaves to have sex; even white domestic servants often found themselves vulnerable to sexual exploitation — thirty-eight years of sexual intimacy would not have to mean that the relationship involved respect and mutuality or was devoid of coercion. In Jefferson's times, wives — let alone slaves — had no right to deny sex to that man to whom they were legally bound" (193).

[15] Significantly, these two epithets come to the minds of her black kinfolk, as well; suspecting her crossing of the color line, Congo Hoango immediately calls her "disloyal traitor," and Babekan calls her "deceitful hussy," anticipating Gustav's verdict (258).

Works Cited

Angress, Ruth. "Kleist's Treatment of Imperialism: 'Die Hermannsschlacht' and 'Die Verlobung in St. Domingo.'" *Monatshefte* 69 (1977): 17–33.

Benthien, Claudia. *Haut: Literaturgeschichte — Körperbilder — Grenzdiskurse.* Reinbek: Rowohlt, 1999.

Blumenbach, Johann Friedrich. *The Anthropological Treatises of Johann Friedrich Blumenbach.* Trans. Thomas Bendyshe. London: Longman, 1865.

Dean, Tim. "The Germs of Empires: Heart of Darkness, Colonial Trauma, and the Historiography of AIDS." In *The Psychoanalysis of Race.* Ed. Christopher Lane. New York: Columbia UP, 1998, 305–28.

Eze, Emmanuel Chewed. "The Color of Reason: The Idea of 'Race' in Kant's Anthropology." In *Anthropology and the German Enlightenment: Perspectives on Humanity.* Ed. Katherine M. Fall. Lewisburg, PA: Bucknell UP, 1995.

Eze, Emmanuel Chewed, ed. *Race and the Enlightenment: A Reader.* Cambridge: Blackwell, 1997.

Fink, Gonthier-Louis. "Das Motiv der Rebellion in Kleists Werk im Spannungs- feld der Französischen Revolution und der Napoleonischen Kriege." *Kleist- Jahrbuch* (1988–89): 64–88.

Fischer, Bernd. "Zur politischen Dimension der Ethik in Kleists 'Die Verlobung in St. Domingo.'" In *Heinrich von Kleist: Studien zu Werk und Wirkung.* Ed. Dirk Grathoff. Opladen: Westdeutscher Verlag, 1988, 248–62.

Fleming, Ray. "Race and the Difference It Makes in Kleist's *Die Verlobung in St. Domingo.*" *German Quarterly* 65 (1992): 306–17.

Gilman, Sander. "The Aesthetics of Blackness in Heinrich von Kleist's 'Die Verlobung in St. Domingo.'" *Modern Language Notes* 90 (1975): 661–72.

———. *On Blackness without Blacks: Essays on the Image of the Black in Germany.* Boston: Hall, 1982.

Girtanner, Christoph. *Ueber das Kantische Prinzip für die Naturgeschichte: Ein Versuch diese Wissenschaft philosophsch zu behandeln.* Göttingen: Vandenhoek, 1796.

Grathoff, Dirk. *Kleists Geheimnisse: Unbekannte Seiten einer Biographie.* Opladen: Westdeutscher Verlag, 1993.

Horn, Peter. "Hatte Kleist Rassenvorurteile? Eine kritische Auseinandersetzung mit der Literatur zur 'Verlobung in St. Domingo.'" *Monatshefte* 67 (1975): 117–28.

Kant, Immanuel. "Bestimmung des Begrifs [sic] einer Menschenrace." *Berlinische Monatsschrift* 6 (1787): 390–417.

Katzew, Ilona. "Casta Painting: Identity and Social Stratification in Colonial Mexico." In her *New World Orders: Casta Painting and Colonial Latin America.* New York: Americas Society Art Gallery, 1996.

Kleist, Heinrich von. *The Marquise of O— and Other Stories.* Tr. David Luke and Nigel Reeves. Harmondsworth: Penguin, 1978, 231–69.

———. "Die Verlobung in St. Domingo." In his *Sämtliche Werke und Briefe.* Vol. 2. Ed. Helmut Sembdner. Munich: Hanser, 1984, 160–95.

Meiners, Christoph. *Grundriß der Geschichte der Menschheit.* Lemgo: Meyer, 1786.

———. "Historische Nachrichten über die wahre Beschaffenheit des Sclaven-Handels, und der Knechtschaft der Neger in West-Indien." *Göttingisches Historisches Magazin* 6 (1790): 645–79.

———. "Ueber die Ausartung des Europäers in fremden Erdtheilen" and "Zusatz zu der vorhergehenden Abhandlung." *Göttingisches Historisches Magazin* 8 (1791): 209–74.

———. "Über die Farben, und Schattierungen verschiedener Völker." *Neues Göttingisches Historisches Magazin* 1 (1792): 611–72.

———. "Ueber die Natur der Afrikanischen Neger und die davon abhangende Befreyung, oder Einschränkung der Schwarzen." *Göttingisches Historisches Magazin* 6 (1790): 385–456.

———. "Von den Varietäten und Abarten der Neger." *Göttingisches Historisches Magazin* 6 (1790): 625–45.

Mielke, Andreas. *Laokoon und die Hottentotten: Oder über die Grenzen von Reisebeschreibung und Satire.* Baden-Baden: Koerner, 1993.

Müller-Salget, Klaus. "August und die Mestize: Zu einigen Kontroversen um Kleists Verlobung in St. Domingo." *Euphorion* 92 (1998): 103–13.

Onuf, Peter. "Every Generation Is an 'Independent Nation': Colonization, Miscegenation, and the Fate of Jefferson's Children." *William and Mary Quarterly* 57 (2000): 153–99.

Rosenthal, Angela. "Die Kunst des Errötens: Zur Kosmetik rassischer Differenz." In *Das Subjekt und die Anderen*. Ed. Herbert Uerlings and Viktoria Schmidt-Linsenhoff. Berlin: Erich Schmidt, 2001, 95–117.

Rupp-Eisenreich, Britta. "Choses occultes en histoire des sciences humaines: Le destin de la 'science nouvelle' de Christoph Meiners." *Ethnographie* 90–91 (1983): 131–83.

Uerlings, Herbert. "Die Haitianische Revolution in der deutschen Literatur." *Jahrbuch für Geschichte von Staat, Wirtschaft und Gesellschaft Lateinamerikas* (1991): 1–47.

——. *Poetiken der Interkulturalität: Haiti bei Kleist, Seghers, Müller, Buch und Fichte*. Tübingen: Francke, 1997.

——. "Preußen in Haiti? Zur interkulturellen Begegnung in Kleists 'Verlobung in St. Domingo.'" *Kleist-Jahrbuch* (1991): 185–201.

Werlen, Hans Jakob. "Seduction and Betrayal: Race and Gender in Kleist's *Die Verlobung in St. Domingo*." *Monatshefte* 84 (1992): 459–71.

Weigel, Sigrid. "Der Körper am Kreuzpunkt von Liebesgeschichte und Rassendiskurs in Heinrich von Kleists Erzählung *Die Verlobung in St. Domingo*." *Kleist-Jahrbuch* (1991): 202–17.

Wünsch, Christian Ernst. *Unterhaltungen über den Menschen. Erster Theil: Über die Kultur und äusserliche Bildung desselben*. Leipzig: Breitkopf, 1796.

Zantop, Susanne. "The Beautiful, the Ugly, and the German: Race, Gender, and Nationality in Eighteenth-Century Anthropological Discourse." In *Gender and Germanness: Cultural Productions of Nation*. Ed. Patricia Herminghouse and Magda Mueller. New York: Berghahn, 1997, 21–35.

——. *Colonial Fantasies. Conquest, Race, and Nation in Pre-Colonial Germany, 1770–1870*. Durham, NC: Duke UP, 1997.

——. "Verlobung, Hochzeit und Scheidung in St. Domingo: Die Haitianische Revolution in zeitgenössischer deutscher Literatur." In *"Neue Welt" / "Dritte Welt": Interkulturelle Beziehungen Deutschlands zu Lateinamerika und der Karibik*. Ed. Susan Cocalis and Sigrid Bauschinger. Tübingen: Francke, 1994, 29–52.

Ripe Moments and False Climaxes: Thematic and Dramatic Configurations of the Theme of Death in Kleist's Works

Hilda M. Brown

> Now more than ever seems it rich to die,
> To cease upon the midnight with no pain,
> While thou art pouring forth thy soul abroad
> In such an ecstasy! (Keats, "Ode to a Nightingale")

RIPENESS AND DEATH are brought into a striking new relationship in the Romantic period. The terms *Todeslust* and *Todessucht* are familiar enough to us in the Baroque, but at that period they signify an entirely different approach to the theme of death. Death obtains a high rating in proportion to the low esteem in which life is held, the latter being variously regarded as a "Vale of Tears," or a "Venusberg" offering vain distractions and illusory aspirations from which escape should be ardently sought in exchange for a blissful afterlife.[1] Placed in a secular, post-Enlightenment world, the Romantic sensibility actively seeks to extract pleasure from the senses, to savor and offer itself up to a whole range of experiences in the here and now. John Keats's "Ode to a Nightingale" (1820) well expresses this hedonistic view, according to which such intensely pleasurable sensations include the anticipation of death itself (Keats 49–51). Instead of antitheses, life and death are, for the Romantic mind, a continuum, contemplation and anticipation of which produces such extreme emotions as ecstasy ("Wollust" and "Entzücken"). In a letter of 1807 Kleist himself refers to death as a "refrain" of life, by which, I think, he means a summation and carrying over of essential elements from the one to the other sphere.[2] A manifold experience spread over the fullness of a lifetime is less important to the Romantic mind than the quality and intensity of this all-encompassing vision of death and life. Coincidentally, many Romantics did die young, among them Novalis, Kleist, and Keats, and it is of more than passing interest that these writers' perception of life was tinged to some extent by an

affirmation and anticipation of death. Paradoxically, this positive evaluation of death adds to and enriches the quality of life itself, death becoming, as it were, a property of life. In the case of Novalis's poem collection
Hymnen an die Nacht (1800) this idea is taken to an extreme point and
leads to an intermingling of life and death in the form of a "Liebestod,"
a Romantic paradox that finds its fullest expression in Richard Wagner's
opera *Tristan und Isolde* (1865).

This affirmative, sometimes openly celebratory view of death was capable of shocking the establishment of Kleist's day, for whom, of course,
suicide was anathema. The extent of the outrage can be gauged from the
various newspaper reports at home and abroad of Kleist's suicide (for
example, that of the *Times* of London of December 1811; cf. Sembdner
1996, 35–47). Even more-liberal minds, schooled on the popularity of
works such as Goethe's *Die Leiden des jungen Werther* (1774), could not
condone the drastic step. The minute recording of the preparations taken
by Kleist and Henriette Vogel at the inn near Wannsee, their festive, even
joyous character (eyewitnesses spoke of the "exaltation" and "enthusiasm" exhibited by the pair), and the deliberation with which they carried
out their plan, to say nothing of the impropriety of the relationship itself,
constituted a scandal of the first magnitude. It also sparked a heated
debate about suicide, and among the many disapproving voices raised,
those of Mme De Staël and the Schlegels stand out.[3] Much has been
written about Kleist's stage-managed suicide and much remains (and will
always remain) a mystery.[4] We can hazard a guess about what may have
precipitated it: the prospect of financial ruin after the censorship of and
government ban on the publication of the *Berliner Abendblätter,* the
wretched political situation, the ostracism by his family, and Henriette's
terminal illness and the perceived need for a mercy killing may all have
been factors. In themselves these factual explanations would all point to
failure rather then to "ripeness," and to Kleist's need to extricate himself
and Henriette from what seemed an accumulation of hopeless disasters.
It is well documented that Kleist had on many other occasions expressed
a wish to die and had even at various points invited his sister, Ulrike; his
cousin by marriage, Marie von Kleist; and his friend Ernst von Pfuel,
among others, to join him. These requests had generally, though not
invariably, taken place at crisis points in his life. A distinctive and unusual
feature of his attitude toward this death, however, is its interactive dimension — it manifests itself most frequently in the form of a "Doppeltod," occasionally as a collective act. Clearly, it was imperative that it
should not be regarded as an isolated act in the Werther mode. The most
familiar form of the alternative "Doppeltod" would be a "Liebestod";

but it seems that in Kleist's case erotic factors were not of paramount importance, and the evidence that he had invited male, as well as female, friends, including close relations, to participate suggests that there were other considerations.

Two major strands can be discerned in Kleist's various attempts to explain his motives for the final fateful decision: one is clearly altruistic, the other more complex. Henriette's needs were only too patent: death was a release for her; she took full responsibility for the act and expressed her gratitude toward Kleist in fulsome terms for carrying out the role of a facilitator, even composing a counterpart to Kleist's own so-called "Todeslitanei" as a kind of thanks offering.[5] Kleist's feelings for Henriette and his attitude toward the act itself were different and much more complex. On the one hand, her compliance in the pact gave him the opportunity to achieve his long-cherished goal of a "Doppeltod" and, thus, inspired gratitude. At the same time, however, he was mindful of the special nature of his own active part as instigator of each death and could articulate the role of the self-denying, sacrificial victim-cum-liberator on both Henriette's behalf and his own. Thus, his gratitude to her was interlaced with something more masterful: the role of the noble martyr for a cause, the undeserving victim of an uncomprehending world. The importance of this self-sacrificial role in Kleist's thinking and literary works has been fully analyzed by Anthony Stephens, who traces it back to Kleist's early identification with and admiration for a number of exemplary biblical figures, including Christ. Kleist may have believed that the deep significance the "Doppeltod" held for him and for Henriette would be clear to others and would send signals to his friends and family of the meaningfulness of the joint act. The desire for understanding and approbation, both as an artist and as a man, and for an "audience" among the friends and the family who had rejected him are factors whose importance cannot be underestimated. As it happened, however, his sensational suicide achieved the opposite of understanding. It damaged his reputation, delayed the publication of his works, and stood in the way of an unbiased appreciation of his oeuvre for at least 100 years.

At the heart of Kleist's complex attitude toward death lies the question of his art: the focus so often of his boundless ambitions as he successively set himself the challenge of mastering virtually every literary form (except poetry) that was then current, from the tiniest anecdote or piece of reportage to full-scale comedy and tragedy. His friend Pfuel's remark that he intended to wrest the laurel wreath from Goethe's brow does not sound apocryphal (cf. Sembdner 1977, no. 112). Soon after the first intimations that he felt destined for a literary vocation (around 1801–

1802), it is symptomatic that he should immediately react with panic lest something prevent this newly found destiny (and replacement for the earlier, failed "Lebensplan") from finding fulfillment. Around then he set up three new aims in life: "a child, a fine poem and a great deed."[6] Of these, the first soon fell by the wayside.[7] The second and third remained more or less intact.[8] For a brief period, however, even the second came under threat. The intensity of feeling invested in the fulfillment of his literary ambitions, boosted by the encouragement of the greatly respected elder statesman of German letters, Christoph Martin Wieland, grew to almost intolerable proportions as Kleist struggled with the recalcitrant material for his grand tragedy, *Robert Guiskard, Herzog der Normänner*. The prospect of failure for this goal produced a sense of panic and a clearly articulated death wish. In a famous letter to his sister, Ulrike (26 October 1803), written from St. Omer, where Bonaparte was assembling his army in anticipation of an invasion of England, Kleist strikes an exalted tone, exclamatory and enthusiastic. He anticipates with pleasure a watery grave, shared with other participants in the Grande Armée (clearly identifying at this point with his hero Guiskard and his Norman warriors; cf. Samuel and Brown 1981, 52): "unser aller Verderben lauert über den Meeren, ich frohlocke bei der Aussicht auf das unendlich-prächtige Grab" (3:321). If the second of the "drei Dinge" to be accomplished before death, "ein schön Gedicht," is to be denied him, he will settle instead for what he persuades himself is "eine große Tat" (even though this single substitution does not correspond to the original three conditions he had set himself). Death becomes linked here with *un*ripeness and lack of fulfillment, the opposite position from Keats's postulation of a fullness of being that tips over into a state of "ripeness for death." It seems that Kleist himself subconsciously realizes this, since the idea is strongly reinforced by his adoption — knowingly, it would appear — of the petulant gesture of defiance typical of a child who cannot obtain what it wants: "Der Himmel versagt mir den Ruhm, das größte der Güter der Erde; ich werfe ihm, wie ein eigensinniges Kind, alle übrigen hin" (3:321).

The position is quite different by 1806, by which time Kleist has completed several "schön Gedicht," including *Der zerbrochne Krug*, and has several more well on the way (*Amphitryon* and *Penthesilea*). In the confessional letter of 31 August 1806 addressed to his close friend Rühle von Lilienstern, which ranges widely over the themes of life and death, we find an abrupt change of mood, a feature typical of Kleist's longer letters. From despairing reflections on the political situation in the immediate post-Jena period and the impossibility of taking effective action ("Der Gedanke will mir noch nicht aus dem Kopf, daß wir noch einmal etwas *tun* müssen" [3:360]) Kleist moves to general observations about human transitoriness ("Wir begegnen uns, drei Frühlinge lieben wir uns; und eine Ewigkeit fliehen wir wieder auseinander" [3:361]) and thence to a daredevil wish to perform some meaningful deed — a kind of gesture of defiance toward Fate — and then die: "Komm, laß uns etwas Gutes tun, und dabei sterben!" (3:361). But in the next breath he can switch to a confident statement about his own literary achievements: "Nun wieder zurück zum Leben! So lange das dauert, werd ich jetzt Trauerspiele und Lustspiele machen" (3:361). The second of the "drei Dinge" is being conspicuously achieved. After the disastrous noncompletion of *Robert Guiskard,* which led to the destruction of the manuscript, he is in control of his art and relishes the sense of achievement being so brings. This all-absorbing activity belongs emphatically to life, not death: "ich dichte bloß, weil ich es nicht lassen kann" (3:362). True, the perfectionist in him can never admit to total satisfaction, but that does not cancel out the excitement of the "first, fine careless rapture," the heady spontaneity, that is experienced when the creative impulse takes flight: "Es gibt nichts Göttlicheres als sie! Und nichts Leichteres zugleich; und doch, warum ist es so schwer?" (3:362). Despite, or possibly because of, a growing "ripeness" in terms of creative experience and achievement, this all-engrossing activity precludes thoughts of its termination.

While the motivational factors behind Kleist's various expressions of "Todessucht" in the letters are often partially hidden from us, one would not necessarily expect the same to apply to his *literary* treatment of the theme. We can speculate endlessly about the impact of various crises on Kleist when thoughts of death are often uppermost: Kant crisis, Guiskard crisis, Jena crisis, as well as the most problematic crisis of all, that of late 1811; but in the case of those literary works in which the theme of death, particularly in the form of "Todesreife," is prominent, we are dealing with artistic constructs that might be expected to contain some inner coherence not present in life. For one thing, they are equipped with characters for whom the writer has had to provide credible motivation, drawing on both his conscious and his subconscious resources. Subject to the vagaries and limitations of our own interpretative powers, theoretically, at least, we might, therefore, expect to be on safer ground untangling the motives behind the attitudes toward death expressed by Kleist's characters than we are with his own. This does not mean, however, that useful comparisons cannot be drawn between the biographical and the fictional planes, although the relationship between the two is rather more complex than used to be supposed in days when the concept of "Erlebnisdichtung" was fashionable. In studies of what was termed

"Kleists Todesproblem,"[9] which were influenced by Wilhelm Dilthey's theory, the connections between life and works were often regarded as axiomatic. When placed in its literary context, however, this theme could be explored from a number of different angles, some of which are additional to or find no counterpart in Kleist's recorded personal utterances on the subject. An obvious example is the phenomenon of the Doppeltod, which is the form in which the theme of death almost invariably appears in the letters. In the literary works a double suicide or suicide pact, as such, does not feature. Penthesilea, for example, a character who to a greater extent than any of the others could be described as "todessüchtig," certainly does not consider a *joint* death or a suicide pact as an option. It is only after she becomes aware that she has killed her lover by mistake that she resolves to *follow* him in death.

Literary examples of the theme of "Todesreife" are significant, although few in number: *Penthesilea* and *Prinz Friedrich von Homburg* provide the most substantial, together with a few passing references in stories such as "Der Zweikampf" and "Michael Kohlhaas." Kleist's so-called "Todeslitanei" occupies a unique and fascinating position between the literary and the documentary levels of discourse. While its motivational pivot is clearly the product of *real* circumstances, it presents itself entirely in literary terms as a poetic effusion. Although it might not at first sight seem to be directed at a wider audience, its careful composition suggests that it may have been written for eyes other than those of his partner, as well. This would accord once more with Kleist's overpowering need for communication with a public and his eye on posterity. Henriette's counterpiece has led commentators to talk of a contest,[10] but we do not know for sure its raison d'être, since in any literary "competition" with Kleist, Henriette was bound to come out as the loser. Recent scholarship inclines, I believe rightly, to link Kleist's "Todeslitanei" with the final letters, whose mood of exaltation it echoes and of which it could be described as the apotheosis (cf. Müller-Salget, in Kleist 3:1038–40). It is a unique document in the annals of world literature. In content and style, it presents itself in unequivocally literary terms, with its antecedents lying in such diverse sources as the Bible (the Song of Solomon and the Psalms of David), hymns, and the poetry of the Baroque, among others. But a literary document that is predicated on a real, not an imaginary plot, that is to say, the mise-en-scène of its author's own death, surely presents the reader with special problems of evaluation.[11]

It is no accident that the major literary examples of the theme of "Todesreife" come from two of Kleist's greatest dramas. For in this genre the question of motivation and causality is at the forefront, and as a dramatist

Kleist always reckoned to be a master of the art of meticulous motivation of his characters — especially in *Penthesilea,* where, because of the potentially shocking subject matter, he was particularly alert to the need for grounding his heroine's behavior convincingly.[12] Romantic lyric poets such as Keats could use the song of a bird to trigger reflections on the theme of "Todesreife." By harnessing all the special effects of rhyme, assonance, imagery, and rhythm he could vividly evoke for his reader the transition from a state of fullness of being to a longing for death. Kleist, by contrast, in his dramatic treatment of the theme, must set up for his audience a chain of causality in which the connections have to be presented in sufficient detail and coherence. In *Penthesilea* there are two iterations of the theme of "Todesreife": the first occurs at the midpoint of the play (scene 14, an important structural crux), the other near the conclusion (scene 24). This installment presentation is structurally important: the first functions as a foreshadowing of Penthesilea's death, the second as an anticipation of its imminent fulfillment. Taken together, the two sections provide cross-referential material and points of comparison that aid the process of elucidation for the audience, doing so with an artifice that has no counterpart in real life. The situations that enclose each of the examples can be seen to differ greatly. In scene 14 Penthesilea imagines that she has triumphed over Achilles, thinks she has achieved — to paraphrase Michael Kohlhaas's final expression of fulfillment in the face of death — her "höchster Wunsch auf Erden." The sober fact is that the reverse is true: Achilles has taken her prisoner but has connived with Prothoe in a ruse whereby he feigns defeat in the hope of gaining time to persuade her to return to Greece with him for a while. At the end of the play the tables are turned. She has, indeed, in one sense triumphed, but barbarically, and in a misguided orgy of violence directed against Achilles' physical person. In both examples, as we shall see, Penthesilea's very perception of her "ripeness for death" is falsely grounded in the light of the developing action by means of which Kleist is creating a context for and building up in the spectator an expectation of a strict motivation. There is a clear mismatch between Penthesilea's sense of achievement and its legitimacy when set against this implied motivation, and Kleist plays on this dramatic conundrum. The character herself is trying to project a meaning on events that accords with her own desires and future expectations, thus forcing what, in strictly dramatic terms, is a false climax. By sheer willpower and the power of her imagination she envisages a dénouement that, in fact, has not happened, and one, moreover, that is complicated by the fact that, on the subconscious level, Penthesilea *knows* that her vision of "ripeness" is falsely based. This is clear from the way in which she describes herself as a sullied child ("ein besudelt Kind") who wishes to purify herself by immersion in pure water. Ideas of impurity and even suppressed self-hatred lurk here. Essentially, she would like to transcend these ignoble feelings and to experience what the effects of a triumph *would be like,* to lay claim to and to savor the state of fulfillment — but without having observed the conditions she has imposed on herself. If this ideal state (to which she gives the name "Elysium") could be achieved, she believes, she would be projected onto a plane of existence that reaches beyond that normally associated with human heroism or mere mortality (with the latter state she prefers to associate the idea of "fragility" ("Gebrechlichkeit"). The emotions to which she aspires all touch on the otherworldly, the vocabulary being familiar from religious, and especially Pietist, literature. Key terms are *Seligkeit,* which is reserved for the departed souls or "Blessed Spirits" of the classical and Christian traditions, respectively; *Wollust,* which carries erotic overtones; and *Entzücken* (religious exaltation). That Penthesilea, in a kind of Freudian slip, compares herself to a child signals to the audience her identification with the immature condition of unripeness and (as at so many other points in the drama) exposes the contradictions in her personality and her situation. At the same time, it reveals the sheer scope of her aspirations and the tragic mismatch between aspiration and achievement.

As we have seen, she would, according to her own criteria for success, seem to have more reason to lay claim to this state of superhuman bliss when for a second time she professes her attainment of "Todesreife," that is, after the ultimate triumph in battle over Achilles, which was the precondition she had set herself for its attainment. "Reifsein zum Tode," "Seligkeit," the sense of having already passed over into the Beyond and into Elysium, together with the appropriate feelings of "Entzücken," sum up her position at this point — and represent for her a supreme emotional climax. But memory has been partly obliterated, and although the end result of the engagement with Achilles was a technical victory, all the accompanying factors, which she knows subconsciously are qualifications for true "ripeness," have been suppressed (Achilles was, after all, unarmed). Again she distorts, fictionalizes the real situation and puts a construction on events that does not correspond to their true reality:

> Ich bin so selig, Schwester! Überselig!
> Ganz reif zum Tod' o Diana, fühl' ich mich!
> Zwar weiß ich nicht, was hier mit mir geschehen
> Doch gleich des festen Glaubens könnt' ich sterben,
> Daß ich mir den Peliden überwand. (24.2894–67)

The nagging doubts already slip out in the concessive "zwar," reinforced by the odd, secretive, and edgy behavior of the Amazon women as they dissemble and attempt to shield her from the sight of Achilles' mangled body.

When the horrible truth comes out, and a full understanding has been achieved on Penthesilea's part of the circumstances leading to Achilles' death, together with her own part in it, there is at first no further reference to the ripeness or fittingness of death. Penthesilea is, in fact, for a time speechless, as if she has reached the limits of language. Neither bliss nor Elysian fields are anticipated as she now, with full knowledge of what she has done and what she must do to atone for it, acts out in almost ritualistic fashion what Walter Rehm has called "einen sühnenden Opfertod" (442). Penthesilea, then, sets in motion the process of fashioning for herself a death that will be appropriate to her particular circumstances and that will be quite different from the ecstatic vision of Elysium that had been associated with her earlier untimely and mistaken anticipation of ripeness. The materials on which she draws are taken from the detritus of the catastrophe she has brought about. Thus, in place of Seligkeit there are "Jammer," "Reue," and a leavening quantum of "Hoffnung." These provide the constituent elements from which she can, in a bold, literal metaphor, fashion her own death out of the material, or the essence, of her life's experience. This supreme effort of will and self-determination achieves at least something close to that level of human heroism she had disdained in scene 14 as being inadequate for her aspirations. It is, Kleist suggests, appropriate, however, for a world or a human condition that, as the characters themselves remind us, is fragile ("gebrechlich") and on which the gods look down from a distance "Auf die nur fern die Götter niederschaun" [24.2855]).

These two "ripe moments" experienced by Penthesilea, and so ardently desired by her, are projected into a timeless vacuum, out of sync with the dramatic action developing around and upon her. As defined by her, such ripeness could only be validated in the postheroic, posttragic realm, where no such time constraints exist. This, to my mind, illustrates the problematic status that Kleist confers on the concept of ripeness and suggests the impossibility of its being attainable within a given time frame. But the twofold articulation of this failed objective produces signposts, structural markers against which the spectator can measure the degree of distance between vision and reality, effort and achievement, between Penthesilea's desired program and aspirations and the destructive momentum she has released in their pursuit.

If the unattainability of "Todesreife" is a key issue in defining Penthesilea's tragic position and in revealing two contrasting attitudes toward death, the "merely" heroic (by which I think Kleist means the stoic, where sheer will triumphs over circumstance) and the postheroic, or sublime, the presentation of the theme in *Homburg* makes a case for suggesting the process by which, first, ripeness might possibly be attainable in more practical terms and, second, the extent to which the protagonist in this work might be thought justified in laying claim to it. When compared to Penthesilea, however, this hero stands out because of his initial refusal to have anything to do with the idea of "Todesreife." The low-key monologue (4.3) reduces life and death to their most basic physical components, the short duration of the former being matched by an awareness of the ignominious process of decomposition of the human body after death ("nur schade, daß das Auge modert" [4.3.1295]), together with a bitter reflection on the illogicality of thinking that images of an afterlife projected by men (such as, possibly, are suggested by the "Elysian fields") could be enjoyed under these circumstances. As has often been noted, the contrast between this materialistic conception of death (almost Büchneresque in its starkness) and Homburg's high-flown rhetoric and apostrophization of immortality in his final monologue (5.10) could hardly be greater. The dramatic miracle is how Kleist can contrive to provide a plausible motivation for such a volte-face. Subtle inner processes are triggered in Homburg's mind after the Kurfürst has offered him a free choice to determine his own fate. This leads Homburg to scrutinize and reassess his situation, to transcend his fear of death, and to affirm his willing compliance with the law and the death sentence: "Der Tod wäscht jetzt von jeder Schuld mich rein" (5.7.1770). The famous "Unsterblichkeitsmonolog" contains all the otherworldly imagery of light, space, and height that is traditionally associated with the Christian afterlife, including the appearance of angelic throngs.[13] But at the same time, Homburg's senses are sharpened to more earthly things, such as the three types of flowers whose scents assail his nostrils in the summer garden at Fehrbellin. This richness of sensory experience reminds us of Keats's almost swooning anticipation of death: "I cannot see what flowers are at my feet, / Nor what soft incense hangs upon the boughs, / But in embalmed darkness, guess each sweet / Wherewith the seasonable month endows / The grass, the thicket and the fruit-tree wild" ("Ode to a Nightingale").[14] The flowers, violas (Nachtviolen), night-scented stock (Levkojn), and carnations (Nelken) — all noted for their long-lasting evening scent — succinctly suggest the otherworldly and the terrestrial levels at one and the same time.

The flower itself is, of course, a symbol of development and growth, being a culminating point in the life cycle of the plant. Networks of plant imagery are common throughout the drama and are often applied to

Homburg himself — for instance, the vine imagery in the scene between Natalie and Homburg (cf. Demetz). Related to this is the motif of the child needing careful tending and control, like a plant: "Natalie: O diescr Fehltritt, blond mit blauen Augen" (4.1.1095). These leitmotifs suggest the idea of potential nurture and development, and in their sheer suggestiveness they contain an ambiguity and richness of association.

It might seem from this that Homburg does, indeed, progress to a point where he attains a true "Todesreife" in that a life-based experience, or crisis, ultimately leads on, by way of a series of complex interactions, to a harmonious celebration of death. Although the term *Reife* itself does not occur, his state of mind is certainly much closer to a sense of fulfillment than it is to "Todessucht" in the sense that the positive acceptance of death is coterminous with an affirmation of the meaningfulness of life. At first sight it might seem difficult to distinguish between Homburg's position and Penthesilea's (misguided) vision, her sense of fullness of being after earthly triumph and her enthusiastic acceptance of death as the next logical step. But on closer scrutiny, Homburg's vision is much less forced and much more inclusive; it is presented as a natural process he believes he is undergoing in his passage from life to death (which is expressed in the familiar metaphor of a ship leaving shore). His belief that he has achieved a kind of transcendence of self is not a chimera; the coincidence between his inner convictions and the demands placed on him by what he now perceives as a higher instance take place within the context of a new and positive appraisal of death. The drama could conceivably end on this note and would then come close to a "Läuterungstragödie" in the best Schillerian manner (cf. Samuel 1957, 37). But in this drama we have a character without a counterpart in *Penthesilea* or, indeed, a Schillerian tragedy: a master of ceremonies and a successful Regisseur rolled into one — the Kurfürst. When events themselves can be manipulated and are subject to human judgment and discretion, a resolution can be achieved instead of a standoff. We then have, in one sense, another false climax, in that the affirmation of "Todesreife," which sounds forth so eloquently in the "Unsterblichkeitsmonolog," ends up being superfluous to the dramatic requirements. This is a rather different dramatic situation from *Penthesilea*, where there is a shortfall, rather than an overshoot, in terms of ripeness. The movement in Homburg's position has been generated by external events — that is, the combination of interventions, principally those of the Kurfürst. With these Homburg moves more and more into phase, until he comes to accept the verdict he believes they embody. Unbeknown to him, however, this verdict itself has been undergoing a process of modification as the Kurfürst, the agent of its implementation, in turn is acted on, principally by Natalie. Homburg's interpretation of the outcome, accordingly, turns out to be needlessly severe: his acceptance of the death sentence would in itself be enough — at the level of plot and situation — to justify his reinstatement and for the rebellious soldiery to benefit from the example he sets. As in "Der Zweikampf," the cancellation of an expected tragic dénouement creates surprise for both character and audience, mentally and emotionally prepared as the latter have been, in their identification with the character's emotional path, for a different outcome. The subsequent turnaround, with its suggestions of a forced "happy ending," seems to undermine the whole meticulously constructed exposition that led to the manifestation and affirmation of "Todesreife" itself. For some commentators the dissatisfaction with this disjunction between dramatic expectation and actuality is transferred to the Elector's "arbitrary" behavior and abuse of his position as head of state.

In interpretations of the drama these issues remain possibly the most debated and controversial feature. "Ripeness for death," to follow our theme, while fully affirmed by the protagonist and with greater plausibility and justification than in *Penthesilea*, is, seemingly, subverted on a whim by an external agency. The uneventful ending might seem to trivialize or even invalidate the significance of the process undergone. But to look at the question in another way: once it has been publicly expressed with this degree of conviction and plausibility, "Todesreife" — a state of mind and attitude that one imagines is of lasting duration and from which there will be no turning back; one, moreover, that the Kurfürst himself has put to a public test — no longer requires the application of that death sentence. Attitude toward death is more important than the physical act itself. The Prince *has to* be taken through the whole psychological experience of being brought to the brink of death in order for this particular death to be rendered superfluous. The logic of this strand of Kleist's motivation is surely clear. Toying with this paradox, he leaves his hero with a short-term problem of adjustment. He flounders between the postheroic bliss of the Elysian fields, whose joys he had imagined he was on the threshold of experiencing, and the rough-and-tumble of the battlefield, between a dream world and a harsh reality. Not surprisingly, he is confused. There is a parallel here with Keats's ode as the poet hovers between the very same two realms of life and death: "Was it a vision, or a waking dream? / Fled is that music — do I wake or sleep?"

Kleist's last letters and the "Todeslitanei" give further food for thought on the themes of "Todesreife" and "Todessucht." Resemblances have often been noticed between the imagery employed in these documents and in Homburg's "Unsterblichkeitsmonolog," despite the lapse of an entire year between them. It is significant that all the last letters (except the strictly factual one to Peguilhen, who fulfilled the task of Kleist's executor) are addressed to women: Marie von Kleist (three), Sophie von Müller, and Ulrike von Kleist. As in his other letters, Kleist is highly aware of the need to adjust his writing to the sensibilities of the particular correspondent (cf. Brown 1998, 41–42); so, for instance, the letter to Ulrike is factual but not confessional,[15] while the one to Sophie von Müller is more effusive and flowery. The latter has several motifs in common with Homburg's "Unsterblichkeitsmonolog,"[16] the "Luftschiff" image being a vertical variant of the horizontal motif of the "Lebensschiff" in *Homburg*, suggesting the passage from life to death, expressed in terms of a movement of ascension heavenward (cf. Nölle 185–86). The three letters to Marie,[17] who for several years had been Kleist's main confidante, are the most revealing about his motives: in that of 10 November similar flower imagery ("wie ein Veilchen aus einer Wiese") to that in Homburg's monologue ("Nachtviolen") is picked up, suggesting the ambiguity and continuity of the relationship between death and life. This imagery is also evident in the letter of 12 November ("mit Blumen, himmlischen und irdischen").

Other points, which are reserved for Marie, include the idea of sacrifice ("aufopfern"), which is embedded in the notion of a Doppeltod. According to Kleist, Henriette is prepared to sacrifice "einen Vater . . . einen Mann . . . ein Kind . . . nur meinetwillen" (4:509). Kleist's construction of events in extremis reflects his conviction, however debatable, that he and Henriette were on equal terms in regard to the sacrifice each was making for the other. The idea of sacrifice invests the act itself with a *moral* dimension reminiscent of the "große Tat" that Kleist had always demanded as the single, most durable criterion for "Todesreife." Henriette's acceptance of the moral challenge gave added justification, in his eyes, to the acts of both of them and simultaneously triggered a sense of elation in Kleist, as can be seen in his reference to his forthcoming death in the last letter to Marie as "der herrlichsten und wollüstigsten aller Tode" (4:510). The relationship between this death and the life he is leaving is now made clear: a freely chosen death is to be a compensation for the suffering and agony of a life such as no other human being has ever experienced: "das allerqualvollste, das je ein Mensch geführt hat" (4:510). Although his literary achievements now carry no weight, because the dimension of appreciation and understanding to which he attaches so much importance has not been forthcoming, he has found in the act of suicide — or, rather, the special significance he has invested in this act, which is confirmed by the almost ritualistic preparations he instigated — more than adequate compensation.

It is only in the letter to Marie of 9 November 1811 that the idea of "Todesreife" is alluded to explicitly: "Nur so viel wisse, daß meine Seele, durch die Berührung mit der ihrigen, zum Tode ganz reif geworden ist" (4:507). These last letters themselves, however, while bearing witness to a state of "exaltation," even religious fervor — "morgens und abends knie ich nieder . . . und bete zu Gott" (4:510) — do not, indeed, cannot expand on the sense of a life of fulfillment but, rather, on the torment experienced. Life is seen as inferior to death and to the afterlife to which he and Henriette are heading: "in jene bessere Welt, wo wir uns alle mit der Liebe der Engel einander werden ans Herz drücken können" (4:510); "wir wollen nichts von den Freuden dieser Welt wissen" (to Sophie Müller, 4:511). At this point Kleist's attitude seems closer to the Baroque "Todeslust" than "Todesreife." The balance between life and death seems to have tipped over completely to the latter.

And yet, when we look at the "Todeslitanei," we are struck by the fact that it is in Kleist's carefully composed and constructed summary[18] of what he feels he has found represented in Henriette (in one brief episode in life) that the whole meaning of "Todesreife" is expressed. The document clearly constitutes a threefold statement, punctuated by the phrases: "o Liebste, wie nenn ich dich?" "Ach, du bist meines zweites bessers Ich," and, finally, "wie lieb ich dich!" (3:450–51). Within the first section are listed a number of earthly goods he failed to achieve in life, such as property ("Hab und Gut," "Schlösser," etc.), as well as less tangible possessions such as close personal relationships ("meine Braut, mein Mädchen, meine liebe Freundin" [3:451]). The second section encompasses solid and tangible signs of achievement, such as worldly power and prestige ("Krone, Königin und Kaiserin"), and domestic stability in the form of a wife and family ("Weib, Taufe meiner Kinder"), as well as literary success ("Trauerspiel und Nachruhm" [3:451]). The final section addresses moral qualities and otherworldly aspirations: Henriette is, for example, an embodiment of the virtues to which he aspires, even an intermediary with the Almighty, the source of forgiveness of sins, equipped with various religious functions ("Himmelstöchterchen," "Gotteskind," "Fürsprecherin und Fürbitterin"), as well as a guardian angel (3:451). In other words, everything Kleist could ever possibly wish to achieve in *life* — physical, spiritual, and transcendental — is now concentrated into this one individual. The plenitude suggested by this evidence, the transfer (in his imagination) of all these worldly and otherworldly aspirations to the person of Henriette and the fact that, by virtue of her relationship to him, her "sacrifice" on his be-half, these at once become accessible, therefore, provides ample justifica-tion for declaring his "Todesreife." It is a narcissistic vision, in that what he is here celebrating is the richness of his own imaginative powers. It is also truly a poet's vision of heaven and earth, a literary accumulation of riches, an extraordinary manifestation — even, one could say, a triumph of the poet's tongue over the bleakness and mean-spiritedness of the empirical reality he had known.

In these various explorations of the theme of "Todesreife" the di-mension of illusion looms large, and the relationship between the attain-ment of the "ripe" state and the given circumstances remains problematic. This is most apparent in the case of Penthesilea in that her visions seem to be pitched at the furthest remove from the reality of her situation and virtually in a timeless vacuum; this extreme disparity is reinforced by her identification of her position and state of *un*ripeness with that of a child. Homburg, on the other hand, starting from a much lower level of aspira-tion, finally seems to his own satisfaction to have worked through to a position where the relative claims of life and death come into something approaching an equilibrium, though the dramatist's deliberate play on the confusion of dream and reality in the final coda section works against any sense we might have of closure. As if to underline the movement toward ripeness, the image of the child, which had been persistently used in association with Homburg in the early phases of the action, yields to suggestions of growth and maturity. In his own "Todeslitanei" Kleist himself transposes the problem of (real) life and death to the realm of imaginative discourse, and, while still clinging to the "rules" of the game he had wagered with life, forces a personal reading onto the disaster of reality, thereby investing it, through the persona of Henriette and against all odds, with a sense of fulfillment and meaningfulness that had been conspicuously absent in his tormented life. His projections of an afterlife, theologically conventional as they are, may also just be part of that imagi-native process of reconstruction, or the poet's traditional armory when addressing matters of life and death. Possibly, as in the case of the "Op-fergedanke,"[19] the attachment of any sense of "transcendental causality" to the concept of "Todesreife" is debatable. That would in no way de-tract, however, from the poetic force of Kleist's vision: in his constant revisiting of the problem and his attempts to define and redefine it ever more closely, he succeeds in communicating its intense significance most eloquently. Even if a number of different approaches are explored, his readers are left in no doubt about its central significance as a theme.

Notes

[1] The titles and individual movements of many of Johann Sebastian Bach's cantatas, based on texts by Baroque poets, encapsulate this attitude toward life and death: e.g. "Komm, du süße Todesstunde" (BWV 161), "Ich steh' mit einem Fuß am Grabe" (BWV 156), "Ach, wie flüchtig, ach wie nichtig" (BWV 26), etc.

[2] To Marie von Kleist, in a passage recalling conversations with his friend Ernst von Pfuel held in the summer of 1804: "in jenem Sommer vor 3 Jahren, wo wir in jeder Unterredung immer wieder auf den Tod, als das ewige Refrain des Lebens zurück kamen" (4:379).

[3] See F. Schlegel to A. W. Schlegel: "Er hat also nicht bloß in seinen Werken, sondern auch im Leben *Tollheit* für Genie genommen und beide verwechselt" (Sembdner 1996, 59) and "eine kürzlich sich zu Berlin zugetragene Begebenheit kann einen Begriff von der sonderbaren Exaltation geben, der die Deutschen sich schuldig machen" (60).

[4] One of the most sober accounts remains Walter Silz's chapter on Kleist's death (271–88).

[5] To a friend she wrote on the day of her death: "so sage ich Dir nur so viel, daß mein Tod *mir ganz allein zuzuschreiben ist*" (Sembdner 1977, 425). In other words, her gratitude stemmed from the fact that Kleist was nobly enabling her to carry out her *own* resolve, and she was anxious that nobody should attribute intentionality in the more fundamental sense to him. For Henriette's own text, see Kleist 4:520.

[6] Letter to Ulrike von Kleist, May 1802: "kurz, ich habe keinen andern Wunsch, als zu sterben, wenn mir drei Dinge gelungen sind: ein Kind, ein schön Gedicht, und eine große Tat" (4:307).

[7] Letter to Ernst von Pfuel, 7 January 1805: "Ich heirate niemals, sei du die Frau mir, die Kinder und die Enkel" (4:336–37).

[8] Letter to Rühle von Lilienstern, 31 August 1806: "Komm, laß uns etwas Gutes tun, und dabei sterben" (4:361).

[9] See Rehm; also, Unger: "die Parallelen von Erlebnis und Dichtung sind zu handgreiflich und aufschlußreich, als daß sich der Kleistforscher nicht immer veranlaßt sähe, das eine auf das andere zu beziehen" (91). For a more modern treatment of the theme, see Bohrer.

[10] "das schöngeistig-litterarische Wettspiel" (Steig 659–61); "ein dithyrambisches Wettspiel" (Sembdner, in Kleist 1965, 1:917).

[11] For a detailed analysis of both Kleist's and Henriette's texts and a thorough investigation of their possible sources, see Sauer. For additional suggestions on influence, including, for example, Protestant "geistliche Kirchenlieder," see Kreutzer 240 and Müller-Salget's commentary in Kleist 3:1038–40.

[12] To Goethe, 24 January 1808: "So wie es hier steht, wird man vielleicht die Prämissen, als möglich, zugeben müssen, und nachher nicht erschrecken, wenn die Folgerung gezogen wird" (4:407).

[13] Kleist's attitude toward the afterlife is a neglected aspect of his works; commentators have suggested the influence on him of various *Aufklärung* writings, such as Wieland's *Sympathien* (1756), which Kleist himself mentions in an early letter (4:250). The theme is obviously relevant to the question of Kleist's attitude toward death and comes strongly to the fore in the last letters and the "Todeslitanei."

[14] Note that both Kleist and Keats invoke summer to suggest plenitude.

[15] Kleist had quarrelled with his sister, formerly a major confidante, on his last, fateful visit to the family in Frankfurt an Oder: see the letter to Marie von Kleist of 10 November 1811 (4:508–9).

[16] For example: "mit langen Flügeln an den Schultern," "lauter Fluren und Sonnen," and "zwei fröhliche Luftschiffer" (4:511).

[17] There is some confusion about the dating of these three letters; see the discussion by Müller-Salget, 4:1071–73. While Müller-Salget preserves Marie's original dating of 9, 10, and 12 November 1811, Sembdner (*Sämtliche Werke und Briefe*) rearranges them as 10, 19, and 21 November, on the grounds that Marie had confused 9 with 19 and 12 with 21. There is also some major rearrangement of sections of text between these letters.

[18] See Müller-Salget's commentary in 3:450–51. I am indebted to Katherine Ebisch-Burton, Oxford, for her helpful discussions of this text.

[19] Cf. Stephens, who says of *Penthesilea:* "die Brüchigkeit des Opferdiskurses in dieser Tragödie ist das Wahrzeichen solcher Anarchie und der einzige Weg, der aus diesem Chaos führt, ist der von der Todeseuphorie Penthesileas vorgezeichnete, nämlich der Befreiungsakt der 'Selbstopferung,' eine Lösung, zu der Kleist selber am Ende greifen sollte" (237).

Works Cited

Bohrer, Karl Heinz. "Kleists Selbstmord." In *Kleists Aktualität*. Ed. Walter Müller-Seidel. Darmstadt: Wissenschaftliche Buchgesellschaft, 1981, 281–306.

Brown, Hilda M. *Heinrich von Kleist: The Ambiguity of Art and the Necessity of Form*. Oxford: Clarendon P, 1998.

Demetz, Peter. "The Elm and the Vine: Notes towards the History of a Marriage Topos." *PMLA* 73 (1958): 521–32.

Keats, John. *The Poems of John Keats*. Ed. Ernest Rhys. London: Dent, 1911.

Kleist, Heinrich von. *Sämtliche Werke und Briefe*. 2 vols. Ed. Helmut Sembdner. Munich: Hanser, 1965.

———. *Sämtliche Werke und Briefe in vier Bänden*. 4 vols. Ed. Ilse-Marie Barth et al. Frankfurt a.M.: Deutscher Klassiker Verlag, 1987–97.

Kreutzer, Hans Joachim. *Die dichterische Entwicklung Heinrichs von Kleist*. Berlin: Schmidt, 1968.

Nölle, Volker. *Heinrich von Kleists Niederstiegs- und Aufstiegsszensarien*. Berlin: Schmidt, 1997.

Rehm, Walter. *Der Todesgedanke in der deutschen Dichtung*. Halle: Niemeyer, 1928.

Samuel, Richard H., and Hilda M. Brown. *Kleist's Lost Year and the Quest for Robert Guiskard*. Leamington: James Hall, 1981.

Samuel, Richard H., ed. *Prinz Friedrich von Homburg*. London: Harrap, 1957.

Sauer, August. *Kleists Todeslitanei*. Prague: C. Bellmann, 1907.

Sembdner, Helmut, ed. *Heinrich von Kleists Lebensspuren*. Frankfurt a.M.: Insel, 1977.

———. *Heinrich von Kleists Nachruhm*. Munich: Hanser, 1996.

Silz, Walter. *Heinrich von Kleist: Studies in His Works and Literary Character*. Philadelphia: U of Pennsylvania P, 1961.

Steig, Reinhold. *Heinrich von Kleists Berliner Kämpfe*. Berlin: Spemann, 1901.

Stephens, Anthony. "Der Opfergedanke bei Heinrich von Kleist." In *Heinrich von Kleist: Kriegsfall — Rechtsfall — Sündenfall*. Ed. Gerhard Neumann. Freiburg: Rombach, 1994, 193–248.

Unger, Rudolph. *Herder, Novalis, Kleist: Studien über die Entwicklung des Todesproblems im Denken und Dichten vom Sturm und Drang zur Romantik*. Frankfurt a.M.: Diesterweg, 1922.

"Mein ist die Rache spricht der Herr": Violence and Revenge in the Works of Heinrich von Kleist

Seán Allan

IT IS HARDLY SURPRISING that in his review of Tieck's *Dramaturgische Blätter* Goethe should refer to Kleist as a writer who filled him with a sense of horror and disgust (Goldammer 53). For no one reading Kleist's literary works can fail to be struck by the wide variety of characters bent on exacting revenge at any price, ranging from the villainous Rupert in *Die Familie Schroffenstein,* who compels his family to swear vengeance against all the members of the house of Warwand, to the outraged Kohlhaas, who styles himself as the emissary of the Archangel Michael and insists, during his initial meeting with Luther, that it is his right to avenge himself against his enemy, the Junker. But despite the many instances of brutality in his works, Kleist goes out of his way to show that violence is not simply an inevitable fact about the human condition. On closer analysis, his fascination with wickedness has its roots in an elaborate theory of aesthetics and moral education and the belief that there is at least as much to be gained from the scrutiny of wickedness as there is from the contemplation of moral excellence. This view is spelled out most clearly in the humorous essay "Allerneuester Erziehungsplan," in which the would-be director of the proposed "Lasterschule" urges prospective parents to shun the mimetic principle of moral education, the practice of trying to copy the behavior of exemplary cases of human virtue, in favor of a system of moral education based on what he terms the "law of contradiction." By exposing his young charges to instances of human depravity, the would-be headmaster hopes to educate them to an understanding of virtue through the active rejection of vice (cf. Nobile 49–74). In devising such a program, Kleist displays his keen understanding of human psychology and, at the same time, shows that what is important in moral education is to dissuade human beings from simply embracing uncritically the moral precepts of others (however exemplary these may be) and, instead, to stimulate and encourage the development of an autonomous moral will. Accordingly, in confronting his readers with a wide range of perspectives on human wickedness in his literary works, Kleist is simply endorsing in his own aesthetic medium the pedagogical principles set out in his essay. And as we shall see, the extreme predicaments in which so many of Kleist's characters find themselves stem not from a failure to understand what virtue is but, rather, from their inadequate grasp of the nature of evil.

". . . fortan kein anderes Gefühl als nur der Rache will ich kennen . . .": *Die Familie Schroffenstein*

Die Familie Schroffenstein suffers from many defects, not least its schematic plot structure and often melodramatic language. Nonetheless, it is striking that even in this, Kleist's first published work, the motif of revenge plays a crucial role. In the opening scene the spectator is invited to reflect on the nature of violent retribution (and its contradictions) in the perverted version of the Eucharist that takes place during the burial of the child in the chapel in Rossitz. This scene — which cannot but strike any sincere Christian as deeply abhorrent — is contrived to fill the spectator with a sense of foreboding regarding the likely outcome of such an enterprise. It is made clear that the deity Rupert worships is the god of his own malign autocracy, a god who demands violent retribution whenever his authority is challenged and who requires unquestioning obedience from his subjects. Nonetheless, in what will be the first of many gestures of *mauvaise foi,* the despotic Rupert styles himself not as the instigator of such a plan of vengeance but merely as an instrument of God, "Dessen Willen, wir vollstrecken" (1.1.9). In purporting to know the will of God, Rupert is, of course, guilty of a blatant act of hubris. For the fact that human beings enjoy only limited knowledge of the motives behind the actions of their fellow human beings underpins the notion that vengeance is the prerogative of God alone: "Vengeance is mine, I will repay" (Rom. 12:19). In addition, the obvious contradiction between the Old Testament concept of a vengeful God and the New Testament doctrine of forgiveness is echoed in the juxtaposition of the stanzas sung by the male choir — "Rache! Rache! Rache! Schwören wir" (1.1.10) — with those sung by the female chorus:

> Nun im Sarge,
> Ausgelitten,
> Faltet blutige Händlein er,
> Gnade betend
> Seinem Feinde. (1.17–21)

This plea for forgiveness, however — a plea that is also implicit in Eustache's question as to how she, qua woman, is expected to take revenge (1.1.38) — makes little impression on the leader of the Rossitz clan. For Rupert's concept of revenge is an all-consuming passion that knows no limits. Not only does he compel all the members of his entourage (including the reluctant Eustache) to take the oath, but, as Ottokar discovers (cf. 1.1.32–34), the oath of revenge is to embrace all the members of Sylvester's family. Finally, as if this were not enough in itself, the unconditional character of Rupert's lust for vengeance is underlined in his intention not just to destroy the present generation of the House of Warwand but to bring about its extinction for all eternity (cf. 1.1.68–73).

Nonetheless, it is, of course, the sheer intensity of Rupert's desire for revenge that proves to be his undoing. In a forlorn attempt to divert her husband from his chosen course of action, Eustache suggests that his passionate rage is likely to constitute an obstacle to the successful outcome of any attempt to avenge himself:

> O Rupert, mäßge dich! Es hat der frech
> Beleidigte den Nachteil, daß die Tat
> Ihm die Besinnung selbst der Rache raubt,
> Und daß in seiner eignen Brust ein Freund
> Des Feindes aufsteht wider ihn, die Wut — (1.1.74–8)

In saying as much, she demonstrates her understanding of the dynamic of revenge — at least in the form in which it is presented in this play — and, in particular, of the way in which passionate anger renders the injured party incapable of rational reflection. For like all extreme passions — including love — the desire for vengeance blinds those who succumb to it. Indeed, throughout the play Rupert steadfastly ignores any account of events running counter to his own and rejects any concept of human nature that would call into question his view of man as essentially evil. Unshakable in his belief that human beings act solely from motives of self-interest, he remains profoundly distrustful of the house of Warwand (who under the terms of the "Erbvertrag" would become sole heirs to the family's fortune) and is convinced that Sylvester's men must have been responsible for the death of his son. So caught up is he in the wild fantasies of his pessimistic ideology that by the end of the play he has lost sight of reality altogether, and his quest for vengeance, once unleashed, becomes an unstoppable force with a life of its own. For having killed what he believes to be Sylvester's daughter, Agnes, he turns to his henchman, Santing, asking:

> Warum denn hätt ich sie gemordet? Sage
> Mir schnell, ich bitte dich, womit sie mich
> Beleidigt, . . . (5.1.2524–26)

These words, however, underline the deluded nature of his quest for vengeance; for even when it appears that he has achieved his stated aim, he no longer comprehends the motives that lay behind it. And while Santing may supply the only answer compatible with Rupert's perverted logic — "Das Mädchen ist Sylvesters Tochter" (5.1.2529) — this explanation only postpones the moment of his master's moral insight. Although Rupert regards man as essentially evil, his fatal error consists in overlooking a residual capacity in all human beings — himself included — for good. Accordingly, when he realizes that the corpse before him is not Agnes but Ottokar, and that he has, albeit inadvertently, murdered his own son, he comes to acknowledge not only the full extent of his capacity for evil but also that he alone is responsible for the crime. As he contemplates his son's dead body, he finally recognizes himself for the devil he is:

> Höllisch Gesicht! Was äffst du mich?
> Ein Teufel
> Blöckt mir die Zung heraus. (5.1.2677–78)

But it is precisely because he is not altogether devoid of a sense of morality that he is able to acknowledge his satanic behavior for what it is — and reject it. And in the provocative ending of the play, significantly, it is he (not Sylvester) who initiates the reconciliation.

While Kleist goes to considerable lengths to suggest a real possibility for self-improvement in a man such as Rupert, in his characterization of Sylvester he demonstrates how a man with essentially benevolent aspirations is capable of descending to Rupert's level of wickedness. Throughout the play Sylvester is confronted with a series of suspicious incidents, all of which appear to have been orchestrated by Rupert. But despite his advisers' demands that he strike back, Sylvester stubbornly refuses, believing willfully that an alternative explanation will emerge, exonerating Rupert and rendering the use of force unnecessary. When it seems that his daughter, Agnes, has been attacked by Johann, however, Sylvester comes perilously close to specifying the circumstances in which he would be prepared to resort to violent retribution:

> ja hätten sie
> Im Krieg mein Haus verbrannt, mein Weib und Kind
> Im Krieg erschlagen, noch wollt ichs entschuldgen.
> Doch daß sie mir den Meuchelmörder senden,
> — Wenns so ist — (2.3.1138–40)

But although he stops just short of naming the necessary and sufficient conditions that, in his opinion, would justify such an act, the tacit admission that such conditions do exist reveals the presence of a crucial flaw in the particular version of the Christian ethic that he espouses. For what Sylvester fails to understand is that no matter how damning the evidence against Rupert may appear, there can never be circumstances in which revenge would be justified, since such acts of vengeance are contrary to the system of ethics underpinning the form of society toward which Warwand is progressing. His failure to appreciate the full implications of the ethical system he purports to embrace shows how flawed his concept of human nature is. Seduced by his doctrine of the perfectibility of man into disregarding his own human limitations, he fails to give due consideration to the possibility that circumstances may arise when even he will be sorely tempted to take revenge, and that he is — as the end of the play underlines — quite capable of giving in to such temptation. Sylvester may hope that the lack of clear-cut evidence against Rupert will always protect him from having to take action, but in adopting this approach, he is deceiving himself. He would do better to remind himself that no matter how great the temptation to take revenge, he must always do his utmost to resist, and that there is no guarantee that he will succeed in this effort. Accordingly, when Sylvester learns of the death of Jeronimus in Rossitz, he loses faith in his ethical system and succumbs to the temptation to take revenge. Mistakenly, he believes that he has seen the error of his previous ways, when, in effect, all he has done is to abandon the benevolent (but flawed) view of human nature he has espoused hitherto in favor of that of Rupert. And as we shall see, in so doing, he anticipates the behavior of the elderly Piachi in "Der Findling," who, in refusing absolution, turns his back on the ethical system in which he had placed his trust: the Catholic Church.

At this point in the play Sylvester imagines that he has learned from the mistakes of the past, whereas, in fact, a much harder lesson lies in store for him. It is only in the final act, when he enters the hell of the lovers' grotto, that he becomes truly enlightened about the nature of evil. There he discovers that he is quite capable of descending to Rupert's level. And when the latter addresses him at the end of the play, asking "kannst du besser nicht verzeihn, als ich?" (5.1.2716), the fact that Sylvester cannot bear to look him in the face (the stage directions indicate that Sylvester offers his hand, averting his gaze as he does so) is not, as some critics have suggested, an indication of the tentativeness of this reconciliation[1] but, on the contrary, an indication of the depth of Sylvester's grief and self-disgust. Just as Rupert recoils in disgust when he sees his reflection — the face of a devil — staring back up at him from the pool of spring water, so, too, Sylvester cannot bear to see his own satanic nature reflected in the gaze of his rival, Rupert. In attempting to do to Rupert what Rupert did to him, Sylvester has come to resemble the opponent he once blamed. By the end of the play a state of equilibrium has, indeed, been achieved, but only at the cost of the extinction of the Schroffenstein family — a damning testimony to the futility of revenge.

"Die Rache des Himmels . . . würde dadurch entwaffnet . . .": "Die Verlobung in St. Domingo"

In "Die Verlobung in St. Domingo" the picture of revenge with which we are presented is considerably more complex than that in *Die Familie Schroffenstein*. In his account of the Haitian uprising Kleist highlights the dangers that ensue when a group of individuals (the blacks) are brutally oppressed and systematically subjected to one injustice after another. As the novella shows — and here its relevance for an understanding of the aftermath of the French Revolution cannot be underestimated — when the prevailing structures of authority collapse, conventional notions of humanity are likely to be swept away in a blood-bath of violent retribution. In his characterization of the Swiss mercenary, Gustav, Kleist shows that while this quasi-neutral outsider recognizes that the behavior of the white plantation owners has been anything but exemplary, he is incapable of understanding what motivates the oppressed to go to such extremes in their quest for vengeance against their former masters. This incapacity is evident in his account of the black woman with yellow fever who, brutally treated by her master on account of her refusal to sleep with him in the past, is presented with the perfect opportunity to take her revenge when the revolution breaks out. Having exploited her sexual charms to lure the terrified man into her bed, she deliberately infects him with the disease. So appalled is Gustav by the calculated manner in which the woman exacts such extreme vengeance that he declares: "keine Tyrannei, die die Weißen je verübt, einen Verrat, so niederträchtig und abscheulich, rechtfertigen könnte" (2:170–71). What makes the woman's behavior so abominable in his eyes is that it represents a complete inversion of human nature (as Gustav understands it). Not only is this heinous act of vengeance carried out by a woman, but the coup de grâce is delivered precisely at the moment when the plantation owner believes himself to be in a position of safety. In short, it is a monstrous act that would not be out of place in the world of Rupert Schroffenstein, a world in which, as the latter puts it, men have become like beasts (cf. 1.1.57–58). Gustav's appalled reaction, however, underlines his status as an outsider in this conflict and the extent to which he has been protected from the kind of brutal excesses to which the majority of the black population has been habitually exposed. Perhaps, like the pupils of Kleist's proposed "Lasterschule" in the essay "Allerneuester Erziehungsplan," he would have profited from a greater exposure to the excesses of human wickedness. Nonetheless, by the end of the story he will have learned at first hand just how powerful the desire for revenge is in those who believe themselves to be the victims of betrayal and humiliation.

The same sense of abhorrence is evident in the narrator's account of Congo Hoango's life — an account that, as a number of critics have pointed out, manifestly fails to situate Hoango's behavior in the social and political context of this cruelly oppressive colonial regime (cf. Horn; Fleming). For although Herr Villeneuve had granted Congo Hoango his freedom many years ago (but only, of course, because the slave had saved his life), the narrator is horrified to report that all these proofs of gratitude had failed to protect Monsieur de Villeneuve from the fury of this ferocious man. As soon as the island is seized by this frenzy of vindictiveness, Congo Hoango wastes no time in executing his former master and setting fire to the house in which the latter's wife and children have taken refuge. Although the narrator is appalled by the indiscriminate murder of the whites, even worse in his eyes is the fact that in slaughtering Herr Villeneuve together with his wife and children, Congo Hoango has failed to honor what the narrator (albeit from his position of bias) clearly regards as an implicit bond of trust between the Negro and the former plantation owner. And thus, in the case of both Herr Villeneuve and the white plantation owner infected by the woman with yellow fever, what makes these brutal deeds seem even worse than they already are is the calculated act of betrayal involved. For in each case, what we witness is not an indiscriminate act of violence but a highly personalized act of revenge.

It is, of course, easy to condemn the blacks for such behavior — as, indeed, both Gustav and the (implicitly white) narrator do. But when we consider the total dominance the white colonists have come to enjoy, together with the inevitable slanting in their favor of the law and its related institutions, it is easier to understand how the blacks, smarting under the arbitrary cruelties and injustices of the regime, should respond with total counterviolence. And significantly, the one question Gustav (and the narrator) never really face up to is that posed by Toni when she asks Gustav, "wodurch sich denn die Weißen daselbst so verhaßt gemacht hätten?" (2:170). The powerful effect of injustice in nurturing feelings of hatred and in promoting a need for indiscriminate violent retribution is particularly well illustrated by the case of Babekan, the mulatto woman whose hatred of everything white harks back to her experiences in Europe with Toni's (white) father, a wealthy Parisian businessman. While pregnant with Toni in Paris, Babekan was betrayed by Herr Bertrand, who, ashamed of his liaison with her and anxious to marry another (presumably white and, hence, "respectable") woman, denied paternity of Babekan's child before the courts. The bitter experience of this humiliating betrayal has been compounded by a further injustice (and corresponding loss of esteem), the flogging administered by Herr Villeneuve. Smarting from her experiences of personal and legal betrayal, Babekan is, of all the characters in the story, the most extreme in her desire for revenge. As an elderly mulatto woman, she has no choice but to resort to "List und den ganzen Inbegriff jener Künste, die die Notwehr dem Schwachen in die Hände gibt" (2:165). For, like the woman with yellow fever (whom Babekan no doubt admires greatly), the fact remains that as an oppressed black — and a black woman at that — she has no other means at her disposal.

Unlike Congo Hoango — who, as the ending of the story shows, is not devoid of a streak of humanity, insofar as he is unwilling to sacrifice the lives of his beloved children, Nanky and Seppy, on the altar of the black cause — Babekan's desire for vengeance knows no such bounds. She takes no account of the moral culpability of the individual whites she succeeds in luring to their doom and has no qualms about exploiting her daughter as an instrument in her vindictive schemes. Toni, on the other hand, has not yet experienced the prolonged exposure to white injustice and brutality suffered by Babekan, and thus, when she reflects on the similarities between the behavior of the woman with yellow fever and her own (unwitting) participation in the execution of the fleeing whites, she has a greater capacity to recognize the immorality of the ruthless pursuit of revenge that drives her mother and makes her incapable of imagining herself in the position of her victims. Now quite incapable of thinking in terms of quasi-Kantian moral categories, Babekan's total commitment to the black cause is perhaps most clearly revealed when, believing herself to have been betrayed by Toni, her unconditional desire for revenge overrides her maternal feelings, and she calls on God to take vengeance on her own flesh and blood (2:191).

Babekan's wish is tragically realized when Gustav shoots Toni — an act of violent retribution for what he believes to be a gross act of betrayal on her part. And just as the two fathers in *Die Familie Schroffenstein* are left to contemplate the self-destructive consequences of their quest for vengeance, so Gustav is forced to acknowledge that his rage has blinded him to the reality of his predicament. But what the story underlines, above all, are the different types of revenge available to the strong and the weak, respectively: Gustav, the white European mercenary, exacts his vengeance by shooting down his chosen victim at point-blank range; by contrast, the likes of the woman with yellow fever cannot tackle their oppressors head on but have to resort to underhanded tactics, exploiting their sexuality to ensnare their oppressors and take their revenge. And while Kleist does not condone revenge in "Die Verlobung in St. Domingo" (cf. Wittkowski), it is striking that he offers an essentially realistic account of the way in which the oppressed have no choice but to avail themselves of the weapons they have at their disposal in their struggle for freedom.

"Die Rache der Barbaren sei dir fern!": *Die Hermannsschlacht*

Like "Die Verlobung in St. Domingo," to which it is often compared, Kleist's revolutionary drama *Die Hermannsschlacht* explores the nature of the acts of violent retribution committed in the struggle to overthrow the oppressive regime of a colonial power.[2] The world of Hermann and his German chieftains is permeated by a longing for violent retributive justice far removed from the moral rectitude underpinning the bloodless revolution of Schiller's *Wilhelm Tell* (1804). In the latter, Walter Fürst may declare that

> Rache trägt keine Frucht! Sich selbst ist sie
> Die fürchterliche Nahrung, ihr Genuß
> Ist Mord, und ihre Sättigung das Grausen. (10:264)

Kleist's Hermann, on the other hand, not only exacts condign vengeance on several occasions in his own right but deliberately encourages the members of his entourage (including his wife, Thusnelda) to give free rein to their desire to avenge themselves against their oppressors.

The difficulty with which Hermann is confronted is that the majority of the German chieftains have little or no understanding of freedom or of the kind of enslavement that is entailed by the occupation of one's country by an alien colonial power. As the opening scene of *Die Her-*

mannsschlacht makes clear, the majority of the German leaders are all too willing to further their own particular interests by coming to local agreements with the foreign power and are oblivious to the loss of personal autonomy that this inevitably entails. As a result, Hermann sees only one remedy: to engender in his fellow Germans a deep-seated hatred of the Romans and a consequent desire for revenge. Accordingly, he sets out deliberately to demonstrate that there is no atrocity that the Romans would not commit and even goes to the extreme of fabricating evidence in support of this propaganda war. The high point of his campaign comes in the Hally episode of act 4, scene 6, when, in a clear biblical allusion (Judges 19:29), Hermann orders the corpse of the girl who has been raped by Roman soldiers to be cut into fifteen pieces and a piece of her flesh sent to each of the German chieftains. Indeed, there is something almost carnivalesque about the Hally episode, which succeeds almost immediately in unleashing a flood of powerful emotions and in prompting the assembled mob to exclaim "Empörung! Rache! Freiheit" (4.6.1621) — a formulation that itself embodies the three stages through which Hermann hopes to guide the oppressed Germans in their journey to freedom from the Roman yoke.

Given the Germans' lack of sophistication, Hermann is aware that his countrymen have neither the diplomatic cunning nor the military muscle to tackle the Romans on the latter's terms. In mobilizing their more primitive capacity for vengeance, he is forced to make a virtue out of a necessity. Nonetheless, the fact remains that, once released, this desire for violent retribution that is so characteristic of smaller, less advanced social units can become a powerful vitalistic force. For this type of retributive justice — in which the injured party is directly involved in the punishment of the offending party — is far removed from the more "civilized" versions of law and order associated with sophisticated societies in which punishments are administered by a third party, usually the state, and then not according to the *lex talionis* but, rather, in accordance with an abstract system of fines and imprisonment.

The opposition between these two worlds is most strikingly illustrated by the exchange that takes place between Hermann and Septimius Nerva in act 5, scene 13. Even though he has firsthand evidence of Hermann's treachery, the "civilized" Septimius feels confident that Hermann will merely take him prisoner in keeping with the Roman version of martial etiquette: "Mein Haupt, das wehrlos vor dir steht, / Soll deiner Rache heilig sein" (5.13.2212–13). But just how poor Septimius's understanding is of the conflict in which he is caught up is underlined when he is forced to recognize that, unlike him, Hermann is not a professional soldier on duty in a remote part of the world but a warrior committed to a life-and-death struggle in which nothing short of his own freedom — conceived as only one in his situation can conceive it, as absolute freedom outside all others' control — is at stake. As such, sophisticated codes of conduct such as Cicero's *De officiis* that have been designed to govern the treatment of prisoners of war in conflicts involving "civilized" nations have no meaning for a man like Hermann. Accordingly, Hermann pokes fun at Septimius's naive hope that he, a German "barbarian," would endorse such a system of ethics: "Er hat das Buch von Cicero gelesen. / Was müßt ich tun, sag an, nach diesem Werk?" (5.13.2209), before condemning the Roman to be clubbed to death, a death that in its humiliating brutality is nothing short of a brutal act of revenge. At the same time, the episode underlines Hermann's grasp of the all-or-nothing nature of the conflict between the Germans and the Roman power and, above all, his realization that the only escape from such a power is to replace it with one's own. In acting as he does, he shows that he is a "true German" and that he places a higher value on his freedom than he does on being regarded as "civilized" by those who would take it away from him. In this respect his behavior mirrors that of Congo Hoango, who, it may be assumed, cares as little about being branded "a terrible old Negro" by his white oppressors as Hermann does at being termed a "German dog."

Throughout *Die Hermannsschlacht* Hermann demonstrates his understanding of the psychology of hatred and, in particular, of the way in which hatred of the Roman invaders, far from being natural, is something that must be consciously cultivated by the freedom-fighter. Thus, when, in act 4, scene 9, his wife, Thusnelda, accuses him of being blind to the decent behavior of certain individual Romans, Hermann cuts her short, alluding to the obvious contradiction between such virtuous acts, on the one hand, and the Romans' involvement in a bitter imperial conquest, on the other hand. Hermann is all too well aware that all human beings are capable of losing sight of the greater picture and, consequently, of overvaluing isolated acts of individual kindness. He recognizes, too, that the enemy of all passions — of hatred no less than love — is time, and that hating one's true enemy requires a concerted effort and a constant renewal of commitment:

> Ich *will* die höhnische Dämonenbrut nicht lieben!
> So lang sie in Germanien trotzt,
> Ist Haß mein Amt und meine Tugend Rache! (4.9.1723–25)

But when Thusnelda pleads with him to spare the life of her beloved Ventidius, it becomes clear to Hermann that she will never be persuaded by
rational means of the extent to which she is complicit in her own downfall.
Only when the full force of her capacity for hatred and revenge is unleashed
will she be able to break free from the spell Ventidius has cast on her by
means of his sophisticated — but essentially exploitative — flattery.[3]

Thusnelda's terrible lust for vengeance is, of course, triggered by the
discovery of Ventidius's letter containing the locket of her hair. Confronted with incontrovertible evidence of his deception of her, she is
filled with a profound sense of humiliation together with a deep hatred
of everything around her, including, most importantly, herself: "Verhaßt
ist alles / Die Welt mir, du mir, ich" (4.9.1819). And thus, once again
in the encounter between her and her lover, Ventidius, we witness essentially the same collision of two diametrically opposed worlds of experience that we saw in the case of Septimius and Hermann. Ventidius's fatal
flaw is that in his self-satisfied sophistication as a member of an advanced
society, he regards the Germans as a race of sub-human primitives incapable of the kind of cunning and sagacity that Hermann demonstrates.
This contempt is revealed most clearly when he is asked by Varus
whether Hermann can be trusted, and he replies smugly:

> Er ist ein Deutscher.
> In einem Hämmling ist, der an der Tiber graset,
> Mehr Lug und Trug, muß ich dir sagen,
> Als in dem ganzen Volk, dem er gehört. (3.6.1250–53)

Similarly, he regards Thusnelda as "merely" a woman — and a barbarian
woman at that. That is to say, he views her, as, indeed, he does all women,
as a weak, naive creature, incapable of resisting the charms of his sophisticated, civilized chivalry. But like Achilles in *Penthesilea* — another Kleistian
figure who subscribes to the view that woman are "by nature" incapable of
intense feelings of rage — the Roman legate is in for a surprise. Protected
from exposure to such raw passion by the conventional trappings of his
sophisticated society, Ventidius remains oblivious to the danger he is in until
it is too late. By contrast, Thusnelda's maid, Gertrud, by virtue of being a
woman *and* a member of a more primitive form of society, has a much
healthier respect for the fury of a scorned (barbarian) woman, and she recognizes the deadly seriousness of the situation only too clearly. At the same
time, Gertrud underlines the fact that the act of revenge is not without
consequences for the avenger. As she says in a final attempt to persuade
Thusnelda to abandon her odious plan:

Die Rache der Barbaren sei dir fern!
Es ist Ventidius nicht, der mich mit Sorg erfüllt;
Du selbst, wenn nun die Tat getan,
Von Reu und Schmerz wirst du zusammenfallen!
(5.15.2317–20)

Gertrud's words underline an important feature of such acts of revenge. For it is one of the paradoxes of the quest for vengeance that, while abhorrent in itself, it is often prompted by motives that are normally regarded as positive — not least the desire for real justice on the part of the injured party. But it is precisely because the perpetration of such acts presupposes a sense of morality that the avenger, whenever he (or she) reflects on the act in retrospect, cannot but be filled with a sense of remorse.

"Ich will nicht selig sein . . .": "Der Findling"

Like "Die Verlobung in St. Domingo," "Der Findling" also ends on a note of extreme violence. Toward the end of the novella the elderly Piachi comes home to discover his adopted son, Nicolo, raping Piachi's wife, Elvire. When he demands that Nicolo vacate the premises, he — not the boy — is thrown out of house and home. Furious at the boy's callous behavior, he turns to the authorities in the hope that they will take formal legal action to put right the obvious injustice he has suffered (even though Nicolo's claim to the property is, under the strict terms of the law, valid). Piachi's hopes are dashed, however, when the corrupt bishop intervenes, and the courts decide in favor of the boy. Let down by the authorities and plunged into despair by the death of his wife, Piachi turns his back on the judiciary and, with no regard for the consequences of his actions, takes the law into his own hands. So extreme is his desire for vengeance that it is incapable of being satisfied in the temporal world. He not only kills Nicolo in a brutal manner but goes on to desecrate the corpse, stuffing the state's decree down his victim's mouth. Through the inclusion of this trivial detail Kleist underlines an important aspect of revenge: by exacting violent retribution, the avenger builds into the punishment an element of the original injury done to him. Even then, however, Piachi's desire for vengeance is not satiated, for he consistently refuses absolution:

> Ich will in den untersten Grund der Hölle hinabfahren. Ich will den Nicolo, der nicht im Himmel sein wird, wiederfinden, und meine Rache, die ich hier nur unvollständig befriedigen konnte, wiederaufnehmen! (2:214–15)

While Piachi's initial violent rage may be comprehensible under the circumstances, his considered rejection of absolution is far more chilling. The extreme nature of his desire for vengeance — his willingness to descend to hell itself in pursuit of Nicolo — is an abhorrent act that compels the reader to reassess the character of "the good old man."

While Piachi's desire to avenge himself against Nicolo is reflected in his violent treatment of the boy, his considered refusal on more than one occasion to take absolution before being executed constitutes a further act of revenge, albeit one directed against a different target. For when he rejects the Body of Christ, insisting "Ich will nicht selig sein" (2:214), Piachi's defiance constitutes an act of revenge against the Catholic Church and the system of ethics he has hitherto espoused. In choosing to reject God and embrace the devil, he closely resembles Sylvester in *Die Familie Schroffenstein,* who decides that the time has come to abandon the more humane version of ethics underpinning Warwand society and strike back at his enemy, instead. This is not the only point of similarity between the two men, however. For although each of them feels that he has been betrayed by his respective ethical system, neither fully understands the true nature of the belief system to which he is committed. In each case, the error consists in the failure to recognize that while institutions incorporating a system of moral views (whether of a religious or nonreligious kind) can play an important role in promoting certain patterns of human conduct, they cannot causally determine the behavior of individual human beings. Sylvester is forced to recognize that while the social organization in Warwand constitutes a considerable barrier to arbitrary acts of violence, it cannot rule them out altogether. For his part, Piachi misunderstands the nature of Christian charity underpinning the ethical system he espouses, believing — mistakenly — that the generosity he has shown toward his adopted son must, of necessity, elicit feelings of gratitude in return. But as he finds to his cost, this is not the case.

Piachi is not the only character to seek vengeance in "Der Findling." In the latter part of the novella the narrator notes that Nicolo's abhorrent — yet highly elaborate — plan to seduce Elvire by concealing himself in her room and dressing up as her beloved Colino stems from a mixture of humiliation, lust, and the desire for revenge (2:212). In this novella — perhaps Kleist's most provocative analysis of human morality — the reader is compelled to ask why Nicolo should respond with such ingratitude to the kindness shown him by Piachi. The answer lies in Piachi's failure to understand what is involved in the psychology of adolescent upbringing, in particular, the delicate mechanisms involved in conferring a benefit on another human being. As we have seen, in the essay "Allerneuester Erziehungsplan" Kleist emphasizes the importance of encouraging the development of an autonomous moral will in the individual. But in "Der Findling" the effect of Piachi's excessively benevolent treatment of Nicolo is to block such a development. His treatment of Nicolo increases the boy's pre-existing sense of his own worthlessness and renders him incapable of loving either himself or others. And having been denied the capacity to love by Piachi's (oppressive) benevolence, Nicolo begins to despise his benefactor and seeks to assert his freedom through the only other channel at his disposal: hate.

Why then does Nicolo select Elvire — and not Piachi — as the object of his revenge? First, he assumes (erroneously, as it turns out) that it is she who is preventing him from continuing his liaison with Xaviera Tartini. Significantly, his desire to get even with Elvire is prompted by the humiliation (and reminder of his essential worthlessness) that he suffers during Xaviera's mock funeral (2:206). Second, since he can discover no conventionally acknowledged flaws in the "good old man," he has no choice but to turn instead to Piachi's young, attractive wife in the hope that she may offer greater possibilities. Convinced that Elvire is, indeed, a hypocrite as a result of what he has observed through the keyhole of her room, he can console himself with the thought that in this ocean of Piachi's boundless generosity he is not alone on his island of wickedness. Finally, he is well aware that Elvire is Piachi's protégé and that by exposing a flaw in her character he can indirectly strike a blow at the old man himself. And in so doing he can evade the disagreeable control to which he is subjected and, albeit in this perverted fashion, reassert himself.

"Der Herr aber, dessen Leib du begehrst, vergab seinem Feind . . .": "Michael Kohlhaas"

While "Der Findling" ends with Piachi's insistence on his right to avenge himself — even at the cost of eternal damnation — the central figure in "Michael Kohlhaas" develops in the opposite direction. Although Kohlhaas tries to persuade Luther that he has a right to hate his enemy, by the end of the novella he rejects revenge and returns to the bosom of the Church. Indeed, the complex relationship between justice and revenge is central to an understanding of the novella.[4] Like that of Piachi in "Der Findling" or Sylvester in *Die Familie Schroffenstein,* Kleist's characterization of the horse dealer is such that we can be sure that in his normal condition he is not a man predisposed to avenge himself on his enemy. Not only is he a sincere Christian; he has a firm commitment to the rule of law and order. At the same time, he subscribes to a commonsense, pragmatic view of the world, accepting "die gebrechliche Einrichtung der Welt" (2:15). Despite the manifestly unreasonable behavior of the Junker, he goes out of his way to be accommodating; and when he questions his groom, Herse, about the fate of his horses, he never loses sight of the possibility that there may be mitigating circumstances that, while not excusing the Junker's behavior, might at least go some way toward explaining it. Part of the reason Kleist goes to such lengths to emphasize the utter reasonableness of Kohlhaas's initial dealings with the establishment is to show that the horse dealer is a man for whom the prevailing social conditions have hitherto offered a more than comfortable existence and that, in contrast to those from the lower orders of society (such as Herse and Nagelschmidt), he has a lot to lose.

The driving impulse behind Kohlhaas's initial quest for vengeance is, as the narrator correctly observes in the opening paragraph of the story, his sense of justice. Even when Kohlhaas follows the approved legal procedures, his attempts to secure justice via the courts fail on account of the intervention of corrupt officials (all of whom are closely connected with the Junker von Wenzel). When his case is finally dismissed, and he is referred to as a vexatious litigant (2:23), Kohlhaas is outraged and is only pacified temporarily when his wife, Lisbeth, offers to intercede on his behalf and present her husband's petition to the Elector of Brandenburg. But when Lisbeth is fatally injured in the process, Kohlhaas reaches the point of no return. The dying Lisbeth may point to the verses in Matt. 5:44, "Forgive your enemies; do good also unto them that hate you," but as Kohlhaas's reply — "so möge mir Gott nie vergeben, wie ich dem Junker vergebe" (2:30) — makes clear, he has but one thought in his head: violent retribution. And while hardly rational — for the death of the Junker will not bring back his wife — Kohlhaas's burning desire for vengeance at this point in the narrative is the understandable reaction of a man driven mad by anger and grief.

Thwarted in his initial attempts to track down the Junker, Kohlhaas recovers a degree of composure and embarks on a more systematic program of rebellion, attracting a small army of malcontents and setting fire to the towns of Wittenberg and Leipzig. But it is at this point that Kohlhaas's mission is transformed from a personal quest for vengeance against the Junker to a wider crusade for justice generally. This shift in emphasis is signaled in one of the proclamations issued by Kohlhaas, in which he styles himself as

einen Statthalter des Michaels des Erzengels, der gekommen sei, an allen, die in dieser Streitsache des Junkers Partei ergriffen würden, mit
Feuer und Schwert, die Arglist, in welcher die ganze Welt versunken
sei, zu bestrafen. (2:41)

And as the authorities discover to their horror, even those citizens who
suffer personally as a result of Kohlhaas's incendiary attacks are willing to
support the rebel's demands. So convinced is Kohlhaas of the essential
justness of his cause that he is stunned when Luther publicly condemns
his campaign. During their ensuing meeting, however, it soon becomes
clear that Luther will have to revise his opinion of Kohlhaas. For the fact
that Kohlhaas threatens to kill not Luther but himself should the latter
call for help cannot but underline the depth of his commitment to his
quest for justice. During this discussion Kohlhaas presents his case as that
of a man who has been systematically denied justice and, thus, cast out
from his sovereign's community (cf. 2:45). Indeed, it is hard to avoid
drawing a number of intriguing parallels between Kleist's "Michael
Kohlhaas" and Schiller's *Die Räuber* (1781), not least because of the
similarity between Kleist's Kohlhaas and Schiller's Karl Moor. Like Kohlhaas, Karl Moor regards himself as a man unjustly cast out of the bosom
of his family and protests defiantly against a society in which such injustice is possible with the words: "Sag ihnen, mein Handwerk ist Wieder-
vergeltung — Rache ist mein Gewerbe" (Schiller 3:71). Karl Moor's
words here underline the extent to which such retributive justice is associated with those more "primitive" social units located on the margins
of "sophisticated" society. Kleist's Kohlhaas, however, remains committed to the rule of law and order and proves quite willing to abandon the
rule of the club if it can be shown that he can obtain justice within the
parameters of conventional society. But Kohlhaas is willing to abandon
his campaign of armed rebellion, he is not, at this stage, prepared to
abandon his quest for revenge in respect of the Junker (cf. 2:48). The
fact that Kohlhaas cannot yet bring himself to forgive the Junker — and
wants the Junker personally to fatten up his horses — is evidence of
Kleist's realistic portrayal of human nature. At the same time, it points
to one of the weaknesses of sophisticated legal systems that operate with
a series of abstract penalties and in which the punishment of the criminal
occurs in isolation from the injured party. Nonetheless, to succumb to
the temptation to hate one's enemy is simply part of human nature, but
to claim that it is one's right to hate one's enemy — as Kohlhaas attempts to do here — is an altogether different proposition and one that
Luther, as a good Christian, has no choice but to reject.

Kohlhaas's refusal to pretend that he is prepared to forgive his enemy in order to obtain absolution is a mark of his integrity (and of the sincerity of his religious belief). In the light of this, the fact that just prior to his death Kohlhaas does receive communion from Luther's emissary, Jakob Freising (cf. 2:100), is of crucial significance, for it clearly suggests that Kohlhaas has undergone a profound change of heart, abandoned his perverse belief that he is right to hate his enemy, and, instead, embraced the Christian doctrine of forgiveness.[5] As we shall see, this has a crucial bearing on the interpretation of the final episode of the story in which Kleist demonstrates that it is not necessary for a man of integrity to resort to baser acts of revenge in order to triumph over the wicked. For when, just prior to his execution, Kohlhaas swallows the paper contained in the mysterious locket, this is not an act of vengeance but, rather, the final confirmation of the fact that he places his quest for justice above his own life.[6] In surrendering his life, he demonstrates before the assembled crowd that he behaved in an altruistic fashion, that what he did was not for the sake of his horses, nor for the sake of personal enrichment, but for the sake of justice for all. At the same time, his acceptance that he deserves the death sentence passed on him by the Emperor as the just punishment for a man who, in attempting to overturn the state, has attacked the very principle of law and order, signals that far from seeking the destruction of the state, he wants to have some of its more glaring deficiencies put right.

In "Michael Kohlhaas" Kleist explores the consequences that ensue when standards of government are allowed to decay beyond a certain point. That the authorities in Saxony should find themselves in such a perilous predicament is largely a reflection of their own weakness, shortsightedness and overconfidence. They are so steeped in the machinations of self-interest that they are no longer able to recognize their corruption for what it is. As a result, they fail to appreciate the grave injustices that individuals suffer on an almost daily basis and the intense feelings of rage that these injustices provoke. In part, the problem can be traced to the way in which in such developed societies the legal system represents not so much a means of ensuring that justice is done as a mechanism for ensuring the maintenance of law and order — and with it, of course, the position of the ruling elite. If the position of the ruling elite is to remain unchallenged, it is essential that the system of law and order over which it presides is shown to be infallible and inviolate. Since Kohlhaas's attempt to secure justice via the courts cannot but expose some of the more glaring deficiencies in the system, those in authority are determined to block it at every turn, regardless of the obvious injustice this entails. But when Kohlhaas reflects that his quest for justice has not only been unsuccessful but also has cost him the life of his wife, he turns his back not only on the rule of law but also on his Christian faith and insists on his right to avenge himself against his enemy. While the authorities are used to dealing with the kind of attacks on the system launched by the likes of Nagelschmidt — and are confident that they have the necessary force at their disposal to deal with him — they are quite unprepared for the sheer ferocity of Kohlhaas's assault. But as the story shows, when injustice is allowed to pass unchecked, numerous pockets of disenchanted individuals are created consisting of people who, having effectively been "cast out" from their society, will seek justice on their own terms and can be effectively mobilized by a resourceful leader such as Kohlhaas.

Part of our admiration for Kohlhaas stems from the fact that his desire for vengeance is not rooted in self-interest but is driven by motives that we would normally regard as positive — notably, a desire for general justice. He does not wish the system to be altered in his favor (although, no doubt, this is something he might well be able to bring about were he to trade in the mysterious locket). And as the end of the story confirms, once it is clear that justice will be restored, he returns to his religion. In receiving absolution from Luther's emissary, Kleist signals a change of heart on Kohlhaas's part that indicates an acceptance of the Christian doctrine of forgiveness. At the same time, in accepting the essential correctness of his execution he signals his return to his sovereign's fold and his acceptance of the rule of law.

Conclusions

In many of Kleist's works revenge is presented in an unambiguously negative light as an act that stands in the greatest possible contrast to the Christian doctrine of forgiveness set out in the New Testament. In *Die Familie Schroffenstein* Rupert's untamed quest for vengeance is shown to be a deluded, self-contradictory act that not only causes the deaths of the two innocent children, Agnes and Ottokar, but also, in bringing about the demise of the Schroffenstein clan, destroys that which it was intended to preserve. Although a state of equilibrium has been reached by the end of the play, the spectator is left with a nihilistic vision of a world with no future. Nonetheless, while Sylvester also succumbs to the temptation to take revenge, it is important to recognize that Kleist clearly favors the more developed social model represented by the house of Warwand over the more ruthless and authoritarian ideology underpinning the Rossitz clan. When Sylvester rejects his preferred system of ethics, he fails to appreciate that while the institution of Warwand represents a considerable advance on its counterpart in Rossitz, no institution can determine individual behavior to the extent of ruling out the possibility for evil absolutely. Accordingly, in abandoning the Christian doctrine of forgiveness in favor of violent retribution, the elderly, mild-mannered Sylvester belongs with those characters in Kleist's works, who, frustrated by the failure of their essentially benevolent systems of ethics to deliver the desired result, turn their backs on those systems and embrace the opposite. It is precisely this transformation, of course, that the well-intentioned Piachi undergoes in "Der Findling" when he refuses absolution and turns his back on God and the Catholic Church.

In stark contrast to the bleak endings of both *Die Familie Schroffen-stein* and "Der Findling," in "Michael Kohlhaas" Kleist shows what it takes to overcome the desire for vengeance. In the novella anger is shown to be an essential motivating force in Kohlhaas's quest for justice — and the actions prompted by the horse dealer's righteous ire are of quite a different order from those committed by the anarchic Nagel-schmidt. For when the law-abiding Kohlhaas — a reasonable man quite prepared to accept some of the shortcomings of human legal institutions — is treated with contempt by the judiciary in Saxony, he comes to see himself as a man "cast out" and, thus, as an individual entitled to seek justice by any means he chooses. At the same time, the convoluted nature of the legal system in Saxony underlines an essential weakness in the judicial institutions of "sophisticated" societies, insofar as they are more concerned with the maintenance of law and order than they are with justice per se. In contrast to more "primitive" societies — in which the injured party is more likely to be involved directly in the punishment of the offender — the members of sophisticated societies are inclined to lose interest in the concept of justice. As a result, whenever an individual's quest for justice threatens to disrupt the prevailing state of public order, he finds himself forced to take on not only the corrupt authorities but also the bulk of the population, who have long since abandoned their love of justice and become devotees of public order instead.

In Kleist's works it is particularly striking that those responsible for injustice are, more often than not, oblivious to the strength of the feelings of hatred they have unleashed in the injured party. Thus, the Junker and the Saxon authorities are caught completely by surprise in "Michael Kohlhaas," and in both "Die Verlobung in St. Domingo" and *Die Her-mannsschlacht* the representatives of the dominant imperial power fail to appreciate — with fatal consequences — the extremes of violence to which their victims are prepared to go in their attempt to redress an imbalance in the scales of justice. Here Kleist offers an acute analysis of the psychology of revenge, pointing out how the desire for violent retribution is intimately bound up with the degree of personal humiliation suffered by the injured party. Perhaps the clearest example is to be found in the characterization of Babekan in "Die Verlobung in St. Domingo." After a life of humiliation at the hands of the "civilized" Europeans, she has been rendered incapable of embracing anything remotely resembling a Kantian notion of morality; as a result, her whole being has been consumed by an insatiable desire for revenge. At the same time, we should not overlook the case of Nicolo, the boy "killed" by Piachi's kindness. Forced to experience one humiliation after another on account of his failure to live up to the virtuous behavior of the good old man (and his impeccable wife), Nicolo seeks to assert his autonomy through the only means at his disposal: taking revenge on his benefactor. And as the unfortunate Piachi discovers, the problem is not that we know too much about human wickedness; it is, rather, that we know too little.

Notes

[1] Anthony Stephens, for example, speaks of "the dubious reconciliation of the fathers" (42).

[2] For an attempt to link the code of ethics in the two works, see Angress. Her arguments are extended by Fischer, who sees the story as offering a critique of a version of Enlightenment Christian ethics dealing only with individual guilt and responsibility and incapable of taking due account of the political nature of an act (Fischer 1988, 100–112, esp. 105–6).

[3] Note the similarity between Thusnelda's attempts to become worthy of Hermann once more (1:616, line 2322) and Kleist's observation that young Prussian women required a "grimmige Rache" to come to their senses and see through the flattery of the flirtatious Napoleonic officers (cf. Sembdner 1984, No. 319).

[4] The question whether the horse dealer's quest for justice is not itself irredeemably grounded in a personal desire for vengeance is one on which Kleist scholars remain deeply divided. For a positive view of Kohlhaas, see Müller; for the opposite view, see Lucas.

[5] Curiously enough, the majority of critics interpret the fact that Kohlhaas does ultimately receive communion as indicative of a change of heart not on the part of Kohlhaas but of Luther. Thus Lucas comments that "Luther, with really culpable inconsistency . . . bestows on him the accolade of a communion he had withheld from the obdurate man as long as he had refused forgiveness: it is Luther, not Kohlhaas, who has given in" (139–40). In a similar vein, Denys Dyer suggests that the subsequent offer of communion "must cast into question Luther's former adamant stand and . . . suggest that Kohlhaas' actions were not at variance with the Christian faith" (144).

[6] Here I am in agreement with John Ellis, who argues that "the punishment the Elector will suffer is certain and is in the future, and Kohlhaas's act [i.e. his swallowing of the paper] has *nothing to do* with bringing that punishment about" (82).

Works Cited

Angress, Ruth. "Kleist's Treatment of Imperialism: *Die Hermannsschlacht* and 'Die Verlobung in St. Domingo.'" *Monatshefte* 69 (1977): 17–33.

Dyer, Denys. *The Stories of Kleist: A Critical Study.* London: Duckworth, 1977.

Ellis, John. *Heinrich von Kleist: Studies in the Character and Meaning of His Writings.* Chapel Hill: U of North Carolina P, 1979.

Fischer, Bernd. *Ironische Metaphysik: Die Erzählungen Heinrich von Kleists.* Munich: Fink, 1988.

Fleming, Ray. "Race and the Difference It Makes in Kleist's 'Die Verlobung in St. Domingo.'" *German Quarterly* 65 (1992): 306–17.

Goldammer, Peter, ed. *Schrifsteller über Kleist: Eine Dokumentation.* Berlin: Aufbau, 1976.

Horn, Peter. "Hatte Kleist Rassenvorurteile? Eine Kritische Auseinandersetzung mit der Literatur zur 'Verlobung in St. Domingo.'" *Monatshefte* 67 (1975): 117–28.

Kleist, Heinrich von. *Sämtliche Werke und Briefe.* 2 vols. 7th ed. Ed. Helmut Sembdner. Munich: Hanser, 1984.

Lucas, Raymond. "Studies in Kleist: 'Michael Kohlhaas.'" *Deutsche Vierteljahrsschrift* 44 (1970): 120–45.

Müller, Richard Matthias. "Kleists 'Michael Kohlhaas.'" *Deutsche Vierteljahrsschrift* 44 (1970): 101–19.

Nobile, Nancy. *The School of Days: Heinrich von Kleist and the Traumas of Education.* Detroit: Wayne State UP, 1999.

Schiller, Friedrich. *Schillers Werke: Nationalausgabe.* 22 vols. Ed. Julius Petersen et al. Weimar: Böhlau, 1943–63.

Sembdner, Helmut, ed. *Heinrich von Kleists Lebensspuren: Dokumente und Berichte der Zeitgenossen.* Frankfurt a.M.: Insel, 1984.

Stephens, Anthony. *Heinrich von Kleist: The Dramas and Stories.* Oxford: Berg, 1994.

Wittkowski, Wolfgang. "Gerechtigkeit und Loyalität, Ethik und Politik." *Kleist-Jahrbuch* (1992): 152–71.

Contributors

SEÁN ALLAN is Senior Lecturer in German at the University of Warwick, U.K. He is the author of *The Plays of Heinrich von Kleist: Ideals and Illusions* (1996), and *The Stories of Heinrich von Kleist: Fictions of Security* (Camden House, 2001).

PROFESSOR HILDA MELDRUM BROWN is a fellow and tutor in German at St. Hilda's College, and a reader in German at the University of Oxford. She is the author of *Kleist and the Tragic Ideal; A Study of "Penthesilea" and Its Relationship to Kleist's Personal and Literary Development, 1806–08* (1977), *Kleist's Lost Year and the Quest for "Robert Guiskard"* (1981) with Richard Samuel, and *Heinrich von Kleist: The Ambiguity of Art and the Necessity of Form* (1998).

BERND FISCHER is a professor in the Department of Germanic Languages and Literatures at Ohio State University. He is the author of *Ironische Metaphysik: Die Erzählungen Heinrich von Kleists* (1988) and *Das Eigene und das Eigentliche: Episoden aus der Konstruktionsgeschichte nationaler Intentionalitäten: Klopstock, Herder, Fichte, Kleist* (1995).

BERNHARD GREINER is a professor of German literature at the Universität Tübingen, Germany. The author of many books and articles on Kleist, his most recent book is *Kleists Dramen und Erzählungen: Experimente zum "Fall" der Kunst* (2000).

JOST HERMAND is the William F. Vilas Research Professor in the Department of German at the University of Wisconsin. He is the author of many books and articles on German literature and culture, including essays on Kleist. His most recent book is *Revolution germanica: Die Sehnsucht nach der "alten Freiheit" der Germanen. 1750–1820* (2002) with Michael Niedermeier.

TIM MEHIGAN is associate professor of German at the University of Melbourne, Australia. He is the author of *Text as Contract: The Nature and Function of Narrative Discourse in the "Erzählungen" of Heinrich von Kleist* (1988) and editor of *Heinrich von Kleist und die Aufklärung* (Camden House, 2000).

Jeffrey Sammons is Leavenworth professor emeritus in the Department of Germanic Languages and Literatures at Yale University. He is the author of many books and articles on German literature. His most recent book is *Ideology, Mimesis, Fantasy: Charles Sealsfield, Friedrich Gerstäcker, Karl May, and Other German Novelists of America* (1998).

Helmut Schneider is a professor of German Literature at the Universität Bonn, Germany. He is the author of many publications on Kleist. Most recently, he edited *Bildersturm und Bilderflut: Zur schwierigen Anschaulichkeit der Moderne* (2000).

Hinrich C. Seeba is a professor in the Department of German at the University of California, Berkeley. He is the author of many publications on Kleist and is co-editor of *Heinrich von Kleist, Sämtliche Werke und Briefe*, vol. 1 (1991) and vol. 2 (1987).

Anthony Stephens is McCaughey Professor of Germanic Studies and Head of the School of European, Asian and Middle Eastern Languages and Studies at the University of Sydney. The author of scholarly works on many aspects of German literature, his most recent book is *Kleist: Sprache und Gewalt* (1999).

Bianca Theisen is a professor in the Department of German at Johns Hopkins University. She is the author of *Bogenschluß: Kleists Formalisierung des Lesens* (1996).

Susanne Zantop † (1945–2001), was a professor in the Department of German at Dartmouth College. She was the author of many articles on Kleist. Her book *Colonial Fantasies: Conquest, Race, and Nation in Pre-Colonial Germany, 1770–1870* was published in 1997.

Index